Portfolio Presentation for Fashion Designers

Portfolio Presentation for Fashion Designers

Linda Tain

Fairchild Publications
New York

Library of Congress Catalog Card Number: 97-061475

ISBN: 1-56367-094-1

GST R 133004424

Printed in the United States of America

Dedication

To the women in my family, who instilled a passion for the art of making clothes.

&

To Robert Basil, my mentor and friend.

Contents

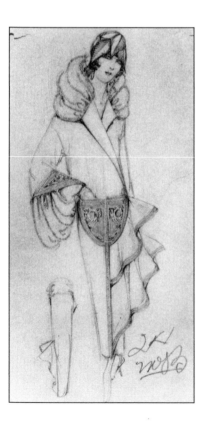

Extended Contents

Preface

The primary goal of *Portfolio Presentation For Fashion Designers* is to provide a fashion portfolio reference to help prepare designers as they begin their fashion design careers. Those already working in the industry or wishing to reenter the job market will also appreciate these new approaches for revising or recreating their portfolios. In addition, this book will help set a standard of portfolio information useful for educators, counselors and employers in the fashion design industry.

In order to address the multifaceted role of the designer in an ever-changing industry, each chapter highlights essential skills and techniques to help designers become competitive within their chosen markets. By focusing on both logical and creative solutions, the designer becomes aware of the process of developing the portfolio—from concept through presentation of the finished product.

Chapter 1 outlines the different types and purposes of portfolios and the importance of media and technique in achieving a unique look. Examples of portfolio/presentation cases are described and illustrated, showing various examples of formats and the advantages and disadvantages of each. Chapter 2 focuses on the history of the designer's sketch from the turn of the century to the present, using archival examples from the Metropolitan Museum of Art and The Museum at FIT–Special Collections. Discussions of characteristic looks in each decade emphasize drawing styles, silhouettes and proportion, rendering techniques and media, demonstrating how fashion design keeps reinventing itself to create relevance to the present. This historical overview provides the designer with a sense of perspective, as well as a variety of inspirational sources.

Chapter 3 shows the importance of focusing the portfolio on a particular customer and market in order to create a consistent design sense from start to finish. The various design markets are detailed and include references to well-known designers for easy identification. Various examples of customer images and profiles are also included for comparison.

Chapter 4 outlines and defines several portfolio formats and discusses their roles in the interviewing process. The organization and contents of each format are described and examples are included. Although this chapter concentrates primarily on the traditional fashion design portfolio and its components, specially targeted presentations are also shown and discussed. The chapter includes a portfolio evaluation checklist and a portfolio evaluation form to assist designers in preparing for the interview. Chapter 5 focuses on the actual presentation formats and outlines the planning process. Orientation, page relationship, figure composition, figure formats and their relevance to design categories are detailed, as are supporting formats such as mood/theme, fabric/color and flats.

Chapter 6 presents an unprecedented analysis and guide to drawing flats and measuring for specs with more than 100 exemplary illustrations by Hong Tan. Because of the critical importance of this essential skill in today's global fashion market, flat sketching techniques for different levels, as well as garment specing, are covered in detail. Special garment silhouettes created for tops, pants, skirts, jackets, coats, dresses and intimate apparel are included to assist the designer in developing his or her own original designs. Variations created from these silhouettes are shown to illustrate how professionals develop a "library" of flats that can be utilized for spec sheets or presentation boards. An illustrated checklist of Do's and Don'ts assists the designer in developing a flat drawing technique that is both accurate and visually appealing.

Chapter 7 discusses the importance of presentation boards as a selling tool and communication vehicle. Types of boards and their uses are highlighted, and designers are also provided with a detailed description of how to plan and create their own presentations. Exercises that specify materials and techniques for achieving professional results are spelled out with illustrated examples.

Chapter 8 acquaints the designer with the computer as a powerful design tool that can enhance design creativity and efficiently execute ideas. Methods of developing concepts and storing information are detailed, as are the important advantages of the computer as a universal communicator. Raster/pixel paint programs and vector/object-oriented programs are compared and illustrated with masterful examples by designer Geoffry Gertz. In addition, the chapter includes information on applications and equipment, as well as a glossary of computer components.

Chapter 9 focuses on the men's wear market, highlighting its specialties and specific portfolio needs. A discussion of color sense and palette, presentation boards and flats is included in this section. In addition, designers will find a specially developed men's wear silhouette with examples of garments created from it. Specialty areas are listed and classified, often in relation to women's wear markets. An award-winning CFDA men's wear portfolio handsomely showcases this special area of fashion design.

Chapter 10 discusses the unique characteristics and requirements of the children's wear designer, as well as the specific portfolio needs of this market. Discussions of age groups and gender shed light on the diverse design areas within children's wear. Specific trends and inspiration sources pertaining to children's wear are examined, including historical inspiration, ethnic influences, children's literature, fabrics and trims and character licensing. Specialty areas are outlined and detailed in relation to specific age groups and gender. In addition, theme orientation, sportswear coordination and stylization are specified as essentials in the children's wear portfolio to help create awareness of professional standards.

A specially developed child's silhouette and garments are included, as is a spectacular award-winning CFDA children's wear portfolio.

Chapter 11 gives an overview of fashion accessories with comments and insight from leading designers in this area. The chapter examines how accessories are bought and their psychological significance. A design exercise that helps create awareness of the relationship of accessories to apparel is also included. Designers will appreciate the discussion of specific portfolio considerations and presentation formats, along with helpful, unique illustrations.

Chapter 12 defines the croquis book, or fashion diary, as a significant companion to the portfolio and stresses its importance in getting an internship or entry-level position. This section discusses how vital quick sketching techniques are for communicating ideas to the various areas of a fashion house. In addition, the croquis book serves to document the designer's distinctive design process through drawing skills, sources of inspiration and color/fabric savvy and sensitivity. Presentation techniques and a suggested exercise are included.

Chapter 13 examines the organizational structure of an apparel manufacturing firm, outlining the functions and personnel responsible for each function in the design hierarchy. The exercise accompanying this section assists in promoting fashion awareness and brings the student into contact with essential merchandising and retail aspects of the fashion business. A glossary of design and manufacturing terms is included in the back of the text to acquaint the student with terminology most often used in these related areas.

Chapter 14 focuses on the importance of the resumé as a tool for marketing oneself and creating an invitation for a personal interview. Resumé preparation is discussed in depth, and examples of chronological and functional resumés are provided. Tips on finessing your resumé are outlined, as well as tactics and information to avoid. Resumé and cover letter strategies are analyzed and illustrated with several samples.

Chapter 15 explores the process of job hunting and interviewing, emphasizing the importance of good preparation and organization. Informational interviewing is explored as a means of making contacts and learning about the fashion industry. Key questions included with this section are designed to facilitate the information-seeking process. How to prepare for the interview is covered in depth, from researching the company to what to wear. In addition, time management, presenting yourself and the portfolio, post-interview follow-up tips, salary negotiation and freelance work are also covered. Samples of an exploratory meeting letter, advertised job response letters, thank-you note and a job search work log are included.

Chapter 16 discusses your first job in the context of the career-building process. You'll find survival techniques for coping with new job jitters, as well as a discussion of what to expect—and what will be expected of you. Included here is information on the importance of maintaining perspective and several tips on creating healthy employer/employee relationships. The section entitled Making it Work focuses on the key ingredients of setting high standards, having a positive attitude and designing your own goals.

With every job the designer strengthens skills, improves techniques, gains critical awareness, increases speed and gains more confidence. The techniques you ultimately choose as a result of your on-the-job experiences are those you will have observed and practiced. What you were satisfied with six months ago can change completely as you continue to work and grow. Your portfolio should reflect these changes and should be continually revised and updated to represent your most current self. Adding and deleting work to accommodate each interview is an accepted practice. The important thing is to allow yourself the exposure and observe what you see around you with a critical eye. Remember, a willingness to experiment with new techniques and materials is crucial to lending freshness and vitality to your work, thus increasing your repertoire of skills.

Creating a fashion design portfolio is a creative process with many possibilities and no simple formula. It can begin with an idea or concept, and in the course of events, things change and evolve. Change is a part of the natural creative process and is what makes it so exciting. View the development of your portfolio as a unique design problem and an adventure in discovering what your special solution will be.

Acknowledgments

Many talented and generous people have contributed both directly and indirectly to making *Portfolio Presentation For Fashion Designers* a reality. I am grateful to Richard, Nick and Joan for their understanding, patience and laughter. To Pauline Stipelman, whose empathy and wonderful meals nourished me throughout the project, my thanks. I gratefully acknowledge Rochelle Rice for helping me reach the physical and mental levels of stamina which this project demanded, for restoring my health, and for helping me fulfill my professional goals.

To those teachers who inspired and helped me develop my talent: a special thanks to Mildred Glaberman, who guided me to FIT to study fashion. To Ruth McMurray, Beatrice Dwan, Ruth Ahntholz, Bill Ronin, Ana Ishikawa, Francis Neady, and Frank Shapiro, who taught me to believe in my talent and encouraged me to share it through teaching, I am sincerely grateful.

Many thanks to Ann Kahn and Nicholas Politis who nursed me through the early stages of learning to use the computer and whose patience and support miraculously remained intact.

I wish to express my appreciation and acknowledge those colleagues who were responsible for gathering some of the outstanding artwork that appears in this book: Richard Rosenfeld, FIT; Karen Scheetz, FIT; and Michele Wesen, FIT. I would especially like to thank Joanne Landis, FIT, for reading parts of the text and reminding me to keep my own "voice." Special thanks to Sandi Keiser of Mount Mary College for her support and encouragement.

Thank you to Dolores Lombardi, Assistant Director of Admissions at FIT, who encouraged this project early on and provided me with substantial background information. In addition, I gratefully appreciate the contribution of the FIT Career Services Office, especially Michele Morad and Juliette Romano, in providing me with valuable information for Chapter 14, Resume and Cover Letter, and Chapter 15, Organizing Your Job Hunt, Mastering the Interview. My gratitude to Gil Aimbez, who was so generous in giving his time and expertise to 25 students regarding the interview process and presenting their portfolios, much of which was the basis of

Chapter 15. Many thanks to Tony Staffieri, President of Savvy Management, Inc., whose excellent seminars relating to the varied aspects of the job search process were most helpful.

I would like to express my appreciation to Camille Aponte, FIT, for her valuable comments and suggestions regarding Chapter 4, Organization and Contents, and Chapter 5, Presentation Formats. To Francesca Sterlacci, FIT, many thanks for the breakdown of the design markets categorized in Chapter 3, Customer Focus, as well as many of the fashion design resources listed in Appendix A. In addition, I am grateful for her input concerning freelance work and many other topics, which she generously shared.

I am also indebted to certain colleagues for their valuable contributions that have influenced the text and illustrations in several chapters. To Steven Stipelman, FIT, whose input, encouragement, and personal vision continually inspired me throughout the project, my deepest appreciation. Many thanks to Dearrick Knupp for his imaginative customer collages created for Chapter 3, Customer Focus. My gratitude to Renaldo Barnette, FIT, for his quintessential croquis books, and for allowing us to share his personal design process. Many thanks to Michele Wesen, FIT, for her thorough research on portfolios and presentation cases for Chapter 1, The Portfolio: A Statement of Style. I would also like to express my gratitude and appreciation to LaDonna Garrett, FIT, for her additions, comments and pre-editing regarding Chapter 13, The Job Market: Basic Organization of Manufacturing Firms.

I am especially indebted to Hong Tan, Design Director for Daniel Caron Sportswear, whose commitment and contribution to Chapter 6, Flats and Specs, went far beyond my expectations. His vast knowledge of the subject and superb illustrative skills are the very core of this chapter and I consider myself fortunate for having had the creative experience of collaborating with him. He has greatly influenced my thinking and has taught me the most about the subject of flats and specs in particular. In addition, I would like to thank Anthony Nuzzo of Mast Industries, Victoria's Secret Division, for his helpful and constructive suggestions in the development of the intimate apparel silhouette and text in this chapter.

I am also indebted to Geoffry Gertz and Chris Musci for their total involvement and enthusiasm in our collaboration on Chapter 8, Computer Design and Illustration. Their creative efforts, coupled with extensive hands-on teaching experience, and great humor resulted in a chapter which invites reading even for those with little or no computer experience. Geoffry's enthusiasm and incredible skill in using the computer as a design tool is evident in his masterful illustrations and descriptions. A special thanks to Lis Bothwell for reading the chapter; her thoughtful and constructive suggestions gave this chapter a broader perspective and focus.

For all their input regarding Chapter 9, Men's Wear Presentations, I gratefully acknowledge the following people: Monique Serena, V.P., Daniel Caron Sportswear; Sal Ruggiero; Vincenzo Gatto, FIT; and Aaron Duncan. In addition, I would like to express my thanks to Andre Croteau, Jason Neil Rovnak, Masataka Suemitsu, and Alan Paul Harris for their dynamic artwork. Alan, a former student, dear friend, and gifted designer, passed on while I was working on this book. Many of our early conversations, philosophies and approaches that we shared are woven through the chapters. His incredible vitality and sense of aesthetics will remain with me always.

I am especially grateful to Susan Cohan, Director of Education, Wood Tobe-Coburn whose comments, suggestions, and pre-editing regarding Chapter 10, Children's Wear Presentations, were invaluable in the development of this chapter. I would also like to thank Joanne Manna, FIT, for her referrals and especially Beth Kay for her overview of the children's wear industry. Special thanks to Chris Tower of Mickey & Company by Donnkenny, who was instrumental in helping me select the incredible artwork done by John Rivoli, and guiding me through the permission process with Disney Enterprises, Inc.

A special thank you to Ellen Goldstein, Chairperson Accessories Design, FIT, for her excellent referrals. I am also extremely grateful to Vasilios Christofilakos, FIT, who so graciously assisted me in the collecting and editing of artwork for this chapter. I especially would like to acknowledge the following people for their insights and anecdotes, so generously given, which brought this chapter to life: Carry Adina, Patricia Underwood, and Sue Siepel for Unisa. Special thanks to Ulrich Grimm for Anne Klein & Company and Renaldo Barnette for their superb sketches.

I would like to express my gratitude and appreciation to The Museum at FIT, for permission to photograph from their archives and to Maris Heller of FIT's Special Collections, Shirley Goodman Resource Center, whose efforts were tireless in helping me gather and select the unique design sketches that appear in Chapter 2, The Design Sketch: A History of Style—many thanks. In addition, I would like to thank Richard Martin and Harold Koda for permission to research and photograph from the archives of the Metropolitan Museum Library, and a special thank-you to Deirdre Donohue for her assistance in the research. The research for me was truly a labor of love. In addition I would like to thank Cotton Inc. for providing the forecast material for Chapter 4, Organization and Contents.

I would like to extend my thanks for the materials and information supplied by Sam Flax, Brewer-Cantelmo and the Art Station. And I especially would like to acknowledge Bill Louie who passed on during the writing of this book and was extremely helpful in providing art supply seminars and samples for me and my students. He had significant input in this text and is greatly missed by all of us.

In addition, I would like to express my appreciation to Stan Herman, President of the CFDA, and Melissa McCarthy, Press Relations Director, who graciously made the award-winning CFDA Portfolios available to me. And special thanks to Peter Som, Masataka Suemitsu and Crystal White for permitting the inclusion of their exceptional portfolios in this text.

My gratitude and appreciation to the staff at Fairchild Publications for their enthusiasm and faith in this project and in me. To Pam Kirshen Fishman, Olga Kontzias and Ilana Scheiner, my thanks for your support, thoughtful comments, and superb editing. A special thanks to Bette Lagow, whose excellent editing added greatly to the book. In addition, I also wish to thank David Jaenisch and Mary Siener, whose keen aesthetics guided the editing and appearance of hundreds of illustrations. To Martin Schwabacher, who adeptly coordinated and directed this project, I wish to express my sincere appreciation for his involvement, attention to detail and commitment to quality. I could not have done it without him.

I would like to thank the following readers and reviewers: Kathy Jung, Brigham Young University; Jacqueline Keuler, Syracuse University; Glenda L. Lowry, Marshall University; Mary Jane Matranga, University of Delaware–Newark; Sharon Rapseik, Wood Tobe–Coburn; Diane Sparks, Colorado State University; Mary St. Hippolyte, Ardis School of the Arts; Richard Vyse, School of Fashion Design–Boston; Trish Winstead, El Paso Community College.

Last, but not least, I would like to thank my students, who over the years have contributed to this book in countless ways—because of them this book is now a reality.

Linda Tain

Portfolio Presentation for Fashion Designers

CHAPTER 1

In today's competitive fashion industry, your portfolio is your ultimate sales tool. It must express the unique qualities that set you apart from others.

The Portfolio:
A Statement of Style

Illustration for Donna Karan, courtesy of Fairchild
Publications.

In today's competitive fashion industry, your portfolio is your ultimate sales tool. It must express the unique qualities that set you apart from others, and should include samples that reflect your best efforts and indicate your range of skills and expertise. In short, your portfolio promotes your most important product—you.

Potential employers are articulate, creative, visually sensitive individuals who work under pressure and tight schedules. Not surprisingly, they seek to hire equally capable designers. A strong portfolio, coupled with an impressive resumé, is your key into the creative business of fashion.

Your portfolio is also an effective interviewing tool. While you can claim certain skills, your portfolio provides the visual evidence, showcasing your creativity, organization, technical skills (knowledge of sewing, draping and pattern making), drawing ability and awareness of fashion trends.

Fashion designers assemble several portfolios over the course of their student careers: one for entry into design school, an internship portfolio and an exit portfolio representing the culmination of their studies, abilities and fashion awareness. In addition, you'll need a portfolio for admission to a graduate program and, as a professional reentering the job market, an updated book including recent samples, press clippings and published work.

The creative fashion portfolio should constantly evolve and never stagnate. You should also make sure to target each company individually by including designs that have their "look," thus promising growth potential and enthusiasm for what they do.

MATERIAL SELECTION AND TECHNIQUE

Perhaps as important as what you choose to include in your portfolio is *how* you choose to present it. Selecting and using the appropriate art supplies demands serious consideration.

Almost any material can be considered an art supply. Sometimes the most unlikely or untraditional materials are used successfully by designers. For example, an illustrator friend uses actual makeup for rendering his drawings, while a designer I know used coffee rings to create a printed fabric for a presentation. Keeping an open mind with regard to your choice of materials can lead to the discovery of unique possibilities and, ultimately, more personal creativity in your work.

It is almost impossible to discuss media or materials without mentioning technique. The two go hand in hand. Media refers to the tools or materials used for artistic expression; technique is the method used to create the desired result via the chosen materials. Consequently, your selection of materials preordains the final "look" you seek.

An additional variable in getting the results you want is your level of skill in controlling the media. You'll want to choose your presentation technique accordingly. First, consider what techniques you have mastered and emphasize these for best results. The more you experiment with new techniques and a variety of art materials, the better you can identify what works best for you and the media with which you are most comfortable. Everyone cannot be good at everything. Some designers love to work in watercolors, others prefer the expediency of felt-tip markers. Still others opt for cut-and-paste techniques instead of actually rendering their designs, and some prefer to use computer-aided design programs. Whatever techniques you choose should reflect what you currently *do* best, and not necessarily what you *like* best. You may love the look of watercolors, but find you get better results with markers.

Discovering what does not work for you is just as important as identifying what does, and may in fact lead to additional training in a technique you would like to acquire or improve.

Another factor to consider in selecting a presentation technique is industry awareness. Industry deadlines require designers to work consistently with speed, cleanliness and accuracy. The techniques and materials used most often in the fashion industry are chosen with this in mind, and are considered "quick media." See Appendix B, Art Supplies for Fashion Designers, for materials most often preferred by designers.

For those who live in remote areas, getting to a good art supplier can be difficult or sometimes impossible. Also, some designers find their local supplier doesn't stock certain brands or types of materials. Few art supply retailers can afford to produce their own catalogs, but most retailers can obtain those distributed by the supply manufacturers themselves. Manufacturers prefer not to take orders directly from customers, but will refer inquiries to the appropriate retailers.

A trip to a large city can be worthwhile for seeking out art supply resources. Once you've seen their selection, you can order supplies by phone or fax. See Appendix B, Art Supplies for Fashion Designers, for a list of major art supply stores that offer catalog sales.

PORTFOLIO CASES

The carrying case for your portfolio can be a design statement in itself. Novice designers often select their presentation case after they complete their pieces and just before they begin to interview. In a way, this is like putting the proverbial cart before the horse. The best time to shop for a case is *before* accumulating a body of work. Case styles and contents lend themselves to different orientations and presentations. While shopping for your case you might be inspired to change your initial ideas about presentation.

Whether you choose a case to accommodate the size and shape of your existing work, or format your work for a specific case, make sure the case is strong and durable. Some designers make their own cases or have one custom-made.

Keep in mind both practical and aesthetic considerations when choosing a case. Case color, finish and detail can help define your professional stance. The case you select will be evaluated along with your portfolio contents and manner of dress. A unique case can affect the perception others have of your work. It communicates how caring and committed you are to what you do.

Make your shopping expedition a quest. Go to more than one source to see the wide range of styles and sizes available. Art supply stores carry large selections, as do mail-order catalogs. (Note: Mail order is not recommended unless you are already familiar with a particular style.) Bookbinders and companies that sell made-to-order cases are worth looking into. These sources offer unique options that can make your presentation special. See Appendix B for a list of stores.

While shopping, examine features such as the hardware, corners, storage pockets and finish. Make sure the case is not too heavy, as it will increase in weight with the addition of plastic sleeves and/or your book. Measure the interior dimensions before you buy a case to be sure it will accommodate your design spreads and any additional inserts. If you allow sufficient lead time, you may be able to buy your case on sale or with a student discount of 10–20 percent.

Another consideration when buying a case is the type of sleeves it accommodates. A beautiful case with unattractive fillers can make for a disappointing presentation. Some cases have loose-leaf spines, others are constructed without spines to accommodate the portfolio book. In either case, the fillers should fit correctly and protect the plates and their corners. Fillers vary in surface coating and access. Know what type is suitable for your case and the plates you wish to show. Uncoated acetate fillers become marked and worn from handling and should be replaced as needed.

An alternative to the loose-leaf case with sleeve fillers is a book-bound presentation. In this form, plates are permanently mounted to light-weight board, allowing the artwork and fabrics to be exposed and free of glare from the acetate. Some designers prefer this method, as they feel it creates a more stimulating interview experience. The exposed pieces invite the viewer to touch and handle both fabric and artwork. Experiencing the fabric "hand" engages the viewer and, at the same time, communicates your knowledge of fabric.

Consider purchasing a shoulder strap for your portfolio case. It can save energy, help distribute the weight and make carrying around more than one case a lot easier. The handy luggage carts used by airline crews and frequent travelers are another option.

Illustrated below are several types of portfolio cases appropriate for fashion design presentation, with a chart illustrating each model's features.

TABLE 1.1 *PORTFOLIO/PRESENTATION CASES*

ZIPPERED PRESENTATION CASE (W/O BINDER)

ADVANTAGES
Can customize with separately purchased binder.

OPTIONS
Retractable or spine-mounted handle, convertible to shoulder strap; brass or nylon zipper; exterior and/or interior pockets; outside identification; available in vinyl, canvas or nylon, with custom options (i.e., leather, suede, cork, velvet).

EXAMPLES
Design NSM Tank; Eberhard Faber/Design Convertible.

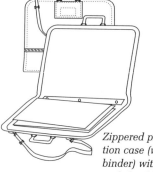

Zippered presentation case (without binder) with handle and shoulder strap.

SEPARATELY PURCHASED BINDER

ADVANTAGES
Can customize with separately purchased case; allows for more than one portfolio.

DISADVANTAGES
Components may not match.

OPTIONS
Multi-ring brass or nylon mechanism; Chicago screw binding with extension posts, expandable from 1/2″ to 3″; cartridge rod binder with inserts that snap in and out of book; easel book; exterior and/or interior pockets; inserts available in vinyl, acetate or polypropylene, multi-punched or welded edge, sealed on one side or three, pebbled or smooth surface.

EXAMPLES
Prat ShowBook with Chicago screw binding; Prat Compact Book; Prat Classic 102; Prat Run 110 Rod Binder; Prat Easel Slimbook.

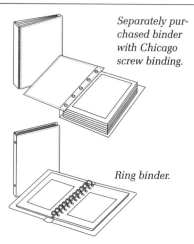

Separately purchased binder with Chicago screw binding.

Ring binder.

TABLE 1.1　*(continued)*

ZIPPERED PRESENTATION CASE (BINDER ATTACHED)

ADVANTAGES
Economical and lightweight.

DISADVANTAGES
No flexibility in binder options.

OPTIONS
Retractable or spine-mounted handle, convertible to shoulder strap; brass or nylon zipper; exterior and/or interior pockets; outside identification; available in vinyl, canvas or nylon, with custom options (i.e., leather, suede, cork, velvet).

EXAMPLES
Design NSM Show case Presentation Case; Design NSM Blackmaster.

Zippered presentation case (binder attached) with spine-mounted handle.

ZIPPERED PRESENTATION CASE WITH REMOVABLE BINDER

ADVANTAGES
Can use portfolio separately. Can buy additional replaceable albums.

OPTIONS
Retractable or spine-mounted handle, convertible to shoulder strap; brass or nylon zipper; exterior and/or interior pockets; outside identification; available in vinyl, canvas or nylon, with custom options (i.e., leather, suede, cork, velvet).

EXAMPLES
Design NSM Presentfolio; Prat Mera 300.

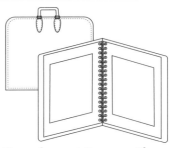

Zippered presentation case with removable binder.

EASEL PRESENTATION CASE

ADVANTAGES
Converts to an easel for hands-free table-top presentations.

DISADVANTAGES
No flexibility in binder options.

OPTIONS
Retractable or spine-mounted handle, convertible to shoulder strap; brass or nylon zipper; exterior and/or interior pockets; outside identification; available in vinyl, canvas or nylon, with custom options (i.e., leather, suede, cork, velvet); landscape (horizontal) or portrait (vertical) orientation; multi-ring, Chicago screw or rod welded binding; inserts available in vinyl, acetate or polypropylene, multi-punched or welded edge, sealed on one side or three, pebbled or smooth surface.

EXAMPLES
Prat Classic - 202; Design NSM Showcase Deluxe Easel Album.

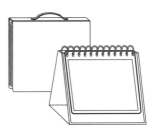

Easel presentation case (landscape orientation).

CUSTOM CRAFTED PORTFOLIOS

ADVANTAGES
Can be made any size, with any material.

DISADVANTAGES
Expensive.

OPTIONS
Unlimited

EXAMPLES
Presentation Box and Portfolio book by Brewer-Cantelmo*; The Elegante, a book and case all in one; The Traygante, a sleek book/box combination.

*Brewer-Cantelmo in New York City has been in the business of making custom portfolios for over 65 years. You can choose from a variety of materials or supply your own.

Custom crafted portfolios.

CHAPTER 2

Just as there is no single, timeless ideal in fashion, there is no one style of portfolio that remains the standard forever. A knowledge of history provides the designer with a sense of perspective, as well as a source of inspiration.

The Design Sketch: A History of Style

Illustrations from Muriel King, FIT Special Collections.

The ideal portfolio is a product of its time. Just as there is no single, timeless ideal in fashion, there is no one style of portfolio that remains the standard forever. A knowledge of history can provide the designer with a sense of perspective, as well as a source of inspiration.

In order to meet the challenge of the workplace today, the designer's portfolio must show a variety of skills and a knowledge of various techniques and technologies. In the past, the designer's work was more segmented and specialized. Today, the designer is involved in both creative and technical aspects of developing a line, which makes his or her role much more challenging. Because the designer's job incorporates many different tasks, these abilities need to be evident in the portfolio.

Gaining a familiarity with the history of the fashion sketch can increase your awareness of different drawing styles and silhouettes, as proportions, rendering techniques and materials used to articulate the fashion design continually change and become reinvented. Looking at past examples will help you sort out what is relevant to the present and figure out how to make it work for you.

Long before the concept of "designer" existed, dressmakers advised society about fashion. Sometimes they used a quick sketch of an idea, but more often than not a fashionable work of art became fashion's inspiration. This was the case for Rose Bertin, dressmaker to Marie Antoinette. She recreated the Queen's image with the help of the court painters Watteau, Fragonard and Boucher. Their renderings of women in exquisite silk gowns were the examples of the fashion of the day.

In the last quarter of the 19th century, Charles Frederick Worth— "the father of couture"—also created clothes for his wealthy clientele based on the artwork of the period. A client might have commissioned a dress inspired by a Velásquez *Enfanta*, while another preferred the swags and rosebuds of a Watteau painting of the ladies of the French court. One day, Worth sent his wife Marie with a sketchbook of his designs to the Princess de Metternick, wife of the Austrian ambassador to France and a close friend of the Empress Eugenie. The princess became intrigued by his designs and ordered two dresses. When she wore one of his gowns to court, it attracted the attention of the Empress, who became a devoted client, as did the rest of society. From then on, Charles Frederick Worth was the court designer and made clothes for the crowned heads of Europe.

The fashion design sketch is a tool to communicate the designer's ideas. It facilitates the production process and records the original intention. Those in the workroom, including the patternmaker and draper, rely on the sketch throughout the technical process to keep focused on the designer's intent. Once the line is completed, the sketches are kept as a record of a specific season, numbered and labeled with fabric and findings information for identification. This procedure has been in place since the early 20th century.

As fashion houses began to spring up, first in Europe and later in America, the sketch became a fundamental part of the design process. In turn-of-the-century Parisian and Italian couture houses, designers sketched their ideas more readily or hired fashion illustrators such as Georges Lepape, Paul Iribe or Erté, a great designer in his own right. In addition to facilitating the manufacturing process, sketches were shown to clients, often tempting them with additional purchases or "must haves."

The design sketch is a reflection of its time. It can be a barometer of the economy or gauge social mores as dictated by the length of hemlines.

It can speak to us of prosperity or austerity, luxury or sparseness, through the application of silhouette and detail. The sketch can herald social change and demonstrate timely concerns, or tell us of domestic and international events. The design sketch encapsulates what is around us. But mostly, it is the creative tool allowing the designer personal expression of his environment and experience.

Each decade has its unique look. Silhouette and design proportion are key elements affecting the carriage and attitude of clothes on the body. Designs constructed away from the body often create an architectural impression; those designs that touch the body can have a sensual and fluid quality. Balenciaga, Dior and Halston, 20th-century masters of design, understood that an understructure, or the lack of it, controls how clothes will appear. Consequently, the body naturally positions itself to accommodate the style of clothing worn. The result becomes each designer's philosophical interpretation of how he sees his design, integrated with the individual style of the woman who wears it.

The design sketches included with this chapter represent a range of styles and techniques from the turn-of-the-century to the present. The sketches do not represent each significant designer or silhouette of their decade, but rather highlight one of the "looks" that was characteristic of its time. Emphasis has been placed on the general style and feeling of the period, proportion of the garment and figure, and rendering technique and materials used to create each sketch. As you continue from decade to decade, observe and compare the differences for each for the following points:

- The garment silhouette: Is there emphasis on a specific part of the body?

- Is the figure proportion natural or elongated?

- Fit of the garment: Were understructures used to create the shape? Is the garment closely fitted or does it fall away from the body?

- The style of the designer's sketch: Is it drawn realistically or in a stylized manner? Are there exaggerations in drawing or gesture?

- What technique and materials were used and what feeling or effect do they communicate?

In noticing these differences, you will become more aware of your own preferences, as well as the many possibilities of drawing style variations. By experimenting with design elements, proportion and techniques, you will achieve a result uniquely your own, ultimately impacting the way you choose to represent your own design concepts. An awareness of both design and sketching styles of the past will help you evolve your own approach. Just as it would be incongruous to dress in the exact manner of a specific decade, sketching styles also need to relate to their own time and fashion proportion while reflecting the designer's fashion point of view.

The sketches included with this chapter are from the Special Collections Library at the Fashion Institute of Technology (FIT) and The Metropolitan Museum of Art Irene Lewisohn Costume Reference Library. These collections are excellent design resources for both students and professionals, and contain an abundance of inspiring examples of garments, accessories and textiles. They are highly recommended for design research.

1900 TURN-OF-THE-CENTURY

As women began to be assimilated into the male-dominated workplace, the need arose for a more tailored and functional working wardrobe. Enter the streamlined hourglass silhouette with leg o' mutton sleeve, giving new emphasis to the shoulderline (Fig. 2.1a). Replacing the crinoline and bustle were multiple petticoats, while the corseted bodice remained. The "Gibson Girl" look for evening, complete with poufed hair knotted on top, was even more detail oriented than its daytime counterpart, aided by the invention of the sewing machine and aniline dyes in the mid-19th century (Fig. 2.1b and c). This look was popularized by the American illustrator Charles Dana Gibson in *Scribner's, Harper's* and *Century* magazines. Using his wife as a model, he drew the idealized American girl in a shirtwaist. Taking its inspiration from men's shirt and tie, the "Gibson Girl" became the look of the late 19th and early 20th centuries.

Style and Technique: Design sketches at the turn-of-the-century showed a shorter figure proportion compared with the leggy ideal of today. The torso and legs were about equal in length, resulting in an 8-head figure compared to the 10-head standard currently used. The hourglass silhouette featured a curvy bosom, tiny waistline and round but smooth hipline. Leg o' mutton sleeves, often exaggerated, brought focus to the shoulderline. Whether tailored or dressy, the silhouette remained the same.

Pencil and wash, or fine-point ink and wash (as illustrated in these sketches), was a popular technique of this period. Sketches rendered in color were mostly done in watercolor with a pencil or fine-point ink outline. These techniques help to emphasize the fine detail work in the garment construction. The sketches have a clarity and realism, making the garment the focal point, thus rendering the attitude of the figure less important.

Figure 2.1a

The Gibson Girl look from the turn of the century shows the new hourglass silhouette, influenced by a man's shirt and tie. The leg o' mutton sleeve gives the shoulderline emphasis.

Figure 2.1b

Even more detail oriented than its daytime counterpart, the Gibson Girl for evening takes on a feminine look. The shoulderline still has prominent focus.

Illustrations from *Humphrey's Onslaw Place/South Kensington S.W.*; Vols. 14 and 8, FIT Special Collections.

Figure 2.1c

As the 20th century got underway, the silhouette became less structured. New design houses began to emerge, competing for the same affluent clientele who demanded luxury and workmanship. The couture became a retaliation of the wealthy to the mechanism of the Industrial Revolution, a way of displaying privilege and appreciation for quality. Fortuny's tea gowns, the lacy lingerie looks and inset details of the Callot Soeurs (Fig. 2.2a), Doucet and Patou and Lucile's fantasy gowns each offered a unique fashion vision. Fashionable women began to trade their corsets for the new brassieres known as *la liberté*, popularized by the "Sultan of Design," Paul Poiret. Influenced by the Empire and Directoire styles (Fig. 2.2b), the waistline became less defined, and orientalism inspired both silhouette and fabric. The fashion focus moved above the natural waistline and the skirt became fluid, revealing a bit of leg.

Style and Technique: By 1914, the fashion proportion had shifted above the natural waist, inspired by the 19th-century chemise revivals of Paul Poiret. Fashion details focused on the bustline, creating a more elongated look in the skirt and legs. Historical details often combined with a new "orientalism." The art of the Surrealists and Cubists, such as Cocteau, Picasso and Matisse, had great impact on fashion design and its art. Sketches of this decade characteristically have a stylized and less realistic quality, such as those of Erté, Georges Lepape and Paul Iribe.

Design sketches also took on a more painterly approach in this decade. Watercolor, tempera and gouache, with a fine-line ink outline, were prevalent and more frequently used to illustrate detail and fabric. Designers used watercolor paper or light-weight board to prevent the water-based media from buckling the paper. These sketches, or fashion "plates" as they were sometimes called, often illustrated several views of garment parts to show all important details (Fig. 2.2c).

1916
PRE-WORLD WAR I

Figure   2.2a
This Empire-styled suit with characteristic insets is a reinterpretation of a design by the Callot Soeurs.

Illustration from Max Meyer, Vol. 3.32, FIT Special Collections.

Figure   2.2b
After 1912, inspired by the Empire and Directoire styles, the focus moved above the natural waistline.

Illustration by the House of Worth, FIT Special Collections.

Figure   2.2c
Fashion "plates" of this period illustrate several views of each garment to show all important details.

Illustration from Max Meyer, Vol. 3.32, FIT Special Collections.

1920s
THE FLAPPER

Inspired by the suffragette movement that resulted in women gaining the right to vote in 1920, the silhouette and posture changed dramatically. Hemlines shortened to reveal a silk-stockinged leg emerging from a "boyish" silhouette, often adorned with long ropes of pearls. Hair was cropped with bangs, sometimes worn with headbands or hats that grazed the eyebrow. Movement in skirts was emphasized with the use of pleats, tongues or fringe. By 1925, the silhouette sparkled with intricate beadwork. The Flapper shimmies and shakes to the dances of the Charleston and Black Bottom. The posture speaks of a new-found freedom and equality for women.

Style and Technique: The boyish silhouette of the 1920s flattened the chest and dropped the waistline to the end of the torso. Once again, the pendulum of fashion changed direction, shifting the emphasis from the breasts to the hipline. The new "Flapper" silhouette for the most part was straight and unstructured. Women bound their breasts and wore slips that duplicated the dress shape. The Japanese kimono was an important stylistic influence both in silhouette and detail, especially sleeves. Sketches often reflected a sense of orientalism in gesture, as well. Macramé, fringe and dangling beadwork were often used as decorative treatments, creating movement to enhance the popular dances of the period. Sketching styles tended to emphasize geometric elements and patterns characteristic of Art Deco.

Watercolor, tempera and gouache techniques were still popular, with designers using either fine-line ink or pencil for definition and detail. This period also saw the introduction of pencil on vellum, a semi-transparent paper with a smooth, coated surface. These fine-quality pencil sketches on vellum are superb examples of draftsmanship and garment detail (Fig. 2.3a, b and c).

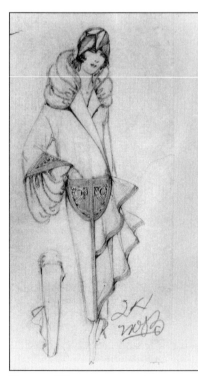
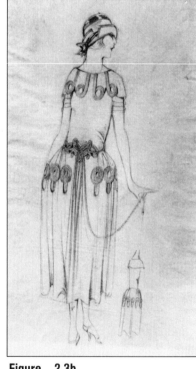

Figure   2.3a   **Figure   2.3b**   **Figure   2.3c**

In the 1920s, when American women won the right to vote, the rapid changes in roles inspired a boyish silhouette that flattened the chest and dropped the waistline to the end of the torso. Macramé, fringe and dangling beadwork were often used as decorative treatments, creating movement to enhance the popular dances of the period.

Illustrations from *Berley*, Vol. Z, FIT Special Collections.

The luxury of long ocean voyages and steamer trunks filled with glamorous gowns—one for every evening—epitomizes the decade of the 1930s, at least for those whose fortunes remained intact following the 1929 stock market crash. Most coveted were the flowing bias gowns with draped halter bodices designed by Madeleine Vionnet or Madame Alix Grès, often in crepe de chine and silk jersey fabrics. Bustlines were softly draped, hipbones prominent, and backbones revealed. The silhouette emphasized fit and flare. Perm-waved hair with bowed dark lips and sultry shadowed eyelids created a haunting and mysterious quality. Women of accomplishment were idolized—Jean Harlow, the Duchess of Windsor, Elsa Schiaparelli.

Style and Technique: The stock market crash of 1929 and the Great Depression that followed made women long for some glamour in their lives. Hemlines lengthened and garments once again sensuously shaped the body. Greta Garbo, Marlene Dietrich and Carole Lombard slinked across the silver screen in bias-cut gowns. Silhouettes were fluid and fabric cascaded over their bodies, often ending in uneven, handkerchief hemlines. Sketches of the 1930s tend toward a more lifelike approach than those of the previous decade. The fit and flare of the bias drapery is often exaggerated on a slouchy figure. Back emphasis, fluttering sleeves and floral patterns were typical, as in the Mainbocher sketch (Fig. 2.4a).

Designers continued to use watercolor and gouache. Brush outline and washes contributed to the softened look of the 1930s' sketches. Emphasis on the fit and flare, created with bias, was enhanced by a varied and contrasted outline. The Muriel King evening dresses are examples of watercolor technique with a pencil outline (Fig. 2.4b).

1930s
THE GREAT
DEPRESSION

Figure 2.4a
Floral patterns were characteristic of the 1930s' gowns, as shown in this Mainbocher sketch.

Illustration from Mainbocher, 1930, FIT Special Collections.

Figure 2.4b
The flowing bias gowns of the 1930s emphasized softly draped bustlines, prominent hipbones and back interest, as in these Muriel King sketches.

Illustrations from Muriel King, 1938, FIT Special Collections.

Figure 2.4c
This Vionnet sketch shows the garment in three views to emphasize the drapery detail. Notice how the dress appears somewhat different from each view, a trait common to bias-draped garments.

Illustration from Madeleine Vionnet, Hiver 29.30, The Metropolitan Museum of Art Library.

Brush and ink is another approach to achieving a similar feeling without using color. The Vionnet sketch of a draped ruffle dress (Fig. 2.4c), shows how dramatic a simple black-and-white sketch can be. Three views of the dress are sketched to emphasize the drapery detail. The dress appears different from each view, a trait common to bias-draped garments.

1940s WORLD WAR II

With production stifled due to the war effort, and cut off from European imports, American designers rallied to fill the clothing needs of the nation. Claire McCardell created a more relaxed way of dressing, pioneering the concept of sportswear. New synthetic fabrics such as rayon and nylon were introduced to fill the gap left by natural fabrics rationed for military use. Hats revealing rolled bangs and exaggerated shoulderlines topped the nipped-in waistlines, accompanied by softly draped skirts that grazed the knee cap (Fig. 2.5a). Ankle-strapped platform shoes often completed the look. Adrian and Schiaparelli suits sporting inserts, cut-outs and dressmaker details were the rage along with big band music (Fig 2.5b). In 1947, with the introduction of the "New Look" by Dior, the silhouette shifted once more. The shoulderline became softer and the bodice and skirt were controlled once again with boning and crinolines.

Style and Technique: An exaggerated shoulderline and upper bodice detail is characteristic of the look of the 1940s and is often the focal point of design (Fig 2.5c). In contrast, the waistline appears small, the hipline smooth, with skirts easy and relaxed. Hemlines are generally shorter than in the previous decade. The ideal figure proportion is natural and not exceptionally elongated, emphasising on the shoulder width. Drawing styles tend toward realism, with some exaggeration of the padded shoulder.

Figure 2.5a

In the 1940s, hats revealing rolled bangs and exaggerated shoulderlines topped the shapely suit silhouette.

Illustration from Bergdorf Goodman made-to-order department, The Metropolitan Museum of Art Library.

Figure 2.5b

This suit features dressmaker details and inserts, which were made popular by Adrian and Schiaparelli in the 1940s.

Illustration from Milton Box 1 1940–45, FIT Special Collections.

Figure 2.5c

During this period, upper-bodice details, often with cut-outs, were frequently the focus of design.

Illustration from Bergdorf Goodman made-to-order department, The Metropolitan Museum of Art Library.

Watercolor and gouache techniques were still preferred for accurate representation of fabric, color and detail. Shadowing lent naturalism to the drape and fit of the garment. Pencil details and backviews were often included with each fashion "plate." Fabric swatches were also a part of the presentation. Even for collections, designers tended to sketch their designs on individual plates, rather than in groups.

Paralleling the "New Look" by Dior, Charles James continued the structured silhouette in America (Fig. 2.6a). The shirtwaist with a cardigan and pearls and the fitted sheath were the popular daytime looks. But the strapless gown, often with a fluted bodice, was the look for gala evenings. Big skirts with yards of tulle and crinolines to support them danced at proms and debutante balls. Hair was coifed and combed naturally, and red lips and a shaped brow á la Elizabeth Taylor were the ideal (Fig. 2.6b). By the end of the decade, the emphasis of the silhouette was ending. The fitted silhouette that molded the body was now moving away from the body. Balenciaga reintroduced the chemise, or H-line, along with the sacque dress and bubble. Yves Saint Laurent popularized the trapeze and A-line/tent silhouettes. Clothes took on their own form, mostly concealing the body underneath.

Style and Technique: The ideal fashion proportion of the 1950s focused on a tiny waist, often "cinched" with a merrywidow corset or elasticized belt. The small waist made the hipline appear rounded, further exaggerated by bouffant skirts (Fig. 2.6c). Crinolines and hoops were worn underneath to create the dome-shaped silhouette. Longer skirt lengths, ranging from mid-calf to just below the knee, kept the figure at a realis-

1950s
FITTED SILHOUETTES

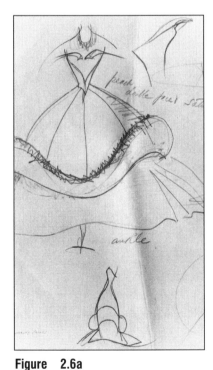

Figure   2.6a
This working sketch by the American designer Charles James illustrates the structured silhouette of the 1950s.
Illustration by Charles James, Fall, 1952, The Metropolitan Museum of Art Library, donated by C. V. Whitney.

Figure   2.6b

Figure   2.6c
The ideal fashion proportion of the 1950s focused on a tiny waist cinched with a corset and exaggerated by a bouffant skirt.

Illustrations from FIT Special Collections, Bergdorf Goodman Box 16, 1953 Imports.

tic proportion of 8½ heads tall. This decade saw understructures molded to popular models such as Suzy Parker and Dovima, creating a pencil-thin appearance. Lady-like poses with glamorous gestures were typically used in designers' sketches.

Both designers and illustrators were primarily working in water-color and gouache. Inks and washes were used as well. The timeless pencil sketch continued to be the fastest way of recording design ideas. These were frequently used in the designer's journal or sketch book. The Charles James pencil sketch is an excellent example of a "working" drawing (Fig. 2.6a). Here, the designer expresses both silhouette and construction techniques for his concept. His thinking process is evident in his notes, which are visible on the page.

The Bergdorf Goodman sketches, by contrast, show fine detail in the fabric rendering through the gouache technique (Fig. 2.6b and c). These sketches suggest an attitude and pose typical of the 1950s. The small waist and full-skirted silhouette complete the look. Elizabeth Taylor and Grace Kelly were often idealized in these sketches.

1960s FASHION REVOLUTION

Eclecticism, inspired by the Kennedy administration, the Beatles, eastern philosophies/Nehru (Fig. 2.7a), cultural diversity (Fig. 2.7b) and space exploration became characteristic of the decade. Early on, Jackie Kennedy's little bias-roll collared suit, designed for her by Oleg Cassini and worn with a pill-box hat, saturated the nation. Givenchy, Valentino and Norell continued the lady-like look. By the mid-1960s, catapulted by a new freedom of self-expression, the fashion revolution escalated and hemlines climbed to new heights. The miniskirt dominated fashion, promoted by the creator of the "Mod Look," Mary Quant, in London, Andre Courreges, Paco Rabanne and Pierre Cardin in Paris and Rudi Gernreich in America. Geometric silhouettes topped with helmeted Sassoon blunt cuts and go-go boots appeared ready for a walk on the moon.

Style and Technique: With the extreme shortening of skirts, legs became the fashion focus in the 1960s. The "little girl look" fostered by the youth movement gave way to an extremely leggy look. Heads appeared larger with the addition of falls, hair pieces and geometric cuts (Fig. 2.7c). Armholes and waistlines were high and bustlines flat, adding to the child-like appearance. Celebrities were given names like "Baby Jane Holtzer." Sonny and Cher sang "I Got You, Babe." Garment shapes were geometric and structured. Fabrics were stiff and worked architecturally on the body (Fig. 2.7d). Double-faced wools and double-knits were often worked with welted seams to define the structure and garment details. Sketching styles became less traditional, more stylized, emphasizing individuality and youth. These Bonnie Cashin sketches reflect the exuberance and energy of the decade, combining a child-like quality with sophistication.

Felt-tipped markers were introduced in the 1960s as the new "quick rendering media." Enamored of their instant drying capacity, designers quickly adopted them for sketching. These single-nibbed Magic Markers and black Flo-master pens are the ancestors of the markers so widely used today. This then-new tool allowed the designer to create a continuous outline without having to dip pen or brush into ink for refills, resulting in a more continuous line quality. The examples here show the spontaneity of the technique. Designers were now able to do many more sketches in a lot less time.

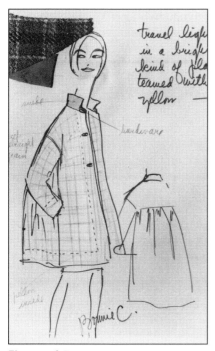

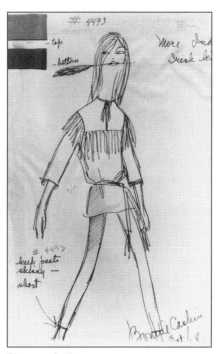

Figure   2.7a

This Bonnie Cashin coat with a Nehru collar reflects America's fascination with eastern cultures in the 1960s.

Illustration by Bonnie Cashin 1966–69, FIT Special Collections.

Figure   2.7b

The 1960s also saw an interest in Native American cultures, which inspired the use of fringed suedes and leathers.

Illustration by Bonnie Cashin 1966–69, FIT Special Collections.

Figure   2.7c

This Bonnie Cashin sketch is a fine example of the geometric influence in both hair and clothing. The garment neckline and silhouette is inspired by costume from the Japanese Noh theater.

Illustration by Bonnie Cashin 1966–69, FIT Special Collections.

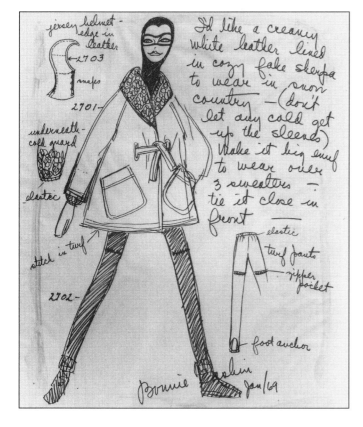

Figure   2.7d

The national obsession with space exploration influenced fashion in the late 1960s, as shown in this space helmet and goggle design. The architectural shaping of the jacket is typical of the period.

Illustration by Bonnie Cashin 1966–69, FIT Special Collections.

1970s LENGTH OPTIONS

Ethnicism of the late 1960s gave way to more elaborate looks, continuing the cultural revolution in fashion. Hemline options from mini to midi (Fig. 2.8a), and then to maxi, allowed for more self expression and creative dressing—a far cry from past decades when designers "dictated" the hemline and everyone followed suit. Layers of clothing continued to reinforce the sportswear concept, exemplified by Yves Saint Laurent's rich and luxurious peasant. Wrapped heads with lots of natural hair, ethnic jewelry and boots completed the look. American designers such as Oscar de la Renta, Bill Blass, Geoffrey Beene and Halston became prominent contenders in the worldwide fashion arena.

With the popularity of the layered look and an abundance of natural hair came the need to elongate the figure proportion. A tall figure was necessary to be able to carry off the multi-layered garments, longer lengths and boots (Fig. 2.8a). The peasant or gypsy feeling ran the gamut from the rich and luxurious to the "hippie" Haight-Ashbury thrift shop variety. Having more than one focal point, the design proportion was broken up and varied due to length options. Pants often answered the question of length when confusion reigned (Fig. 2.8b). Sketching styles were bold and dramatic, emphasizing an exuberant mixture of colors and patterns. These sketches by Gloria Sachs interpret the ethnic look for the American designer market.

Style and Technique: Although watercolor and gouache techniques prevailed, Magic Markers became the popular new rendering media. However, many designers also used an eclectic mix of materials, often "layering" the media to get a desired effect. Experimentation allowed the designer to "do his own thing." Breaking away from traditional approaches gave way to an individualism and the emergence of many different styles.

Figure   2.8a
Originally popularized by Yves Saint Laurent, the "Luxurious Peasant" style of the 1970s featured multi-layered garments, midi skirts and boots.

Illustration for Gloria Sachs, FIT Special Collections.

Figure   2.8b
When confusion reigned over whether to wear mini, maxi or midi lengths, many women rejected skirts in favor of pants.

Illustration for Gloria Sachs, FIT Special Collections.

The soft, flowing looks of the 1970s were still prominent at the beginning of the decade. Perry Ellis continued with the maxi proportion, adding his cropped, baby-cabled sweater with a "dimpled" or puffed sleeve. Japan became an important design resource. Issey Miyake and Rei Kowakubo of Commes de Garçon experimented with architectural approaches in design. Often they combined ancient Japanese traditions and techniques in fabric making with western concepts. For the first time, eastern and western design philosophies became one and received worldwide acceptance. The London scene introduced "punk" fashion to the world and inspired designers such as Zandra Rhodes. Rainbow hair colors, safety pins with chains and slashed garments defined the look, promoted by the Sex Pistols, Boy George and other rock stars. Jean Paul Gaultier, Claude Montana, Kenzo Takada and Azadine Alaia led the Paris fashion scene. Calvin Klein, Ralph Lauren, Norma Kamali and Donna Karan dominated American design. Padded shoulders and short skirts defined the look of the decade. Opulence and drama prevailed, as seen in this evening gown by Bob Mackie (Fig. 2.9a). Fashion moved away from the soft femininity of the bedroom and into the boardroom. Giorgio Armani in Milan pioneered the new, softly tailored suit, skillfully translating men's wear to the feminine form.

The hemline of choice continued to influence proportion and individuality in the 1980s. Looks ranged from soft to hard edged, from refined to tattered (e.g., slashed jeans). The economy boomed and luxurious clothes reflected prosperity and extravagance. Television offered shows such as Dynasty, Falcon Crest and L.A. Law. America was mesmerized by new superheroines wearing "power suits" and living extravagant fantasy lives. This Jonathan Hitchcock sketch reflects the glamour of the Joan Collins CEO image (Fig. 2.9b).

1980s
POWER DRESSING

Figure 2.9a
This evening gown by Bob Mackie shows a taste for opulence and excess associated with the 1980s.

Illustration by Bob Mackie, courtesy of Fairchild Publications.

Figure 2.9b
Television shows such as "Dynasty" inspired glamorous "power suits" for women, typified by Joan Collins' CEO image.

Illustration by Jonathan Hitchcock, Linda Tain private collection.

Figure 2.9c
These sketches by Jennifer George emphasize the padded shoulder and dynamic silhouette that predominated in the 1980s.

Illustration by Jennifer George 1987, Linda Tain private collection.

Style and Technique: Marker and colored pencil continued to be popular among designers as the quickest and most spontaneous media available. Almost architectural, this pencil sketch by Jonathan Hitchcock cleanly illustrates both fabric and detail (Fig. 2.9b). Most designers were not yet acquainted with computer technology, nor did they foresee the incredible advances it would bring to their daily lives as designers. This sketch by Jennifer George (Fig. 2.9c) emphasizes the padded shoulder and dynamic silhouette that predominated in the 1980s. Although the garments are represented on a figure, they have the look of a flat. Clean and simply rendered, this approach brings one's focus directly to the clothing.

1990s
RETRO REVISITED

Dressing softens once again in the 1990s as women become more confident and secure in their accomplishments. Having proven themselves, a more feminine quality begins to resurface. Introduced by Giorgio Armani, Calvin Klein and Victor Alfaro, the "slip" dress becomes a new classic. Ralph Lauren and Donna Karan for DKNY take activewear dressing out of the sports arena and into our everyday lives. Hemlines, no longer an issue, allow for the "do your own thing" approach to dressing, along with other 1960s concepts. As priorities shift to other lifestyle needs, the customer longs for some of the fashion direction associated with earlier decades. As we approach the 21st century, designers look to previous decades to understand where we have been and where we are headed. Collections are filled with a variety of influences from the '20s, '30s, '40s, '50s, '60s and '70s. Karl Lagerfeld, Christian Lacroix, Gianfranco Ferré, Gianni Versace and John Galliano continue to keep the European couture alive. Young designers such as Byron Lars, Victor Alfaro, Anna Sui and Tom Ford for Gucci search for a fresh interpretation of design, one that acknowledges both past values and modern sensibilities.

Figure   2.10a
The 1990s reflect great diversity in style and media. This sketch by Hermès exhibits a cutting-edge classic sophistication.
Illustration by Hermès, courtesy of Fairchild Publications.

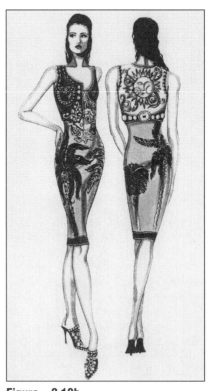

Figure   2.10b
This computer-generated sketch is typical of Versace's richly embellished, body-conscious designs.
Illustration by Versace, courtesy of Fairchild Publications.

Figure   2.10c
Calvin Klein, a master of minimalism, brings a timelessness to his clean, modern designs.
Illustration by Calvin Klein, courtesy of Fairchild Publications

Style and Technique: The proportion of the 1990s suggests a mix of long and short, layered and spare. The importance of the undergarment, popularized by Madonna, draws the eye to the shape of the body once again. The torso is rediscovered and revealed, from midriff to belly button. Lingerie fabrics and floating sheers worn for daytime with Doc Martens continue to relay an eclectic fashion message. There are no rules to follow. It's up to the individual to create her own style and make it work.

Design sketches of the '90s demonstrate great diversity and individuality. Drawing styles and media vary and are as eclectic as the mixture of fashion styles. Media and technique help the designer convey and market his or her fashion image. The flat and graphic use of markers and silhouette create a modern sophistication in this Hermès sketch (Fig. 2.10a). Computer-generated techniques, such as in this Versace example (Fig. 2.10b), reflect a feeling of future technologies. The pencil sketch for Calvin Klein is simplified and minimal both in technique and fashion message (Fig. 2.10c). Soft pastels, ink and wash by Karl Lagerfeld have a subtle, hand-wrought quality associated with the couture (Fig. 2.10d). The Donna Karan sketch conveys a fluid and impressionistic sense of luxury (Fig. 2.10e).

The design sketch is a statement of style in several ways. It reflects the silhouette and proportion of its time, as well as attitude and feeling. It documents body posture, hairstyles, makeup and accessories, all of which contribute to the total fashion look or message. The design sketch can communicate our technological progress through its media, which affects and enhances style. It is a tool in which the designer's philosophy, image and personal style will prevail as the fashion industry develops and evolves. Currency in style, media and "look" will continue to be vital elements of the fashion portfolio in the 1990s and beyond.

Figure   2.10d

The prolific diversity of Karl Lagerfeld is evident in the four distinct lines he produces for KL, Chanel, Fendi and Chloe.

Illustration by Karl Lagerfeld, courtesy of Fairchild Publications.

Figure   2.10e

Fluid lines and luxurious simplicity characterize the personal style of Donna Karan.

Illustration for Donna Karan, courtesy of Fairchild Publications.

CHAPTER 3

The mark of a professional portfolio is its focus. Targeted to a specific customer and market, its design sense should be consistent from start to finish.

Customer Focus

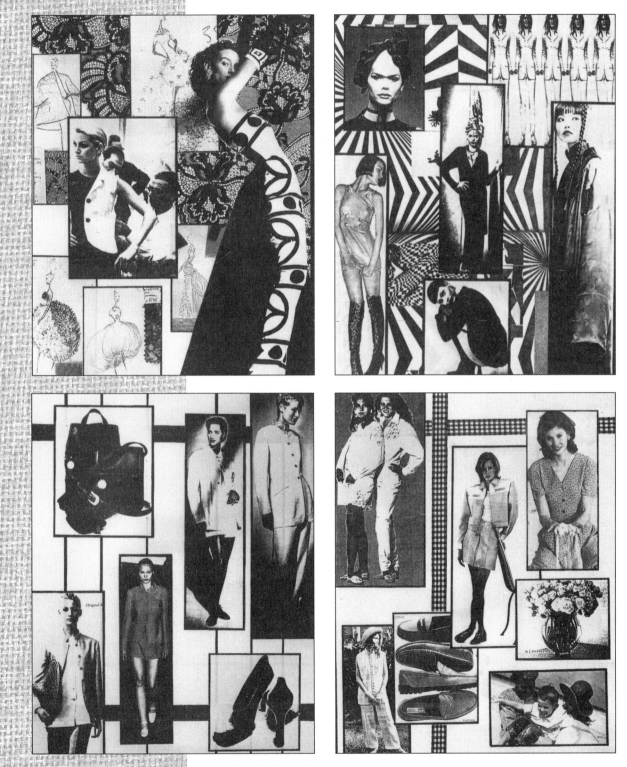

Collages by Dearrick Knupp.

The mark of a professional portfolio is its focus. Targeted to a specific customer and market, its design sense should be consistent from start to finish. This is not achieved instantly, but is instead a gradual process that begins with an early excitement and awareness of fashion. Often, a student's motivation for entering a design program is the dream of dressing glamorous women in expensive clothing. While this is a great start, it is essential to understand the clothing requirements and lifestyle of the customer—and how much she is willing to spend for clothing—in order to make a success of it.

As you broaden your fashion knowledge, you discover the many potential markets and customers, as well as design areas. The combination of these on which you ultimately focus your portfolio should depend on what you do best. Each individual must decide what area of design he or she is most excited about and work within that area and price point. The area you initially choose is not necessarily where you will remain. Experience and fate will play a role in guiding your career decisions.

FOCUSING THE PORTFOLIO

The importance of focusing on a specific market and customer is directly linked to the job search process. Each clothing company has a reputation for a particular kind of clothing. This is not to say a company cannot make more than one product. Those that have divisions or licensees most certainly offer a variety of merchandise. When interviewing for any company, it is essential to research that company to better understand its range of products, look, fabric/color direction and price point. Thorough preparation will ultimately impact your decision as to what pieces to include for each portfolio interview. We will discuss research techniques later in this chapter.

As a rule, when reviewing a portfolio, most companies expect to see the same type of clothing they manufacture. Specifically, sportswear companies are not interested in bridal or eveningwear and vice versa. However, sportswear companies often do manufacture knitwear, thus making its inclusion in your portfolio appropriate. Novices to the interview process often make the mistake of including pieces from a variety of design areas and semesters of study in school. A mixture of this kind makes for a confusing and uneven presentation. Therefore, relying on your company research gives you the advantage of presenting those areas of design the reviewer most wants to see.

Every designer has a unique vision of his or her customer. The most successful designers can maintain this vision collection after collection, yet still give their customers something new each season. For example, pure, clean, modern clothes are unmistakably the trademark of Calvin Klein. An untraditional mix of luxurious fabrics that strategically follow anatomical lines is associated with the collections of Geoffrey Beene. Coordinated, well-tailored, American sportswear with a sensual, sophisticated spirit is identified with Donna Karan. Bold color and a mixture of unusual patterns and proportion are the unmistakable signature of Christian Lacroix.

Each customer is devoted to the designer who will best give her the look she wants in a specific design market. These markets are broken down in the following way in women's apparel. (Children's wear, men's wear and fashion accessories will be discussed separately in their respective chapters.)

SPORTSWEAR DESIGN CATEGORIES & MARKETS

Sportswear/Coordinated Separates
- Career
- Casual/Weekend
- Missy
- Junior

Knitwear/Sweaters
- Sweater sets
- Pull-overs
- Outerwear
- Bulky
- Jacquard
- Pointelle
- Novelty
- Intarsia
- Dimensional

Activewear/Sports
- Golf
- Swimwear/ Cover-ups
- Exercise/Aerobics
- Tennis
- Bicycling
- Skiing
- Rollerblading

Coats/Suits
- Dressy
- Casual
- Rainwear
- Wardrobe— Jacket/Skirt/ Pant

Daytime Dresses
- One- or Two-Piece
- Dress and Jacket

Eveningwear
- After-Five/Cocktail
- Prom/Party
- Clubwear
- Special Occasion
- Gowns
- Bridal/ Mother-of- the-Bride/ Bridesmaid

Intimate Apparel
- Foundations
- Daywear— Camisole/ Tap Pants/ Slips/Teddies

Sleepwear
- Nightgowns and Pajamas
- Sleep-sets
- Robes
- Nightshirts

TRUNK SHOWS

Successful designers and design houses continually research their customers. They hire marketing experts or have their own marketing departments survey customers to determine information such as preferences in style, fit, fabric/color and price. Higher sales figures are positive proof of the importance of this research.

Designers also stay in tune with their customers by holding trunk shows after a collection is presented. This idea began around 1910 when Madame Paquin, of the House of Paquin in Paris, sent her collection across the Atlantic in steamer trunks—along with one dozen mannequins—to tour the major American cities. However, trunk shows did not become standard practice until after World War I, when many designers used this method to learn first-hand what their customers wanted to buy, or more important, what they didn't.

Today, designers travel to trunk shows throughout the country. These events are advertised in the local papers, playing up the celebrity status of the designer. Customers are often invited to come into the store to try on the new line, sometimes with the bonus of personal expertise from the designer. Salespeople personally invite regular customers to attend informal modeling sessions.

Designers who take this opportunity to work with as many customers as possible, participating in fittings and answering questions as to what color, proportion or style suits each person best, discover an honest and candid opinion often sells more garments than flattery. Designers do well to consider the long-term aspect of keeping customers coming back season after season. Personality, enthusiasm and a gift for gab are essential for doing the trunk-show circuit. Consequently, not all designers do these shows, but those who have an aptitude for them do, as ultimately they encourage and boost sales.

GEOGRAPHICAL FACTORS

Customer needs can vary from one area of the country to another, and from continent to continent. California, Texas and Florida have different clothing requirements than New York. As a result, companies may prepare lines to accommodate geographical requirements. Stylistically they may remain the same, simply refabricated or colored more suitably for a specific region. For example, a designer may choose a lighter weight fabric for a warmer climate even though the season may be fall/winter. Or the color palette might be softer or less somber than its eastern version, in keeping with climatic and geographical factors. Lower necklines and shorter sleeve lengths are additional style adjustments that would be considered to suit the region.

LEARNING FROM RETAIL

Buyers and salespeople are also an important source for knowing what the customer wants, as they consistently deal directly with the consumer. Their input counts for much in the way the designer styles the line. Customers confide in salespeople and often rely on their opinion for what to buy. Quality stores such as Bergdorf Goodman and Neiman Marcus are known for excellent service and maintain a personal relationship with customers. When new merchandise arrives, salespeople call certain customers they know are interested in getting a first peek at the collections. They then assist them with their selections and send out their orders, followed by hand-written thank-you notes.

Department and specialty stores are also excellent resources for both the professional designer and the beginner. Professionals know that in order to stay aware of their competition, they need to "shop the stores," as it is referred to in the industry. Seeing collections in their retail environment allows one to view seasonal groups or segments, as well as the whole.

Design students have much to learn from retailers, for instance, by observing the way in which stores display their merchandise according to design categories and price points. This is done for the convenience of the customer. You might find that the designer sportswear floor contains only those designers falling into that category and price point, which could include American designers such as Calvin Klein, Donna Karan and Ralph Lauren. European designers of a similar price point are often located on the same floor, but in a separate area. Bridge sportswear is located on another floor, etc.

Listed below is an overview of categories within the American sportswear market. While every design market has its specific categories, sportswear was chosen here because it is the largest and has the most varied categories.

By becoming familiar with design markets and how retailers categorize them, design students can better see their own work in this context and know where they fit in. By observing shoppers in a specific store, checking price tags and becoming aware of merchandise and how it is displayed, students can accumulate important information that will later be useful in the design process.

The American apparel industry consists of several different categories/markets, each separated by their "look," price and target customer.

DESIGN MARKET OVERVIEW

COUTURE

The most expensive clothes money can buy, with fabrics ranging from fifty to hundreds of dollars per yard. Couture is generally associated with the European market; there are very few American designers making custom-made clothing. The customer can be 30 to 90 years of age and might be a public figure, socialite or performer. Price point for a jacket is $2,500 and up. Established designers such as Oscar de la Renta, Bill Blass or Geoffrey Beene may do custom work for special clients, but this is an accommodation, not the mainstay of their ready-to-wear business. Galanos is one of the few American designers in the couture market.

DESIGNER

Usually a well-known designer, using expensive fabrics ($10–40 per yard). The "look" is sophisticated and refined and caters to an affluent customer. The customer ranges in age from 25 to 60 and is status conscious. These clothes are not trendy. The average price point for a jacket is $500–1500 retail. Designers in this category include Donna Karan, Bill Blass, Ralph Lauren, Calvin Klein, Oscar de la Renta and Geoffrey Beene. Stores carrying these collections are Saks, Bergdorf Goodman, Barneys and Neiman Marcus.

YOUNG DESIGNER

Either an up-and-coming designer or one who has been around for a few years using moderate to expensive fabrics ($10–30 per yard). The "look" appeals to a trendy customer approximately 20 to 40 years old who is very status conscious. The press calls this category "fast fashion" due to its trendiness. The average retail jacket price is $300–800. This category is most often found in specialty stores, but some department stores feature young designer shops. Examples in this category are Zang Toi, Gemma Khang, Marc Jacobs, Todd Oldham, Christian Francis Roth, Cynthia Rowley, Victor Alfaro, Anna Sui and Byron Lars.

BRIDGE/BETTER

Sportswear geared to a broader audience than designer. This category also encompasses secondary lines of "designer collections," hence the word bridge. The look is somewhat trendy and focuses on the 20-to-50 age group. Designers use fabrics in the $5–20 per yard price range and a jacket might retail from $250–425. These clothes are mostly found in department stores such as Macy's, Bloomingdale's, Saks, Nordstrom and Lord & Taylor. Examples of bridge lines are DKNY, CK, RRL, A-Line and Anne Klein II. Examples of better lines are Andrea Jovine, Ellen Tracy, Susie Tompkins, Adrienne Vittadini and Tahari.

CONTEMPORARY

Sportswear that appeals to the widest audience, with fabrics used ranging from $3–10 per yard. The look is not too trendy and the customer is not overly status conscious. She prefers value and price to paying a lot for a "designer label." This customer is usually 18 and up; the average price of a jacket is $150–225. These lines are sold mostly in department stores and sometimes in their own free-standing stores. Examples include Leon Max, Calvin Klein (not Collection), Liz Claiborne, Carole Little, Jones New York and Evan Picone.

UPPER MODERATE/LOWER BRIDGE

More fashion-forward and updated than traditional moderate. Prices are 10–20 percent higher than moderate, with fabrics in the $3–10 per yard range. The look is a bit more forward, filling the void between moderate and bridge/better for the under-40 customer. Jackets range from $100–120, with pants around $70 and skirts $68. Department stores carrying these lines are Macy's, Rich's and Bon Marche. Examples in this category are Nipon Studio, Chaus, Karen Kane, Jones New York, Pamela B and SK by Jessica Tierney.

MODERATE

Extremely price-conscious, volume sportswear. Fabrics range in price from $2–5 per yard. The "look" can range from "missy" (a mature, non-trendy customer 20 years and up) to "junior" (a trendy 15 to 35 year old). Jackets are approximately $70–100. This category is sold mostly in department stores. Examples of moderate missy are Alfred Dunner, Leslie Fay, Counterpoints, Raffaela and Norton McNaughton. Some moderate junior lines are: Necessary Objects, Rampage, Judy Knapp, Guess and Esprit.

BUDGET

Promotional merchandise, sometimes using promotional fabrics, usually polyester blends in the $1–4 per yard price range. This category covers missy and juniors. Customer ages range from 15 to 50. The look for juniors is trendy; missy is more basic. The price of a jacket ranges from $50–75 retail. This customer is strictly price conscious. Carrying this merchandise are department stores, chain stores and discount stores such as Kmart, Conway and Target. Examples of these lines are: Bauer, Body Focus, Details and Andrew Sport.

PRIVATE LABEL

Merchandise that a store manufactures itself or in collaboration with a branded manufacturer. Advantages for the store are flexibility in pricing, control over production, cost, advertising, exclusivity, in-house design and a bigger chunk of the margin. Private-label brands contribute 50 percent more initial markup than branded items. The downside is more inventory ownership, no markdown money and increased management responsibilities. Some stores, such as Saks and Barneys, work directly with factories, while others, like Ann Taylor, work through manufacturers such as Cgyne Design. Private label covers all markets from bridge to moderate and can cost 50–99 percent less than the same item from a branded label. Examples of stores with private label programs are The Limited, Saks (labels include "The Works," "Real Clothes" and "Saks Fifth Avenue Collection"), Barneys, Macy's ("International Concepts," "Morgan Taylor" and "Charter Club"), Kmart ("Jaclyn Smith") and JCPenney ("Arizona," "Worthington" and "Hunt Club").

MASS MARKET

Off-price retailers that account for approximately 10–12 percent of all women's apparel sales. These retailers offer merchandise purchased as closeouts from branded manufacturers. Sometimes they order directly from these companies. Merchandise ranges from designer to budget. Examples of these stores are: Marshall's, TJ Maxx, Annie Sez, Daffy's, Filene's Basement, Vale City, Ross Stores, TJX Cos., Dress Barn, Clothesline, Inc. and Century 21.

CUSTOMER PROFILES

Samples of five customer profiles have been included in this next section, along with a photo/collage of each of the five customer types. Identifying a customer through a visual image is an excellent way to keep focused on your customer as you design.

Executive Professional–Couture/Designer (Fig. 3.1)
Avant-Garde–Young Designer (Fig. 3.2)
Young Professional–Bridge (Fig. 3.3)
Working Woman–Moderate (Fig. 3.4)
Student–Moderate (Fig. 3.5)

Exercise

CUSTOMER IMAGES

Clip out photos of different customer types from your favorite fashion magazines. *Vogue, Bazaar, Elle* and *W* are excellent sources. Group the photos together in their suggested categories, such as student, avant-garde, young professional, moderate or couture, or create your own. Consult the Design Market Overview for examples of appropriate designers. Use the sample images included here for identifying customer type. You may want to edit the photos, using just a few, or create a collage of the customer type with many images. Each approach typifies a different style of working. Use the blank customer profile form (Fig 3.6) to help you further pinpoint your customer's identity.

Creating a customer image and biography makes her "real" and enables you to think more tangibly in terms of design. The customer profile and image become your personal design "contract" with yourself and are an effective way of keeping your designs on track and targeted to your customer.

CUSTOMER PROFILE
EXECUTIVE PROFESSIONAL—COUTURE/DESIGNER

Name:	Barbara Barry
Age:	40+
Occupation:	Anchorwoman on a major television network
Annual income:	$500,000
Education/Degree:	Yale University, B.S., M.S./Political Science
Residence/Type & Location:	Town House, Sutton Place, N.Y.C.
Marital Status:	Divorced
Spouse's Occupation:	
Children/Ages:	None
Leisure Activities:	Personal Trainer
	Fund-Raiser/Chairperson for Diffa
	Season Box at Metropolitan Opera
	On Board of Trustees of MOMA
Vacation/Travel:	Country Estate in Provence
	Flat in Chelsea, London
Favorite Designers:	St. John Knits
	Chanel
	St. Laurent
	Carolina Herrera
Favorite Stores:	Bergdorf Goodman
	Nieman Marcus
	Saks
	Chanel Boutique

Figure   3.1

Executive Professional—Couture/Designer. Collage by Dearrick Knupp.

CUSTOMER PROFILE
AVANT-GARDE—YOUNG DESIGNER

Name:	Darby Kirk
Age:	27+
Occupation:	Sells erotic Slavic art in a Soho Gallery
Annual income:	$23,000 + $80,000 Family Trust Fund
Education/Degree:	Sarah Lawrence, B.F.A./Painting, M.A./Philosophy in Eastern Culture
Residence/Type & Location:	Tribeca Co-op
Marital Status:	Single
Spouse's Occupation:	
Children/Ages:	None
Leisure Activities:	Barnes & Noble Bookstore
	Gold's Gym
	Tower Records
Vacation/Travel:	Italian Riviera in August
Favorite Designers:	Todd Oldham
	Byron Lars
	Anna Sui
	Dolce & Gabanna
Favorite Stores:	Barney's
	Charavari

Figure   3.2
Avant-garde—Young Designer. Collage by Dearrick

CUSTOMER PROFILE
YOUNG PROFESSIONAL—BRIDGE

Name:	Molly Lewis
Age:	31
Occupation:	Magazine Editor
Annual income:	$140,000 (combined)
Education/Degree:	George Washington University, B.S./Journalism
Residence/Type & Location:	Brookline, Mass.
Marital Status:	Married
Spouse's Occupation:	Architect
Children/Ages:	Kimberly/age 6
Leisure Activities:	Skiing
	Mountain Biking
	Boston Symphony
Vacation/Travel:	Summer Cottage/Cape Cod
Favorite Designers:	DKNY
	RL Ralph Lauren
	Ellen Tracy
	CK Calvin Klein
Favorite Stores:	Emporio Armani
	Nieman Marcus
	Bloomingdale's

Figure   3.3
Young Professional—Bridge. Collage by Dearrick Knupp.

CUSTOMER PROFILE
WORKING WOMAN—MODERATE

Name:	Marci Breen
Age:	30+
Occupation:	Day Care Center Assistant
Annual income:	$55,000 (combined)
Education/Degree:	A.A.S. degree, Queens College
Residence/Type & Location:	2-family home, Bayside, NY
Marital Status:	Married
Spouse's Occupation:	Plant Manager, B.S./ Liberal Arts
Children/Ages:	Jennifer 10, Jason 8, and Jonathan 4 $\frac{1}{2}$
Leisure Activities:	Shopping at the mall
	Hockey/Ranger games
	Gardening
Vacation/Travel:	Summer Bungalow in the Pocanos
	Visiting Family in Albuquerque
Favorite Designers:	Express
	Chaus
	Jennifer Moore/Macy*s
	Jones New York
Favorite Stores:	Macy*s
	Old Navy
	Annie Sez/Daffy's

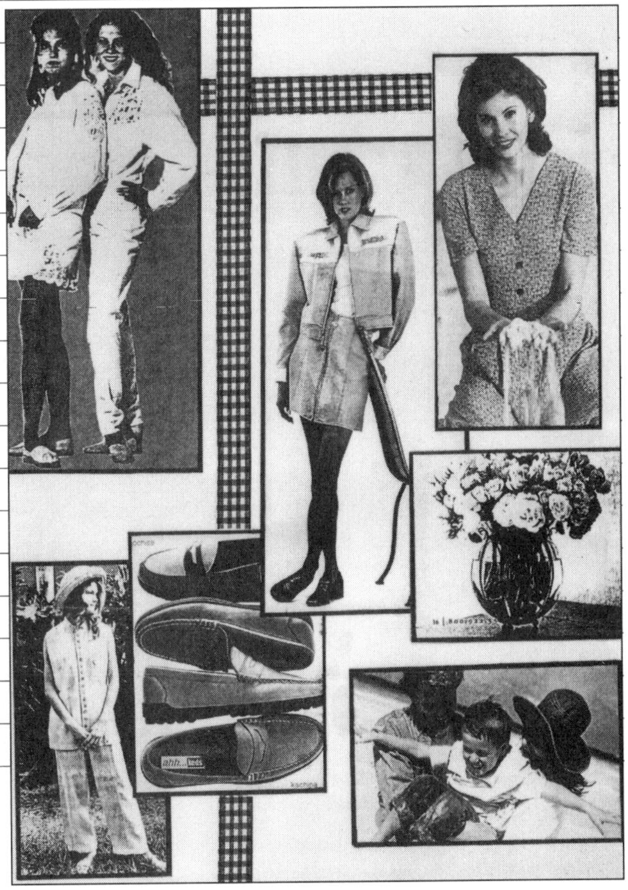

Figure   3.4
Working Woman—Moderate. Collage by Dearrick Knupp.

CUSTOMER PROFILE
STUDENT—MODERATE

Name:	Sarah Gilbert
Age:	19
Occupation:	Student
Annual income:	Family assisted tuition $16,000 room & board, Work Study $5.00 per hour
Education/Degree:	University of Wisconsin, Madison
Residence/Type & Location:	Family residence: Cleveland, Ohio, On-campus dorm
Marital Status:	Single
Spouse's Occupation:	
Children/Ages:	None
Leisure Activities:	Co-ed Volleyball Team
	Shopping
	Hanging out with friends
	Football games
Vacation/Travel:	Florida during Spring Break
Favorite Designers:	Brand Names:
	Levi Strauss
	Gitano
	Guess Jeans
Favorite Stores:	Victoria's Secret
	Express
	Gap

Figure   3.5

Student—Moderate. Collage by Dearrick Knupp.

CUSTOMER PROFILE

Name:

Age:

Occupation:

Annual income:

Education/Degree:

Residence/Type & Location:

Marital Status:

Spouse's Occupation:

Children/Ages:

Leisure Activities:

Vacation/Travel:

Favorite Designers:

Favorite Stores:

CHAPTER 4

Most of us want to put our best foot forward when we interview for a job. One way to do this is by choosing a presentation format that will communicate our strengths while minimizing our weaknesses.

Organization and Contents

Presentation format by Hong Tan.

Most aspiring designers think of their portfolio, or "book," one-dimensionally, as a collection of design sketches accompanied by a variety of other spreads—mood/fabric formats, flats, etc. However, there is a great variety of portfolio presentation formats available to best show your work's scope and your skills as a designer. While these other formats do not replace the traditional portfolio, you may want to consider some of them to supplement your primary book.

This chapter will outline several presentation formats and discuss their roles in the interviewing process. Most of us want to put our best foot forward when we interview for a job. One way to do this is by communicating our strengths and minimizing our weaknesses. Choosing a format presentation or presentations that express your creativity and abilities is a good way to start.

This chapter will concentrate primarily on the traditional components of the fashion design portfolio, since the skills demonstrated in it are essential to initial job placement. We'll look at specially targeted presentations at the end of the chapter.

TRADITIONAL FASHION PORTFOLIO

The entry-level portfolio should consist of a variety of formats to demonstrate design and rendering skills. All that you have learned through your education, exposure and practice should be evident here. Your interviewer will be looking for drawing ability, creativity and imagination, individuality/style and an awareness of trends. These are the criteria you will be measured by, so include only your very best work. This is not to say this portfolio should be ordinary. On the contrary, whatever presentation format you choose should express who you are creatively. The traditional fashion portfolio might contain the following formats:

- Introductory page
- Four to six fashion-group formats with mood/fabric page
- Flats
- Awards/photos, press, etc.
- Fold-out presentations
- Board presentation reproductions
- Croquis sketchbook

Before deciding on which pieces you want to include in your portfolio, you will want to consider several things. To achieve a unified body of work you will need to objectively edit out irrelevant pieces that might confuse the focus. As said before, only your very best goes into the portfolio—that is, the very best pieces selected from a larger body of work. Sometimes you might have to rework pieces or make adjustments in order to meet professional standards. Initially this may seem like a lot of work, but it will pay off in the long run. This is your opportunity to show your talents and skills and apply all you have learned thus far. Neatness counts! Originality counts! Creativity counts! An important rule in evolving your portfolio is that there are no hard and fast rules. Commitment and desire is what it takes to make it happen!

WHAT TO INCLUDE

Ideally, the traditional portfolio consists of four to six concepts or themes that are related to a whole collection. The number of designs, as well as pages included for each concept, should vary. A portfolio using identical formats with the same number of designs and pages is monotonous and lacks creativity and excitement.

Some sections might consist of as little as two pages or as many as eight, depending on the design market you are targeting. For example, in the sportswear market, it is essential to show how pieces coordinate with one another. To do this effectively you need to show the various combination possibilities, which would necessitate a larger spread in the portfolio. Because flats are extremely important in the sportswear market, they often accompany the more glamorous illustrated designs on a figure to illustrate technical construction and accurate drawing ability. Including flats with figure-design presentations expands the size of a design concept. Flats can either be shown as part of a concept or can stand on their own.

Few designers can show their talent and skills with 10 or fewer pieces. On the other hand, showing too many pieces (more than 25) can give a creatively weak impression, show a lack of editing ability and be repetitive. Industry professionals have tight schedules. Presenting too many samples infringes on their time and may give the impression you do not know how to prioritize your work. The reviewer might also lose confidence in your ability to stay focused. Presenting a large number of pieces with the idea that your reviewer will respond to what he likes can jeopardize a valuable interview. The more focused candidate will clearly stand out to a prospective employer who has already looked at dozens of portfolios.

Aim for eight to ten concepts that can be rotated in and out of your portfolio according to the interview focus and target market. The more concepts you have to choose from, the better you will be able to customize your portfolio for each interview. (Review Chapter 3 for a breakdown of customer types and their respective markets.) If you are interviewing in more than one market or design category, you will need a separate portfolio for each, i.e., children's wear or sportswear. Four to six concepts are the standard for a single interview. Be prepared to replace pieces that did not receive a positive reaction. As you continue to interview, you may become aware of gaps in your work or areas you did not cover. Take time to work up replacements or additions, keeping your portfolio flexible and adjusting it to each interview. Remember, your portfolio is only as strong as your weakest piece. And no excuses or apologies can make either you or the reviewer feel good about it!

FOCUS AND UNITY

A cohesive portfolio consists of a unified body of work targeting a particular market and customer and showing a range of design seasons. In addition, each concept in the collection should feature clothing in one price range, for one season, targeted to a specific group of consumers. A knowledgeable professional is able to maintain this focus. Those new to the job search discover how important this is to employers along the way. Chapter 3 discusses customer focus in depth and suggests methods for creating focus before finalizing your presentations.

A frequent mistake in presenting a portfolio is the inclusion of irrelevant pieces. Focus and unity are the hallmarks of an effective fashion design portfolio. All personal work, such as life drawings, non-fashion photographs, sculpture, illustrations, cartoons, etc., should be eliminated. Even though these pieces may have strong merit on their own, they differ from fashion design and may dilute the impact of your presentation.

The point of a portfolio is to show intent. The fine art world is an important, unending source of inspiration to the fashion designer and is deeply rooted in the history of fashion. Yet there is a fundamental difference between fashion and fine art. The artist identifies a problem and seeks a personal visual solution. Fashion designers, working alone or in a team, resolve design solutions for a design house. They create ideas for apparel, either on paper or dimensionally, which target a "look," market and audience. They are hired to create designs that are wearable, salable and appropriate to their customer—not to make clothes that solely express the designer's own personal fantasy.

However, those with strong skills in photography, textile surface design and graphic design can integrate these skills into the fashion design portfolio, which can help show off your versatility and present a more unique product. Selecting beautiful photographs for your mood pages or personally photographing a select group of designs demonstrates your ability in this area. Showing original textile renderings with your design pages also enriches a presentation. Many designers today design and recolor textiles.

Showcase your graphic design ability in your approach to the layout and design of each page. Imaginative lettering choices, background papers and figure arrangements will express graphic skills and creativity. Even covering a traditional portfolio with a unique fabric and tying it into your presentation demonstrates artistry.

HIGHLIGHTING SPECIAL SKILLS

Sometimes, designers prefer to highlight their special skills in a separate portfolio or journal. Although the same standards of quality apply, the samples do not have to relate to the portfolio itself and can stand on their own. Evaluating what skills will best showcase your talent and ability will help determine if multi-portfolio presentations are for you. Different types of fashion portfolios are discussed and outlined at the end of this chapter.

Use an auxiliary portfolio to demonstrate a special skill or to highlight a large number of press clippings or photographs. Make a clear distinction to delineate the two portfolios. Use separate cases and presentation mountings, or a single case with an insert. In the latter, make certain there is a distinct visual difference between the two. Achieve this with size and color or perhaps smaller inserts. Multiple presentations are more commonly used by experienced designers as they accumulate printed samples of their work. Those just entering the market might have one or two awards or published pieces worthy of inclusion that would not necessitate a second portfolio. Instead, place these pieces strategically within the portfolio to invite a dialogue with the reviewer.

In an interview, show the fashion design portfolio first, followed by a second portfolio, if permitted. Reviewers are extremely busy people with limited time; being considerate of this shows awareness and sensitivity. Present a second portfolio only if you feel it will be an enhancement. A lesser-quality second portfolio can jeopardize your chance of landing the job you want.

In addition to your targeted portfolio, you may have "fantasy" designs you might be thinking of including. Showcase these in a separate presentation format or portfolio to make a distinction between the two. All too often, beginners integrate their designs and confuse the issue. Separating your fantasy designs from the others demonstrates your savvy in distinguishing the two. Interviewers tend to be put off by fantasy samples because they often see them as unrealistic and unadaptable to the commercial world. However, if those designs are what you truly believe in, don't give up. Instead, create a presentation that will communicate the personal significance of these designs.

SIZE

Most professional designers prefer a portfolio size that is convenient and practical. For interviewing purposes, you need a portfolio that is comfortable to carry and will fit easily on a desk without disrupting the contents. For this reason, sizes larger than 14″ × 17″ are difficult to handle and too large in proportion to the design sketch. Recommended sizes are 9″ × 12″, 11″ × 14″ (most popular) and 14″ × 17″.

Some designers prefer to have a portfolio made to their own specifications and will customize the page sizes to suit the case. But this is the exception rather than the rule, especially for those beginning their fashion design careers. Remember, the portfolio's contents are more important than the case.

As you gain design experience, you will accumulate printed pieces and press clippings that can be organized in a separate portfolio. Some professionals take several different portfolios to an interview (a good rationale for preferring the smaller sizes). Presentation size is both a practical and personal choice that should be determined by each individual's skills and need for creative expression.

VARIETY

Creativity can be demonstrated by your design skills and through your ability to vary presentations in your portfolio. (This will be discussed in more depth in Chapter 5.) However, apart from size, orientation and quantity of pieces, several factors can make for a more interesting and varied presentation:

- Fabric type/color
- Figure number, size and composition
- Techniques: i.e., marker, pencil, film transfer, watercolor
- Number of pages per concept
- Designs on the flat vs. figures
- Varied presentation formats: i.e., boards, flats, figures, fold-outs

FLOW

Determine the sequence of your groupings within the portfolio once your work is edited. Each interview will require specific groups from your "pool" of work. Knowing this will help you order your presentation. You might ask yourself, "What is most logical, most impressive or most unusual? Which groups will leave a positive, lasting impression? Which pieces will I be remembered by? Which groups represent what I do best?"

The flow of the groups within the portfolio is sometimes compared to a musical score. As with music, your portfolio can unfold dramatically in several ways, illustrated in the following diagrams:

DRAMATIC START/FINISH SEQUENCE

Beginning with a dramatic opening, the portfolio continues to evolve, ending in a powerful conclusion (Fig. 4.1a). With this sequence, first and last impressions count for a lot. But be sure the middle groupings continue to build and heighten to a strong and dramatic ending. Otherwise, the presentation can feel uneventful and bland.

DRAMATIC START/MIDDLE/FINISH SEQUENCE

This sequence utilizes your three strongest groups, placing one at the beginning, one in the middle and one at the end of your presentation (Fig. 4.1b). Make a strong initial impression, reinforce that impression, then conclude with a strong finish. This is an effective presentation strategy even if the reviewer chooses to thumb through the portfolio from back to front. Each of the three key groups should be significant in their own right. Competition or award-winning pieces are good choices as they naturally evoke prolonged discussion.

KNOCK-THEIR-SOCKS-OFF SEQUENCE

This approach begins the presentation with three of your very best groups (Fig. 4.1c). The reviewer is bombarded in quick succession with these powerful pieces and is immediately won over. The remainder of the portfolio is quickly examined, ending with a visually dramatic group, which reinforces the book's early strength.

As you interview, you will become aware of your best and weakest groupings. Remove the "weak links," since this work leaves an uneven and inconsistent presentation and, consequently, a poor impression. The most important pieces in any portfolio sequence are the first and last. Test the impact of these "key" pieces on several reviewers before finalizing the sequence of your portfolio. Instructors and placement counselors can give you valuable feedback even before the interview process

Figure   4.1a, b and c

Flow and sequence options.

Flow/sequence illustration by Geoffry Gertz.

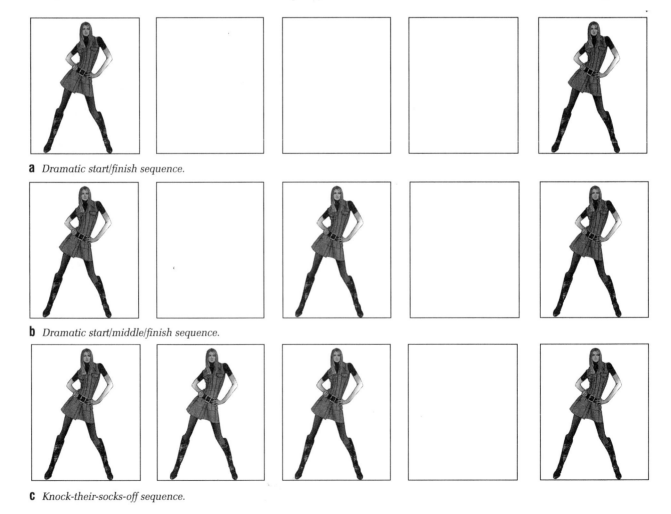

a *Dramatic start/finish sequence.*

b *Dramatic start/middle/finish sequence.*

c *Knock-their-socks-off sequence.*

begins. Never show anything you need to apologize for. Excuses belittle the listener and degrade the teller. Remember that your portfolio represents you, and you should include only your best work.

Once a reviewer has seen your portfolio, it often remains open to the last pages as you chat during the interview. A visually strong piece will continue to attract the eye, reinforcing your strengths and skills. This spread can make a lasting impression and should be representative of your unique design ability and style.

INTRO PAGE

While many presentation formats begin with a blank page, it is more effective to create an introductory page that says something unique about you. A personal logo incorporating your name with a graphic image is one practical option, as the logo can be repeated in your letterhead or business card (Fig. 4.2a). Using a specific garment as part of the design is not recommended, as it will date itself quickly. Sometimes a particular design category can inspire the graphic. In this example (Fig. 4.2b), the outdoor/sailing theme identifies the targeted area of design. Cultural references or symbols are other options that lend a more personal, less generic feeling. Those gifted in calligraphy have an additional means of creating a personal image. The next example (Fig. 4.2c) utilizes a bold Chinese calligraphy character representing the designer's name to dramatically introduce the portfolio.

CONTENTS

Figure   4.2a
Using a personal logo incorporating your name with a graphic image is a practical option for your intro page. The logo can also be repeated in a letterhead or business card.

Intro page and business card by Yukie Takizawa.

YUKIE TAKIZAWA

Figure   4.2b
This example using an outdoor/sailing theme identifies the targeted area of design.

Intro page by Heather De Natale.

Figure   4.2c

Incorporating your cultural background and experience can add a unique and personal touch. This example utilizes a bold Chinese calligraphy character, representing the designer's name, to dramatically introduce the portfolio.

Intro page by Nancy Chen.

Figure   4.3

The intro page can serve a dual purpose: by reducing it to 8 ½″ × 11″ you can convert it to a leave-behind piece—a visual memento of your interview.

Leave-behind piece by Kris Brescoll.

Placement: The intro page is the first, right-hand page in a vertical presentation, turning the portfolio as you would a book. In a horizontal presentation the intro page is the first singular page used in a "flip format." Refer to Chapter 5 for a more detailed discussion of orientation.

LEAVE-BEHIND PIECE

The intro page can serve a dual purpose. By reducing it to 8 ½″ × 11″ you've converted it to a leave-behind piece—a visual memory of your interview (Fig. 4.3). This is relatively inexpensive, even for color copies, and well worth the second interview possibilities it might initiate. Keep copies in the side pocket of your portfolio along with your resumé.

MOOD/THEME/CONCEPT

The purpose of this page, often referred to as either the mood, theme or concept page, is to "tell your design story" (Fig. 4.4). Designers mainly use a variety of photographic images to accomplish this, although anything that sparks the designer's creativity and imagination is appropriate inspirational material. Research photos, both historical and current, may be used to show the designer's creative process. These can vary according to how literally the designer wishes to express the "mood." Fabric/color swatches are often included with the research and tied into the overall color story of the photos, indicating both color sensitivity and coordination ability. An image of the customer is also frequently included to show the customer "type" and targeted market.

Placement: Mood pages are generally placed before design spreads to introduce the group.

FABRIC/COLOR

Design groups should be accompanied by appropriate fabric/color stories (Fig. 4.5). Most job descriptions in fashion design mention the need for applicants with "excellent color sense," the ability to "create colorways," "check lab dips" and "recolor prints." Your choice of fabrics and colors demonstrate how you meet those requirements. (The textile section of the glossary in the back of this text defines these frequently used terms.) An ability to design screen prints or graphics for your clothing is also a big plus in certain markets.

Because of their inherent importance in design, fabrics should be highlighted and arranged accordingly throughout the portfolio. Develop a separate fabric/color page if you do not plan to include swatches with your mood page. Some designers prefer to show their fabric/color story separately, especially if it is extensive and involves different fabric types and trims. A professional fabric page will include findings, i.e., specific trims, passementarie, buttons, ribbon, special closures, zippers, even samples of small garment details constructed in fabric or muslin.

Occasionally, designers prefer to include a drawing of their own trim design. Professionals often like to show an inspirational reference along with their drawing. Without a reference, original samples tend to have a "made up" quality and lack professionalism. Fabric stories can be accompanied by a descriptive picture, if it makes an obvious connection and does not overwhelm the fabrics.

Although every effort should be made to include luxurious, high-quality fabric samples, sometimes you may not be able to find the fabrics or colors you want. Substituting paper renderings or recoloring a print in the colors you need is a better solution in these cases than using mismatched fabric swatches. A local paint store is a good source for samples if you are doing a group of solids and do not have the actual fabric. Use their wallpaper department in a similar way for a variety of print samples. When featuring prints, show larger swatches so the repeat is sufficiently visible. Additionally, for certain price points, it is essential to show colorways (the same item of clothing in different colors). This might involve three to five samples of a print, as well as coordinating solids.

The fabric/color page is often labeled or titled, with the theme and season indicated. Avoid specific dates, such as "Spring 1998," or the piece will date quickly. Professional designers use letra-set or computer generated type for all lettering purposes, which also might include indicating fabric type and content. Both actual fabric and hand-painted swatches should be cut neatly and uniformly. To prevent fraying, many designers use a "pinked" edge and also cut paper swatches in this manner to create a fabric look-alike quality.

Some designers prefer to show their fabrics on top of acetate sleeves so they can be handled during the interview process. For fabric display, place an acetate fold-over insert into the sleeve so fabrics can be touched. Avoid taping fabrics directly to the sleeve to prevent fraying. Instead, mount fabrics on a sturdy paper or light board and position them on the acetate sleeve with Velcro® dots. Fabrics can then easily be removed or changed to accommodate different presentations.

Professional designers do extensive fabric/color research for a specific season months before they begin to work on their collection. Much of this research is done at various fabric forecast services,

Figure 4.4

The mood, theme or concept page "tells your design story."
Mood page by Hong Tan.

Figure 4.5

Design groups should be accompanied by appropriate fabric/ color stories. Your choice of fabrics and colors demonstrates creative ability and color sense—important requisites in the job market.
Fabric/color page by Hong Tan.

Figure 4.6

Designers may purchase forecast books for researching fabric/color.

Forecast books courtesy of Cotton Incorporated.

which specialize in both style trends and color (Fig. 4.6). Fabric shows, both European and American, are frequented by designers who wish to identify trends and purchase goods well in advance of their design season. A list of forecast services, fiber councils and libraries and fabric/color shows is included in Appendix A, Fashion Information Resources.

Placement: The fabric/color page generally follows the mood page of any design group. In any case, the fabric/color page precedes the design group with or without a mood page. Fabric/color pages should not be shown solo unless accompanied by designs on the figure or flat. To do so is like serving an appetizer without the main course.

FIGURE DESIGN SPREADS

These spreads appear in most traditional portfolios, as it is easier to see the proportion of a design on the figure than in a flat sketch (Fig. 4.7). Although some markets prefer flat sketches, most value the ability to see the design in relationship to the body, as this explains the design proportion. These spreads also communicate the "look" the designer wishes to convey. The pose or attitude can contribute greatly to this effect. Chapter 5 discusses both page orientation and a variety of figure composition options.

Figure 4.7

Figure design spreads communicate the "look" and proportion the designer wishes to convey.

Figure design spread by Hong Tan.

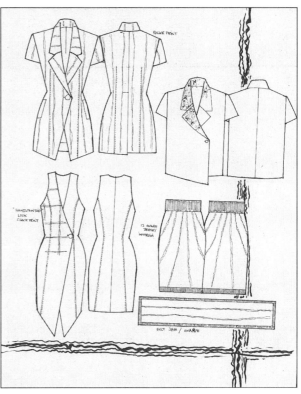

Figure 4.8

The ability to render technical flat sketches accurately is one of the most important skills considered in job placement.

Flat sketches by Hong Tan.

Placement: Figure design spreads can be placed throughout the portfolio, but usually follow a mood page and/or fabric/color page.

FLATS/SPECS

The ability to render technical sketches accurately is one of the most important skills any beginning designer brings to a job, and all portfolios should demonstrate this ability (Fig. 4.8). Many moderate, contemporary and better markets work almost exclusively with flat drawings for production purposes. Flat drawings, which are discussed in Chapter 6, also play a big part in product development programs. Most designers do not show a portfolio composed exclusively of flat sketches, as it is unnecessary and repetitive. However, a good command of flat sketching techniques can almost ensure job placement. Most fashion companies use flats for a variety of purposes, ranging from designing to selling their product.

Flats should be done on separate pages from your figures. Place backviews on the same page as figures only if the back of the garment is very important and it would be impossible to understand the design without it.

Judge flats as if you had to make patterns from them. Employers request a knowledge of patternmaking and garment construction even if it is not part of the job, feeling the applicant will be able to do production sketches with greater accuracy and speed. An employer might even ask you to draw flats on-the-spot, as part of your job interview, to test your speed and skill.

Figure   4.9
Flat spreads are often placed in the portfolio to correspond to figure design spreads. This is especially valuable in sportswear design, where it is necessary to see detail and coordinated pieces.

Flat spread and figure design spread by Hong Tan.

Training yourself to do good flats takes practice and a few simple tools. Use a ruler, french curve and fine-line markers for professional results. Several techniques for executing flats are discussed in Chapter 6.

Placement: Two design groups in the portfolio should include flats. It is not necessary to do flats for every group. Flat pages are often placed to correspond to figure design spreads (Fig. 4.9), or can be spreads unto themselves. This is especially valuable in sportswear design, where detail and coordinated pieces should be easily seen.

You may want to include samples of spec sheets, with accurate measurements, to demonstrate your technical ability. Especially effective is transposing a design taken from a figure or flat spread onto a spec sheet. Place the spec sheet after the spread, at the end of the group.

FOLD-OUT PRESENTATIONS

A designer often chooses the fold-out format to present a special project that is independent of the portfolio and, as such, does not have to conform to it in any way (Fig. 4.10). This format is also used when an employer is interested in an applicant and needs further proof of his or her ability to design in the mode of that company. Chapter 5 details this approach.

Placement: Being separate and portable, the fold-out presentation can be shown at the discretion of the designer during the interview process. It

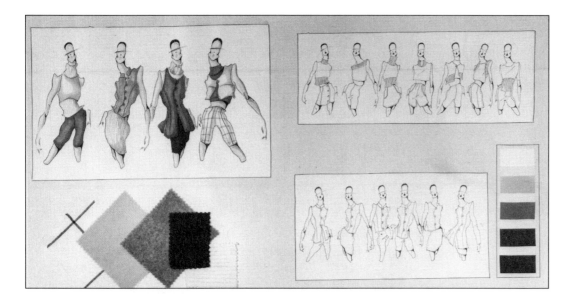

Figure 4.10

The designer often chooses a fold-out format to present a special project that is independent of the portfolio. Or, a prospective employer may ask an applicant to create one, as further proof of his or her ability to design in the mode of that company.

Fold-out presentation by Ashish Batra.

can be easily retrieved from the back of the portfolio or its pocket and introduced to spark a dialogue with the reviewer. If your portfolio doesn't seem to have the "look" the reviewer is after, your fold-out format may be just the thing.

Beginners are often hesitant to show formats they may have done for other design firms. But because these were done for a "real" company and are thus most current, they are most likely your best work. Telling who you did the design group for is further proof you are aware of their market.

SALON BOOK

Most apparel companies produce a salon book in some form or another (Fig. 4.11a and b). This is essentially a catalog and contains the styles offered by the company for the current season. Garments are either photographed or sketched. Fabric and colorways are included along with the wholesale price of the garment. Often, inspirational visuals are included to explain the theme or style direction. These books are created for buyers, as well as customers, so they can review the line. When the line is taken on the road, the salon book can be used to generate orders in the absence of the actual clothes.

Keep the salon book in a side pocket of your portfolio and take it out for review. Creating a salon book incorporates not only drawing and rendering skills, but layout and packaging, as well. It is a unique way of showing your versatility as a designer.

MAILER

When apparel companies wish to announce the viewing dates of their collection, they often send out mailers to important buyers and customers (Fig. 4.12). These can be as simple as a card or as complex as a

MISCELLANEOUS PRESENTATIONS

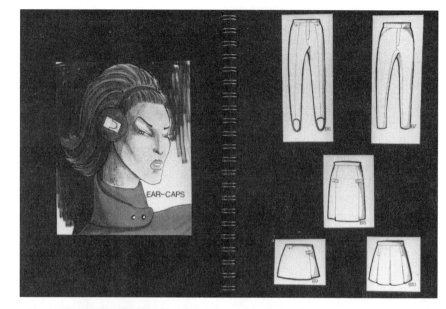

Figure 4.11a and b
The salon book is produced by most companies, either in the form of photographs or sketches. It is essentially a catalog containing the styles, colors/fabrics and wholesale prices of the garments offered for the current season.

Salon book by Karl Aberg.

mini-catalog. The mailer could feature a single photograph of a style representative of the collection or a sampling or portion of the line. The graphics of this piece are very important. Color, unusual paper, dynamic art and interesting packaging intrigue the customer.

Like the salon book, make the mailer easily accessible for viewing. Part of the excitement of this product is the element of surprise it generates upon opening it.

CROQUIS SKETCHBOOK

The fashion sketchbook, or journal, is a great supplement to the portfolio (Fig. 4.13). As a documentary of your thinking process, it demonstrates quick drawing skills and color/fabric sensitivity. It can include accessory ideas, makeup and hairstyles (generally the model's look for the collection). After reviewing a portfolio, most reviewers will ask to see a croquis book because it shows your ability to generate and communicate ideas quickly. The sketches often are not perfectly drawn, nor need they be to get a concept across. This sketching technique is essential to a variety of areas within a fashion house and is considered a "must" by employers.

Figure   4.12
Mailers are sent to buyers and customers to announce the viewing dates of a collection. This creative example, constructed with acetate overlays, features a sampling of the collection and the mailing envelope. Intriguing graphics are important in the design of these pieces.

Mailer by Yukie Takizawa.

Placement: Place the croquis book in the back of your portfolio case for easy access. Some designers carry them in attaché cases or backpacks. Or insert the croquis book into the portfolio binder and work it into the portfolio presentation for variation.

PHOTOGRAPHIC FASHION PORTFOLIO

This presentation format can be used to highlight strong technical skills in garment construction (Fig. 4.14a, b, c and d). Those who need to compensate for weak sketching ability might consider this format. You can use photographic design spreads to supplement your traditional portfolio, or you can set up your entire portfolio in this way.

There is a downside, however. This format can be expensive since it involves the cost of a photographer, model, film and developing. However, several students can share these costs and model their own garments, as was done in the accompanying example.

SPECIAL PRESENTATIONS

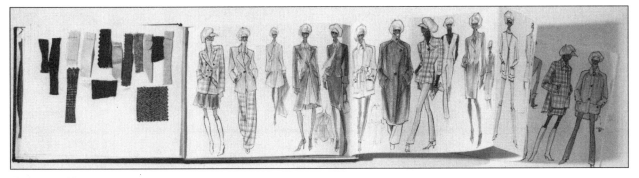

Figure   4.13
The croquis sketchbook, or journal, documents your thinking process and demonstrates quick drawing skills and color/fabric sensitivity.

Croquis sketchbook by Renaldo Barnette.

Essence of Siam
Awarded Outstanding Sportswear Collection 1994. Right, tassel- trimmed mandarin-collar vest with frog closure and slim pant, polyester/rayon. Following pages, left, silk/linen suit with lapped seam detail and frog closures with wrapped skirt. Right, button-front blouse over gilet with lapped-seam detail and frog closure, pant with lapped-seam detail.
Mystic Earth
Landscape Mosaic

Figure 4.14a, b, c and d

The photographic fashion portfolio format can be used to highlight strong technical skills in garment construction. It may either be used to supplement the traditional portfolio, or your entire portfolio can be set up this way. It is an especially viable option for those whose technical skills outweigh their sketching abilities.

Photographic fashion portfolio by Donna M. Parker.

Through computer technology, photographs can be scanned and manipulated to achieve special graphic effects, as well as page design. This sets your presentation apart and shows a creative flair. (See Chapter 8 for further discussion of the computer's role as a design tool.)

If you decide to use the photographic format exclusively, keep in mind you will not be demonstrating your sketching ability as a design applicant. This could hurt your position, as excellent drawing skills have a high priority with interviewers and are important for various phases of the design process. Be advised this format should be used only if your sketching ability will not speak for your skills and talents.

The photographic portfolio may contain the following formats:

- Introductory page
- Photographic design spreads with mood/fabric page
- Awards/press, etc.

PRESS/PRINT PORTFOLIO

This format is used mostly by professionals with years of design experience (Fig. 4.15). The press/print portfolio may feature work from one or several design positions and can be used in any design category. If the designer has worked for several firms, the portfolio is divided accordingly, with a section devoted to and featuring each company. Designers at this level have a track record and a reputation within the industry. Portfolio expectations are different at this level, because these designers have already proven themselves. The press/print portfolio documents the designer's career from season to season. This format may accompany the traditional design portfolio or stand alone.

The press/print portfolio may contain some or all of the following formats:

- Press clippings
- Store ads

Figure 4.15

A press/print portfolio is used mostly by professionals with years of design experience. It may feature work from one or several design positions and can be divided accordingly.

Press/print portfolio by Jennifer Elk.

- Magazine articles/editorials
- Salon books
- Mailers/catalogs

SPECIALTY PORTFOLIO

This presentation format can be an excellent supplement to the traditional portfolio because it allows the designer to feature a unique specialty (Fig. 4.16a and b). For example, a sportswear designer may have knowledge of knitwear technology and might like to create new yarn combinations as a hobby. Formatted in an attractive presentation, this makes a great addition to the traditional portfolio, since it highlights a special skill. Artistry and creativity can also be demonstrated in the unique way you invent your supplement. In the accompanying example, the color story is shown with yarns and color-coordinated visuals to the left of the spread. The facing page imaginatively shows the knit pattern in the color story, seen through a die-cut in the shape of a figure.

Other specialty portfolios might include the following:

- Knitting swatches
- Hand-painted textiles

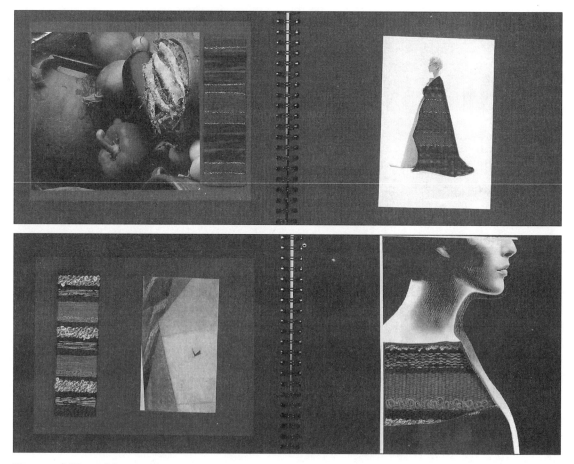

Figure   4.16a and b
The specialty portfolio allows the designer to highlight a unique skill or specialty. This example demonstrates artistry and creativity in the presentation of knit samples seen through a figure-shaped die-cut. The color story is shown with yarns and color-coordinated visuals to the left of the spread.

Specialty portfolio by Gisele Ferrari.

- Beadwork
- Embroidery designs
- Weaving samples
- Accessory designs

The specialty portfolio holds unlimited possibilities for showcasing your individual qualities as a designer. This type of portfolio can help you stand out from other applicants and get you the job.

The portfolio you use for a serious job search should not be a collection of all the work you have ever done. Only your best will do. Everyone has pieces that hold sentimental value or earned them a high grade in a course. However, these may not work with the other pieces you wish to include and could appear disjointed or out of place in the context of the portfolio as a whole.

PORTFOLIO EVALUATION

DO'S & DON'TS FOR SELECTING ILLUSTRATIONS

Do choose a definite orientation for viewing the portfolio (vertical or horizontal).

Do use a practical portfolio size for presentation (usually 11" × 14" or 14" × 17").

Do include only your best work.

Do begin and end with your most dramatic pieces.

Do include fabric swatches in your presentations to show appropriate fabric use and color sensitivity.

Do target each group in the portfolio for one market, one season and one group of customers.

Do research the company you are interviewing with to familiarize yourself with their look, customer and price range.

Do rotate your design groups to customize each interview.

Do show your versatility by highlighting additional skills in your presentations.

Do present a "second" portfolio if it demonstrates additional skills or professional accomplishments.

Do make a visual distinction between portfolios.

Don't overwhelm the viewer with too many groups (four to six concepts per collection is sufficient).

Don't include pieces that have not received rave reviews from several interviewers.

Don't include irrelevant pieces that may alter the focus.

Don't go off on design tangents unless you plan on showing your "fantasy" clothes in a separate portfolio.

Don't finalize your portfolio without feedback from a professional "eye."

Don't use isolated mood/fabric pages without design pages to support them.

Don't label pages with specific dates, such as "Spring 1998."

Don't use hand-lettering unless your calligraphy is flawless.

Deciding what to include can be a tough job, as it is difficult to be objective about your own work. For this reason, it is a bit risky to go it alone without the input of a seasoned editor. Ask your fashion design professor or a design professional for constructive feedback. Their high standards and critical eye could make a measurable difference in your portfolio presentation. Plan for critiques to run one-half to one hour.

Bring all potential portfolio pieces with you for the critique. Be prepared to identify your design market and goals. If you are preparing for a specific interview, make it known so your evaluator knows how best to guide you. Organize your pieces into design categories and presentation types so they may be viewed at the same time. Your best work will be more apparent when compared in this way. This method is more efficient than showing a portfolio that you have already edited, and saves the reviewer the time of going back and forth between unrelated pieces.

Include pieces in all design areas in which you are interested. To round out a presentation, include a variety of work, such as award and published pieces, presentation boards, flats and specs, fold-out presentations and croquis sketchbooks. Although original sketches are preferred for interviewing, some designers have transparencies or slides they wish to include. Determine their relevancy and content with the help of your evaluator.

Write down your evaluators' comments and suggestions. The evaluation form provided at the end of this chapter will help you remember relevant comments about potential portfolio pieces. Copy this form and reuse it with the addition of new pieces for each interview. Or, you may want to devise your own system for evaluation. Relying on your memory can prove undependable if you want to retain the critical points of the evaluation.

The portfolio evaluation will reveal your strengths and weaknesses. It will certainly enlighten you as to what you have, where you stand and what you need to do to create your ultimate portfolio. Your work will fall into four distinct groups. Group One will contain pieces that are ready to show or need slight refinements. Group Two will consist of strong concept pieces that require reworking to make them portfolio-ready. Group Three will be discards. Group Four might consist of additional design concepts and supporting work that is needed to fill in gaps and strengthen areas of the portfolio.

Each portfolio has individual strengths that set it apart from another. Although spreads can be rotated to target a company and market, each designer learns to focus and feature the skills at which he excels. A keen awareness of your strengths can expedite your job search. Renewed direction creates excitement and momentum.

EVALUATION FORM

This sample evaluation form is formatted to cover the most important points in the process. Since no one has total recall, refer to this while you are in the process of readjusting and reworking your portfolio. Whether you choose to use this form or create your own, do use some type of checklist during the critique process. Sensitive people sometimes reject criticism of their own work. An evaluation form helps you deal with criticism in a constructive and memorable way.

The bottom portion of the form serves as a checklist in preparation for the actual interview.

PORTFOLIO EVALUATION FORM

Description	# of Pieces	Rework	Complete	Comments & Revisions
1.				
2.				
3.				
4.				
5.				
6.				
7.				
8.				
9.				
10.				
11.				
12.				
13.				
14.				
15.				
16.				
17.				
18.				
19.				
20.				

Portfolio Contents Checklist

❏ **Portfolio Case I**

❏ **Portfolio Case II**

❏ **Croquis Book**

❏ **Resumé**

❏ **Leave-behind Piece**

Figure 4.17
Sample Portfolio Evaluation Form.

CHAPTER 5

The format includes the shape, size, binding, orientation, layout, number of pages and general makeup or arrangement of a portfolio. The method of presentation you choose is limited only by your personal preferences, special skills and the focus of your interview audiences.

Presentation Formats

CFDA 1996 Scholarship Design Competition
portfolio by Peter Som.

The format includes the shape, size, binding, orientation, layout, number of pages and general makeup or arrangement of a portfolio. The method of presentation you choose is limited only by your personal preferences, special skills and the focus of your interview audiences. Before deciding what kind of presentation formats are best for you, consider the body of work you wish to include. For example, if you are interviewing in the sportswear market, you will need four to six design concepts or themes illustrating your ability to design coordinated separates. By contrast, bridal and eveningwear markets tend toward one-of-a-kind design thinking. But since most design markets develop design concepts in groups, designers prefer this format. So, choosing a portfolio or page format ultimately depends on your design category and portfolio focus.

If you are creating a portfolio with existing pieces, maintain consistency with the format you choose. However, if you decide to take a brave approach by scrapping your old work and starting anew, you have the opportunity to create a portfolio that will speak of your personal design vision. Either way, use creativity and imagination. Think about how you want to present yourself to the design community and what you want your portfolio to say about you, both as a designer and a potential employee.

Be both practical and creative when compiling your book. There is no single formula or approach, as each individual's needs and skills vary. There are, however, standard elements to consider.

GETTING STARTED

Although most fashion design programs work toward the completion of a portfolio, the best time to actively create and assemble your book is in your last semester. By this time you've honed your skills and fine-tuned your focus. You have acquired both technical skills and fashion awareness that you are now able to demonstrate. You have been incubating, waiting for everything to fall into place. Now it's time for you to take control and create a product uniquely your own.

Professionals are quick to recognize a "school," or novice, portfolio. Students often make the mistake of including work from different levels of study which, when thrown together in a portfolio, creates an uneven impression and raises doubts about the designer's ability to focus and prioritize. It stands to reason that most people generally improve and reach their greatest potential upon the completion of a program. Projects that looked good to you in prior semesters may not meet your current standards. Consequently, this may mean editing out some of your favorite pieces for the sake of the whole. However, you can still use early projects that have merit by reworking them to meet your current standards, ultimately giving your portfolio a consistent, even quality.

Planning is an important key to a successful portfolio, beginning with the style and casing of the portfolio itself. Research your options; choose the right case and orientation that will best showcase your work. Strive to create an impression by setting yourself apart with some unique feature of the portfolio. Avoid over-sized cases; they are clumsy on a busy person's desk. And for fashion design interviewing, they are a definite mark of an amateur.

Deciding what to include in your portfolio is an important part of the planning stage. Will you need to create new portfolio formats? Which formats of your existing work should you keep? Do your formats look current and show an awareness of budding trends? How will you organize the "flow" of your formats, and how many pieces or themes will there be? Will you have enough variety for the jobs for which you will be interviewing? Answering these questions will help you compile a focused, creative portfolio.

Vary the formats within the portfolio to create interest and diversity. You can do this by varying the type of format, as well as the number of pages. Entry-level portfolios should demonstrate both a range of skills and a variety of formats. By contrast, the seasoned designer's portfolio need not have as broad a scope. Reputation and a proven track record are additional evidence of their accomplishments. This is often documented in a separate portfolio containing press clippings and published work (see Chapter 4).

Formats are categorized as follows and developed in groups to show design concepts. Any format may be used in combination with another to show variation and diversity of skills. Your creativity and imagination can lead you to the discovery of combinations that work for your special needs.

- Figure formats
- Flat formats
- Presentation board formats
- Fold-out formats

 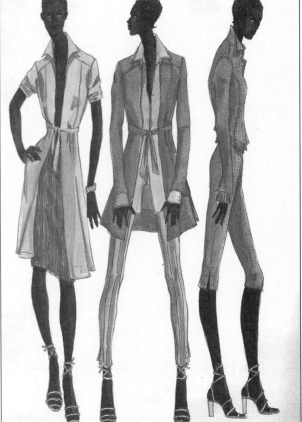

Figure   5.1a and b
Vertical/portrait orientation.

Presentation format by Nicole Benefield.

FORMAT SPECIFICS

Since Chapter 7 is devoted to presentation board formats, this chapter will primarily deal with figures, flats and fold-outs.

The formats you choose should demonstrate what you do best. If your drawing skills are exceptional, choose formats that will highlight this ability. Figure formats and cropped-figure formats are an excellent means of featuring this talent. If fabric renderings are your specialty, showcase this skill in your presentations. Strong rendering skills enhance any presentation and create variety and dimension.

ORIENTATION

The first aspect of the format involves the direction in which the portfolio is to be viewed, or what is known as its orientation. Formats where the designs are shown vertically are known as portrait orientations. This type of format can be shown in either a typical book format, one in which the pages are turned from left to right (Fig. 5.1a and b), or in a flip format, described below.

Formats where the designs are horizontally arranged, known as landscape orientation, work best in a flip format. Here the portfolio is placed with the opening parallel to a desk or table edge, and the pages are flipped upward (Fig. 5.2). The orientation you select will depend on the direction of your best samples.

In both instances, consistency is important. The viewer should not have to turn the portfolio because of a change in your page orientation. This can disturb the organizational "flow" of your presentation and create a disjointed impression.

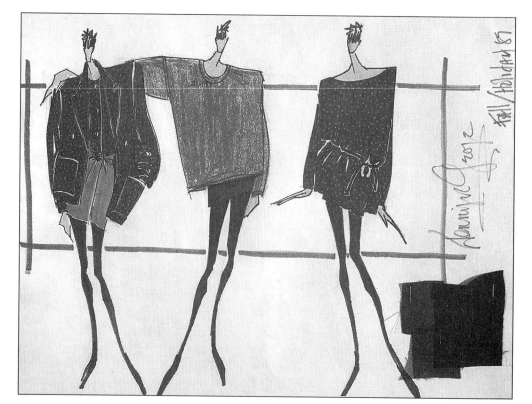

Figure   5.2
Horizontal/landscape orientation.

Presentation format by Jennifer George.

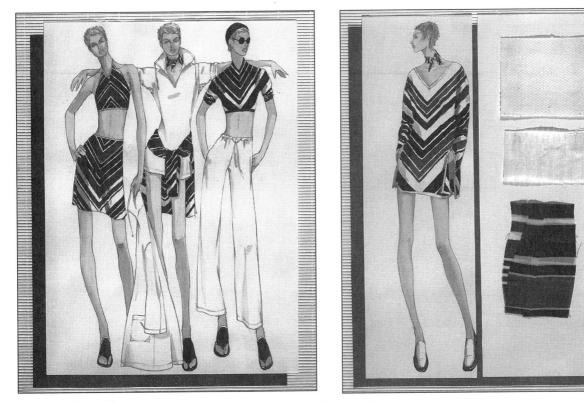

Figure   5.3a and b

The viewer sees a double-page spread as one concept. The fabric/color story is one means of creating a relationship between the two pages, as in this striped grouping.

Presentation format by Nicole Benefield.

Figure   5.4

Designers often like to relate their flats to their figure formats to show how garment proportion is translated from the figure to the flat sketch. Showing pieces on the flat isolates each piece, as garments tend to "blend" together on the figure.

Presentation format by Hong Tan.

Figure   5.5a and b
The positioning of heads and bodies in multiple-figure compositions can contribute to the "flow" of your design pages. The following elements should be considered for "flow" and figure composition: heads looking at one another, bodies turned toward one another, overlap of figures (garment or body part).

Presentation format by Nicole Benefield.

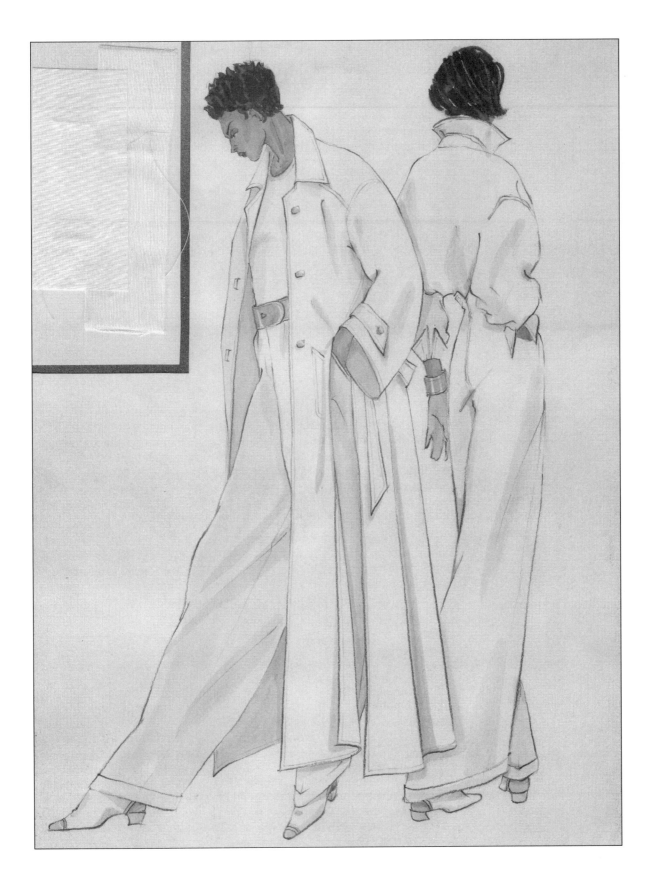

PAGE RELATIONSHIP

The second aspect of the format is the relationship of the pages to one another. Sometimes a design unit contains several pages, such as mood/fabric, fashion figures and flats. Arrange these pages together in the portfolio so their common link is obvious. It is always best to have an even amount of pages for each design spread, which can be as few as two or as many as eight. Having an even amount of pages automatically helps you resist the temptation to put together two different themes in one double-page spread. In student portfolios, it is not uncommon to see the end of one theme on the left-hand page and the beginning of a totally unrelated one on the right-hand page. But a viewer sees a double-page spread as one concept (Fig. 5.3a and b). If the pages do not relate, this can result in a confusing, unattractive presentation. In addition, consider design principles such as balance, flow and composition when any two pages are placed side by side in this manner.

FLAT FORMATS

Showing flats in portfolio formats is important because of their extensive use in the industry. Many professionals will attest to the fact that today at least 80 percent of design sketches are flat sketches. However, you need not show flats with every design concept, unless you are looking for a position as a technical designer. Showing flats exclusively can become boring and repetitive. Aim instead for two flat formats or spreads that demonstrate your ability and technique. Many designers like to relate their flat formats or spreads to their figure formats to show how garment proportion is translated from the figure to the flat sketch (Fig. 5.4). Presentation board formats are also an excellent way to show flat drawing skills. Combining formats adds variation to the portfolio and helps to maintain the viewer's interest.

FIGURE COMPOSITION

Creating strong page relationships in all portfolio formats can be enhanced by your ability to arrange figures on a page. This can be especially effective when your design concept shows a group of garments rather than a single item. The following elements can help you create a relationship in a composition of two or more figures (Fig. 5.5a and b):

- Heads looking at one another
- Bodies turned toward one another
- Overlap of figures (garment or body part)

Figures positioned at or facing toward the spine of the book are considered best because the eye focuses toward the center of the portfolio, rather than on the outer part of the pages. Avoid having the head of the figure on the left page looking out off the page, as the viewer's eye will follow in that direction. However, there are more options for the figure on the right-hand page (Fig 5.5b). The head may look in toward the center, relating to the figure on the left-hand page, or look out toward the far right, which can prompt the viewer to turn to the next grouping. Consequently, the position of the head of your figures can contribute to the "flow" of your design pages.

FIGURE FORMATS

Figure formats are the arrangement of single or multiple figures on a page. Several possible figure formats are:

- Single-figure format
- Double-figure format

- Triple- and multiple-figure format
- Cropped-figure format

Single-Figure Formats

While single-figure formats can be used in any category, they are most evident in bridal, eveningwear and outerwear (Fig. 5.6a and b). These areas are more item-oriented; designs are most likely conceived separately and are not meant to be shown in groups, as is sportswear. For example, in bridalwear, even though the bridesmaids' dresses are meant to coordinate with the bridal gown, they are more appropriately shown on separate pages as "related," rather than grouped together on the same page.

Apart from the bridal category, single-figure formats are less commonly used because they do not show theme development, which is important in most areas of the industry. However, an isolated figure on a page that is part of a larger design group can be quite dramatic when facing a page with multiple figures.

How the figure is positioned on the page is often determined by the clothing being illustrated. For example, evening or bridal gowns tend to take up more space on a page and may require more central placement. Coats and suits, however, allow for more flexibility. Sometimes, you can achieve a more dramatic effect by positioning your single figure off center, creating exciting shapes or negative space around the figure (Fig. 5.7). At the same time, too much negative or white space toward the spine of the book can draw the viewer's eye, hence taking the focus away from the designs.

Figure   5.6a and b
Single-figure formats are most popular in bridal and eveningwear as these areas emphasize design individuality. Note how the pages of this bridal spread are related by positioning the figures facing in toward one another.

Presentation format by Randy Fenoli.

Figure   5.7
A dramatic effect can be achieved by positioning a single figure off center, creating exciting shapes or negative space around the figure.

Presentation format by Troy Surratt.

When using single-figure formats, fill as much of your page as possible. Avoid too much white space around the figure, which comes from using small-scale figures. Professional designers generally show their designs on large figures because the garment silhouette and details are more visible and dynamic. However, if you prefer a small-scale figure, use a horizontal landscape orientation, as it will more readily fill the page. Or, if your natural tendency is to draw smaller, don't fight it. Use a copying machine to enlarge your smaller figures.

Double-Figure Formats

Double-figure formats are most effective when you need to show coordination of garments. Two designs placed close together on a page immediately create a visual relationship between the two (Fig. 5.8a). When two pages are viewed together in a double-page spread, that relationship is expanded to the additional figures (Fig. 5.8b). This format is preferred in sportswear, where design coordination is essential and separates need to be mixed and matched in a variety of ways. Sometimes garments are repeated and paired with different tops or bottoms to show coordination.

You can also use double-figure or multiple-figure formats in other design categories when showing a common design theme. For example, in a dress line, using 1960s silhouettes and details and grouping these designs together (Fig. 5.9a and b) will create a common

Figure   5.8a and b
Two designs placed close together on a page immediately create a visual relationship between the two. When two pages are viewed together in a double-page spread, that relationship is expanded to the additional designs, as in this example.

Presentation format by Hong Tan.

theme. In an intimate line, a particular type of lace or trim used throughout can become the theme and be logically arranged in a group format (Fig. 5.10a, b, c and d).

It is generally a good idea in double- or multiple-figure formats to have the heads looking at one another. This brings the focus to the designs and gives the impression of a related group. Slightly overlapping the figures reinforces this as well, and further creates a feeling of coordination between the designs.

Triple- or Multiple-Figure Formats

Triple- or multiple-figure formats are used most often in the sportswear category, as they readily show coordination in a collection, often in a fabrication for an expanded line group (Fig. 5.11a and b). Nevertheless, this format is appropriate for any category that is not item-oriented. Multiple-figure formats are an excellent vehicle for showing theme and relation within a design category. Visually, multiple-figure formats appear richer and more exciting, since the figures fill the page and suggest activity.

Use decorative background papers to add interest and dimension to figure formats. Texture, color and pattern can unify the composition and link the designs. Even a simple shape placed aesthetically behind the figure composition can add visual excitement to a page.

When the designer needs to show a design group or line segment, decorative background papers reinforce the message. Be careful, however, not to let these papers overwhelm or compete with the designs; their effects should remain subliminal. The example (Fig. 5.12a and b) shows a composition of designs mounted on a background using an original

Figure   5.9a and b
This dress line shares a common theme, based on 1960s silhouettes and details.

Presentation format by Tina Liu.

Figure 5.10a, b, c and d

Often fabric, color and trim can be a unifying theme, as in this intimate line. Notice how the use of lace throughout this group becomes the design theme. A common background graphic further unites the grouping.

Presentation format by Paul Chan.

Figure 5.11a and b

This junior sportswear group shows coordination through the use of striped fabric. Visually, multiple-figure formats appear richer and more exciting, since the figures fill the page and suggest activity.

Presentation format by Ilka Reyes.

Exercise

DOUBLE- OR MULTIPLE-FIGURE COMPOSITIONS

Using a fashion catalog or magazine, select a photograph with two or three figures grouped together and draw the figure composition as it appears in the photograph. The composition for these figures has already been determined by the photographer and saves you time in finding poses that work well together.

You can vary your arrangement by reversing, or flopping, the entire composition. Work on tracing paper, then turn the page over to get the transposed version of the same composition. For more variety, change the position of a head or arm, especially if you are creating a double-page spread and desire less symmetry. Varying poses can add visual interest and showcases drawing skills in your presentation formats. An ability to draw a variety of poses well demonstrates a high level of drawing proficiency. Collect poses from magazines and catalogs on a regular basis to add to your repertoire.

Figure   5.12a and b

This example shows a composition of designs mounted on an original, coordinated print. The border reinforces the "mechanical" theme. Through this presentation, the designer demonstrates skills in both apparel and textile design.

Presentation format by Isabel Castoldi.

coordinated print. The print, visible only as a border, is just enough to suggest the "mechanical" theme the designer wants to convey. Through this presentation, the designer shows abilities in both apparel and textile surface design.

Cropped-Figure Formats

Cropped-figure formats are usually used when it is not necessary to show full-length figures, such as in knitwear, intimate apparel or swimwear. A cropped figure is an excellent way of zooming in on a garment or detail in order to highlight its design aspects. Since garments in these categories tend to be smaller, you can enlarge cropped figures to make the garment appear fuller and more dramatic.

Arrange cropped figures in single- or multiple-figure formats and pair with smaller, full-length figures (Fig. 5.13) to create a dramatic look. The main advantage of this format is that details, which might ordinarily appear small and insignificant, are magnified and emphasized, providing the same effect as a zoom lens on a camera. Drawing skills must be at their best when using cropped figures, since enlarging the image will magnify any drawing flaws.

Figure 5.13

A cropped figure is an excellent way of zooming in on a garment or detail in order to highlight its design aspects. Cropped figures are often paired with smaller, full-length figures to create a dramatic look.

Presentation format by Donnell Walker.

MOOD/THEME FORMATS

Mood/theme formats are used to introduce a design group in the portfolio. The visuals should clearly represent the idea or theme and correspond to its design group (Fig. 5.14).

Sometimes mood/theme formats also include a photo of the targeted customer to show the "look"—hair, makeup, accessories, etc. This allows the viewer to focus on the market and identify the customer type. For example, if you are designing for a young, trendy customer, both the photo of the customer and the clothes you design should reflect this image. And make sure the customer in the photo is dressed in the appropriate category, i.e., sportswear, eveningwear, etc.

Using a customer image photo is optional. If you choose this route, take caution not to go overboard with too many photos, as this can confuse the issue.

As a space-saving feature, include fabrics and trims in your mood/theme format. The coloration of the photos and fabrics should coordinate to create a unified page.

It is generally a good idea to title mood/theme formats. This communicates the intent of the design group to the viewer. And inventing titles is another means of creative expression and demonstrates your

Figure   5.14
Mood/theme formats are used to introduce a design group in the portfolio. The visuals should clearly represent the theme and color-coordinate with the designs, as they are often shown together. Notice how the hand-lettering in this example adds to the mood or feeling of the "seaweed" theme.

Presentation format by Hong Tan.

Figure   5.15
Fabric/color formats can be used alone, as an introduction to a design grouping, or as an accompaniment to a mood/theme format. Creating a separate page enables you to show a larger quantity and variety of fabrics and trims. This format includes the fabric and color story represented in the design group.

Presentation format by Hong Tan.

language skills. Double-check to make sure grammar and spelling are correct. Titles should be simple; three words or less is most effective.

Use letra-set type or computer-generated lettering (no larger than half an inch) to create a professional look. Hand-letter only if you are especially skilled in calligraphy, and make certain the hand-lettered style adds to the mood or feeling of your page.

FABRIC/COLOR FORMATS

Fabric/color formats can be used alone, as an introduction to a design grouping or as an accompaniment to a mood/theme format. The purpose of creating a separate page is to show a larger quantity and variety of fabrics and trims. This format also includes the fabric and color story represented in your design group (Fig. 5.15). In addition, this is the place to highlight findings such as trim, braid, buttons, lace, special zippers or even an original drawing of your own trim design.

Press and uniformly trim fabrics before arranging them neatly on the page. Pink the edges to prevent fraying. Solid swatches sized $2'' \times 2''$ or $3'' \times 3''$ are standard; print swatches can be larger to show repeat of pattern. If you have a large or border print, you may want to reduce it and make a color copy so more of the pattern can be seen. Each fabric and color story is unique and should be handled on an individual basis.

If the fabrics you want are unavailable, recolor a print or paint your own fabric. Pinking painted paper samples will make them appear more like actual fabric. Use paint samples from a local paint store to represent solid fabrics if you can't find the color fabric you need; wallpaper swatches can be substituted for prints and stripes, etc. However, it is to

your advantage to use beautiful fabrics in the portfolio, as they speak to your knowledge and fashion savvy. The substitutions mentioned above should be used only if fabric resources are unavailable to you.

Titling the fabric/color format is optional, since your accompanying mood/theme format may already have one. However, you may want to label your fabric/color format with the season. Just indicate the season without designating the year to extend the use of your format and keep it from becoming dated. Label and identify all fabrics, especially those that are rendered. This communicates your ability to recognize and co-ordinate fabrics for a specific season.

FOLD-OUT FORMATS

Fold-out formats are often assigned following an interview. If a company is interested in hiring you, you may be asked to create a special project for that company so they can see if you can design in their "look." You'll be asked how long you'll need to complete the project. Completing it in a few days will show your ability to follow through quickly, as well as your interest in the job. You may be given fabric samples or asked to research their line in a particular store and create designs based on your research. Your designs should reflect the company's look without copying them line-for-line. Adding your own point of view and spirit creates a fresh approach, which is what they are seeking.

Fold-out formats usually consist of a mood/fabric page with two or three progressive design pages. These can include multiple-figure designs or flats depending on the company or market. Render your pre-

Figure   5.16

The fold-out format makes a great supplement to the portfolio. Designers sometimes use this format when they want to show a design group that is inconsistent with the "look" of their portfolio. Also, if a company is interested in hiring you, you may be asked during the interview to create a special project to show that you can design in their "look." A fold-out is often a perfect solution for this assignment.

Fold-out presentation by Hyun Jeong Chang.

sentation in color, as it will demonstrate your ability to coordinate and design creatively with fabrics.

Carefully attach the pages along the edge with tape, preferably in the same color as the paper. The tape should extend the full length of the page for a fold-out presentation (Fig. 5.16). The paper should be sturdy and easy to handle. If you prefer to work on a lighter weight paper, mount your finished pages on a sturdier paper. Use a proper adhesive, such as Spray Mount™ or Studio Tak™, to secure the pages.

These formats make excellent supplements to the portfolio. Retain them whether you get the job or not. You can recycle the presentation for another interview. Companies respond positively to this form of presentation because it is a mini-version of what you would actually be doing on the job as a designer.

CUSTOMIZED PRESENTATIONS

Customized presentations can be created for a variety of purposes, such as interviews, supplements and contests or competitions. They may demonstrate a unique style of design thinking, a different design specialty that is not included in the portfolio, or a customized presentation format. The packaging is often as important and unique as its contents and often unfolds in a dramatic way. This award-winning example (Fig. 5.17), created for the CFDA Scholarship Design Portfolio Competition, uses a fold-out format and is totally coordinated, from casing to design fabrication, in a windowpane check pattern. It is a unique example of design excellence and presentation technique.

DO'S & DON'TS

Do use different formats to add interest and variety to the portfolio.

Do vary the number of designs or figures per page.

Do maintain a consistent orientation throughout the portfolio.

Do group pages together that relate to the same theme.

Do use a cropped-figure format when you need to have a garment or detail appear larger, as in intimate apparel or swimwear.

Do use clear photos that are directly related to the subject of your theme and design category.

Do use press-on lettering or computer-generated type for titles and labels in a style that works for your presentation.

Do make sure all lettering is in a legible typeface.

Do press and trim fabric swatches evenly with pinking shears or scissors before mounting.

Do use appropriate glue for the weight of fabric (i.e., one that will not bleed through).

Do use color for more effective fold-out presentations.

Don't create isolated designs on a page that are "pretty pictures" and look like a school portfolio.

Don't use too much negative space between the spine of the portfolio and the figure in single-figure formats.

Don't use too much negative space between the figures in double-figure formats.

Don't overlap figures to the degree that the clothes and garment details are hidden in multiple-figure formats.

Don't use photos that are small and insignificant when choosing photos for mood/theme formats. A few large, dramatic photos are best.

Don't use photos that are not directly related to your design category and theme. For example, don't use an evening gown for a sportswear mood/theme format.

Don't hand-letter presentation formats unless you can do it beautifully.

Don't date fabric/color formats, as dating them shortens the life of their use. Fabric/color page may be labeled with the season.

Figure 5.17

In this customized portfolio, the windowpane fabric used in the designs has been incorporated into a handmade cover. The look is totally coordinated and extends from day to evening in an eight-panel fold-out, based on a New York theme.

CFDA 1996 Scholarship Design Competition portfolio by Peter Som.

CHAPTER 6

To get a job in today's industry, you must know how to create flats and specs. Your drawings and spec sheets must be clear, accurate and exacting in every detail.

Flats and Specs

ILLUSTRATIONS BY HONG TAN

To get a job in today's industry, you must know how to create flats and specs. This is especially true of the sportswear market, where the majority of flat work is done. Accurate flats with specs (short for specifications) are necessary to facilitate communication for the production of garments made off-shore. The spec is considered a binding contract between the manufacturer and the factory producing the garment. Today, virtually every region is represented in global garment production, including North, Central and South America, Eastern Europe, the Caribbean Basin and the Far East.

Although English is the universal language used on spec sheets, in most countries that produce contract garments the flat sketch with specs is the primary means of communication between the designer and place of production, whether directly or through a merchandiser, buying office or agent. As such, spec sheets must be clear, accurate and exacting in every detail. Each design is photocopied and reduced onto a spec sheet, which also includes the measurements and all pertinent information required in the production process. Even the "attitude" of the sketch must capture the designer's proportion and concept. This is especially important when designers are not there to supervise the first sample and must rely on the sketch to speak for them. In addition, these documents need to be as detailed as possible for the purpose of costing the garment.

The spec sheet must include assembly instructions, technical illustrations, measurements and descriptive instructions on sewing, pressing, cutting, after-treatment, fabric, trim, care and fusing. The merchandiser is most often responsible for the follow-up details of production.

Another important reason for the spec sheet sketch to be as clear and accurate as possible is that an unsuccessful outcome of the first sample can cancel or reduce orders. Too many correction samples will also result in a loss of production lead time and possible order cancellations if delivery schedules cannot be met.

Spec sheets may vary from company to company depending on their individual needs and preferences. Some are more detailed than others, ranging in size from one page to several pages for a single garment, depending on the format a company prefers. These examples (Fig. 6.1 and 6.2a and b) show garments in both single- and multiple-page formats.

Part of the designer or spec-tech's responsibilities in creating a comprehensive spec sheet with the accompanying technical minutiae is to communicate the design and construction details in as concise a manner as possible. If specific brand-name trims are desired, i.e., buttons, zippers or interfacings, specify them so they can be costed in to avoid later up-charges (price adjustments).

Use logic to organize the information on a spec sheet. Work from top to bottom when describing garment construction and detail. This enables the merchandiser to read your instructions and correlate them to the sketch in a systematic way. This is especially helpful to the merchandiser trying to set the initial price quotation of the garment. Top-to-bottom detailing also facilitates "eye-flow" from one design detail to another. For example, describe the hem facing, the hem finish (top-stitch, blind-stitch, etc.) and then jump to the collar finish. This method also ensures that all construction details are covered.

Consolidate repeated construction details like top-stitching or hem finishes in the same sentence for easier comprehension and to save space.

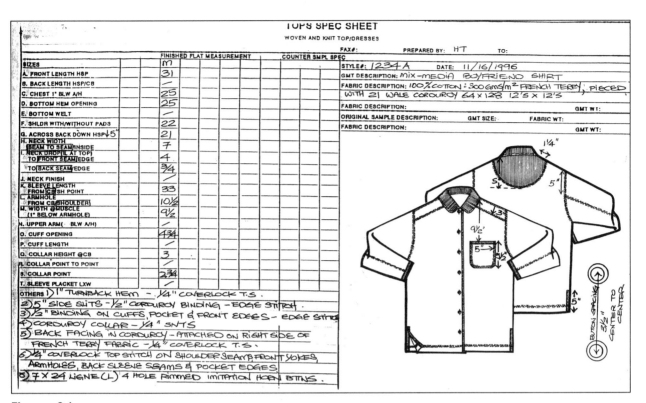

Figure   6.1
Tops spec sheet.

Creating good-looking, well-proportioned flats takes practice. Designers who constantly draw flats claim that, with time, they acquire consistency in technique and speed in execution. The following exercises, techniques and supply list are designed to assist the beginning, intermediate and advanced student in drawing flats.

FLAT SKETCHING TECHNIQUES

Recommended Supplies:

coated copy paper

light box

6″ and 12″ plastic ruler with graph

french curve

templates for stenciling: circles, ellipses

eraser (blue/white)

tracing paper

white-out liquid/correction pen

correction tape: $\frac{1}{8}$″ and $\frac{1}{4}$″ widths

copying machine

electric pencil sharpener

2H or 3H pencil

cool grey markers for shading

Letra-set film sheets

Sharpie black marker (fine point for outline)

Sakura Micron Pigma markers: .08 and .05 (for garment details, collars and pockets), 03 and .02 (for top-stitching and fine detail)

BOTTOMS SPEC SHEET
WOVEN AND KNIT PANT/SHORT/SKIRT

			FINISHED FLAT MEASUREMENT						COUNTER SMPL SPEC	

FAX#: _____   PREPARED BY: HT   TO: _____

STYLE#: 5678B   DATE: 11/16/96

GMT DESCRIPTION: FAUX WRAP SKIRT W D RING SIDE TAB

FABRIC DESCRIPTION: T/C 65/35 CREPE 290 GMS.

COUNTER SMPL REQUIREMENTS: GMT SIZE: ____   FABRIC WT: ____   GMT WT: ____

FABRIC DESCRIPTION:

ORIGINAL SAMPLE DESCRIPTION: GMT SIZE: ____   FABRIC WT: ____   GMT WT: ____

FABRIC DESCRIPTION:

SIZE	M
A. LENGTH(BLW WB)	19
B. OUTSEAM(EXCL WB)	/
C. INSEAM	/
D. WAIST RELAXED	13
E. WAIST STRETCHED	/
F. WAISTBAND FINISHED	/
G. WAIST DROP FRONT	
BACK	/
H. HIP 4" BLW WB	17
I. HIP 8" BLW WB	19
J. THIGH(1" BLW CROTCH)	/
K. KNEE(14" BLW CROTCH)	/
L. FRONT RISE(EXCL WB)	/
M. BACK RISE(EXCL WB)	/
N. BOTTOM HEM OPENING	17
O. BOTTOM HEM FINISH	/
OTHERS:	/

1) 1" TURNBACK HEM – 1/4" DNTS.
2) 1/4" SNTS ON CENTER BACK SEAM & FRONT WRAP EDGES.
3) 2X ANT. GOLD D RINGS – 1" WIDE
4) 1½" FLAT ELASTIC SEWN TO WAISTLINE. 1/4" SNTS ON ELASTIC AT WAISTLINE
5) 1½" SELF-FABRIC FACING FOR FRONT WRAP EDGES –MARROW FINISH.
6) SEE SEPERATE PAGE FOR MORE CONSTRUCTION DETAILS.

WRAP DIST. 10"

Figure   6.2a and b

Bottom spec sheet—multiple-page format.

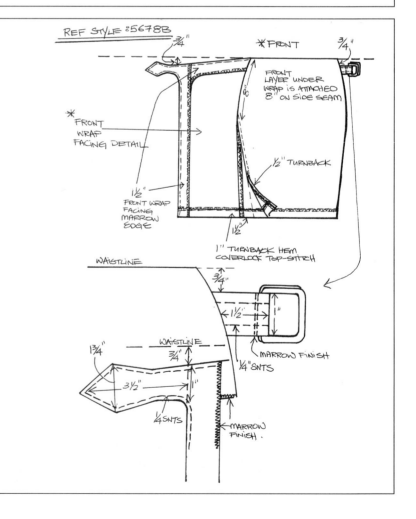

REF STYLE #5678B

FRONT

FRONT LAYER UNDER WRAP IS ATTACHED 8" ON SIDE SEAM

FRONT WRAP FACING DETAIL

½" TURNBACK

1½" FRONT WRAP FACING MARROW EDGE

1" TURNBACK HEM COVERLOCK TOP-STITCH

WAISTLINE

MARROW FINISH

1/4" SNTS

WAISTLINE

MARROW FINISH.

1/4 SNTS

IMPROVING LINE QUALITY

Practice drawing a straight line freehand, connecting two points without using a ruler. Use a marker outline pen so you won't be tempted to erase. Make the points different lengths apart, trying for greater distance each time. Literally cover a page with the practice lines. As you experiment using different pens you will discover which ones you prefer. With enough practice, you will improve and acquire a confident line quality. Once mastered, you will find this technique invaluable for improving line quality.

PRACTICING CURVES

Using a curve stencil, find the size and shape of the curve that corresponds to the curve you want to draw. Place the stencil on top of your rough pencil sketch and redraw the curve using the stencil's shape as a guide. With practice, you will become familiar with the various sizes and be able to judge which works best for necklines, pockets, curved seams, etc.

The idea is to allow these tools to assist you in creating a more professional result than you can freehand. Most professionals use a combination of both freehand and mechanical drawing techniques to execute flat sketches.

Developing these skills will provide other advantages that can be applied in the workplace. For example, quick sketching techniques are a great asset at merchandise meetings when design development concepts are being discussed. A quick sketch of an idea saves time and can be given to the design room to be put into work immediately.

Often a quick sketch serves as a substitute when the actual garment is unavailable; a sketch can be used to create a variation on an existing garment. On shopping trips or during market surveys, sketches can save companies money since they need to buy fewer samples to bring back for design development.

After several seasons, you will acquire a library of sketches that can be used for inspiration to facilitate design development. Companies often repeat the same silhouettes or "bodies," and update from these.

CREATING FLATS

There are a variety of techniques to create flats. Each will be outlined in this chapter. However, before selecting a specific method, take into account your own level of experience in drawing.

Most beginners are intimidated by the prospect of drawing flats. One way to dispel these fears is to become familiar with what will be required of you and what the end product should look like. Most companies have samples of flats and specs available. Use these as your guide until you feel more confident. Be creative, experiment. Be open to what can happen. With exposure to different flat styles and techniques your own style will evolve and change, even if only as a defense against boredom. You will become faster and more fearless as you gain confidence in your own ability. With practice, your approach, execution, line quality, proportion and detail drawing will improve immeasurably. The desire to create something new will continually give your approach freshness and make the experience worthwhile.

Before selecting a flat drawing technique, identify how and where your sketches will be used. For example, flats used for presentation boards require different rendering and finishing techniques than flats used for production purposes. However, the sketching approach is fundamentally the same.

There are as many "styles" of drawing flats as there are designers. Consequently, selecting the right technique for your drawings will depend on your proficiency and their purpose.

DEVELOPING FLATS FROM A CROQUIS

This method is recommended for those with little or no experience executing flats. You can develop your own croquis figure to work over or use one provided by your instructor. You can also photocopy and enlarge the croquis provided in this book. Use realistic proportions developed from the 10-head fashion croquis, as seen in Fig. 6.3a. In Fig. 6.4, you see the comparison between the fashion croquis (Fig. 6.3a) and a flat silhouette (Fig. 6.3b). Since the average accepted fashion figure height is 10 heads tall, most people make the mistake of working on the same elongated figure to create flats. Fig. 6.5a shows distorted garments from an elongated croquis.

The cardigan and pants (Fig. 6.5b) are shown with these garments to illustrate the difference between using the newly developed flat silhouette and the fashion croquis. On the latter, the garments become distorted, especially in the lower torso and leg areas. Understand that the figure for any of the flat drawing methods is used as a "base" to develop garments and is eliminated in the finished stage. Therefore, don't be alarmed if your developed silhouette appears hefty and even a bit overweight. This figure type is best for creating strong, silhouetted garments and gives good end results.

Note: The new flat silhouette (Fig. 6.3b) is symmetrical and positioned for a frontal view; it is straight with feet shoulder width apart. This figure will be used to show how to create the following four basic silhouette/shapes. Illustrations will show garments progressing from fitted to loose, comparing the distance from garment to body. Direction of hemlines, seams, collars, buttons, pockets and center front will be discussed in each garment type.

The croquis you work on need not be a perfect example of finished art. It is there as a guide, or under-drawing, to help you establish correct proportion in your flats. You can draw in either pencil or fine point marker with whatever guide lines you feel are necessary to get an accurate result. The end product should, however, consist of the following features, which will adapt to a variety of garment types.

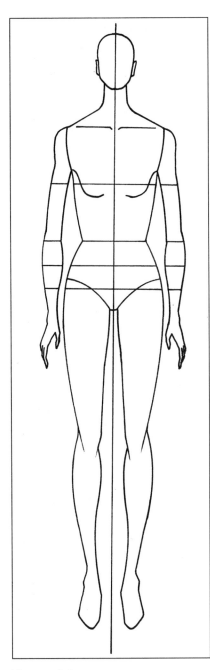

Figure 6.3a
The female fashion croquis.

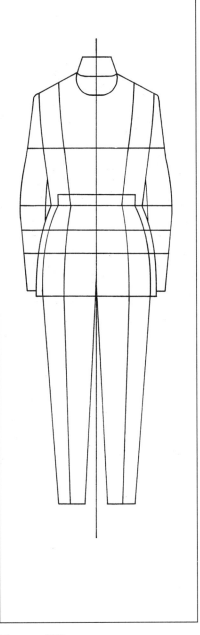

Figure 6.3b
The flat silhouette.

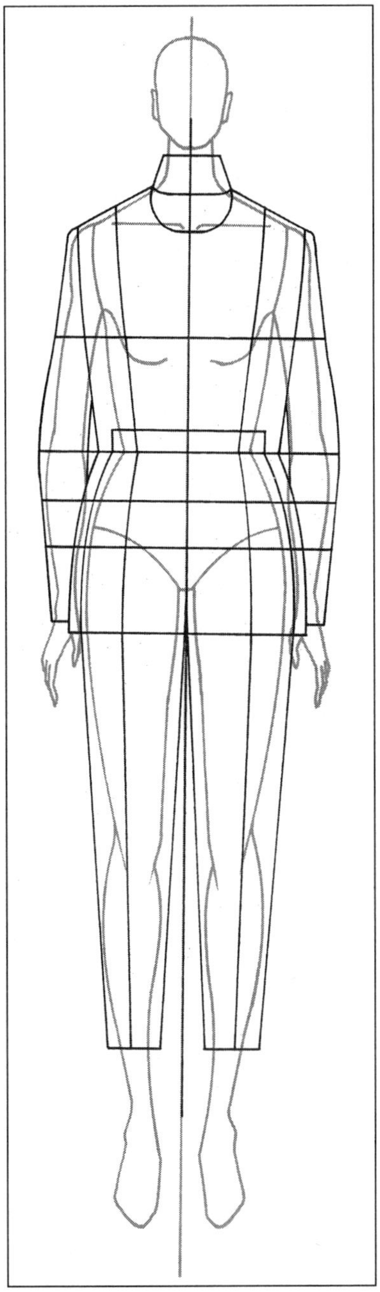

Figure 6.4
The croquis superimposed with the flat silhouette.

Figure 6.5a
Distorted pantsuit created from the croquis.

Figure 6.5b
Correctly proportioned pantsuit created from the Flat Silhouette
(Fig. 6.3b).

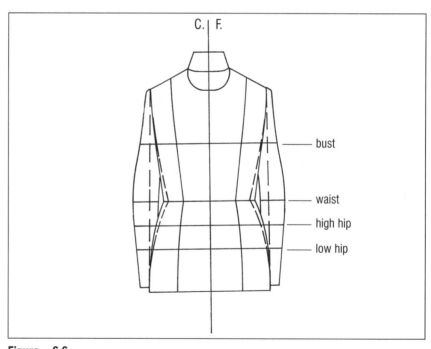

Figure 6.6
Top/Fitted Silhouette—Set-in Sleeves
Straight, arm down for all set-in sleeves, i.e., jackets, blouses.

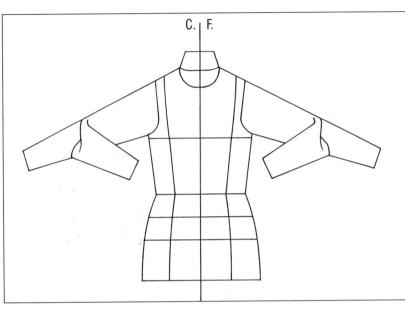

Figure 6.7a and b
Top/Fitted Silhouette—Action Sleeves

Bent arm for action sleeves, when it is necessary to show detail on lower part of sleeve, i.e., jackets, coats, T-shirts, blouses. Straight arm out from shoulder for silhouettes and underarm details, i.e., dolman, kimono and gusset.

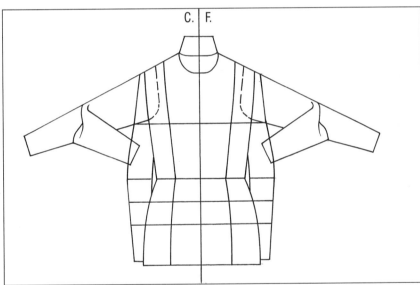

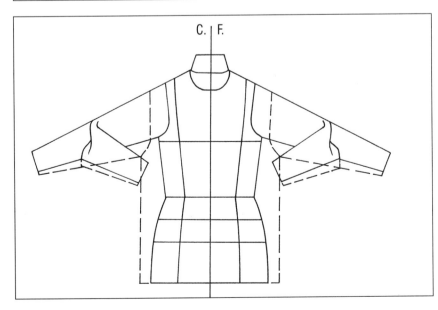

Figure 6.8
Top/Boxy Silhouette—Action Sleeves

Garments can be built over existing silhouette for sweatshirts, coats or any loose-fitting garments.

You are not limited to the two dotted lines shown here for silhouettes. You can extend a line to flare the silhouette, shorten or lengthen the garment on the silhouette, as well as change necklines.

Figure 6.9
Pants/Shorts Silhouette

This garment was derived from the bottom half of Fig. 6.3b. You can create different pants silhouettes from this basic flat silhouette. Start flares for shorts or pants from the lower hip line. Flare lines can be as full or narrow as desired, just be careful to maintain moderate spacing between the legs for pants silhouette development. The croquis should stand with legs shoulder width apart, not spread out. The silhouette developed here automatically establishes correct spacing between the legs.

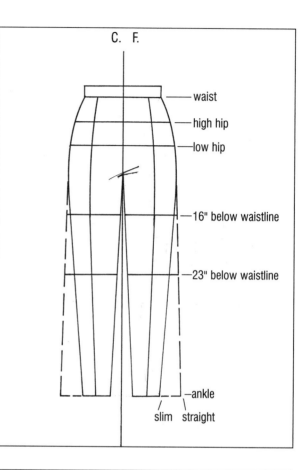

Figure 6.10
Skirt Silhouette

The slim skirt silhouette is derived from the outline of the slim pants silhouette, minus the inseam but with the addition of a continuous hemline. Start the fullness from the lower hipline, as in the pants. As a skirt gets fuller, don't make it wider at the sides, but rather show fullness in the folds. The pattern maker or draper can calculate the amount of fullness by the number of folds you draw in your flat sketch. (See eight-gored skirt in Fig. 6.17).

Note: flared skirts need curved hemlines and cone-shaped folds with dimension at the hemline.

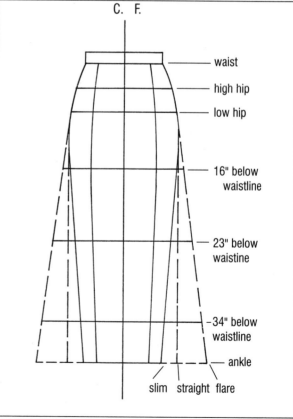

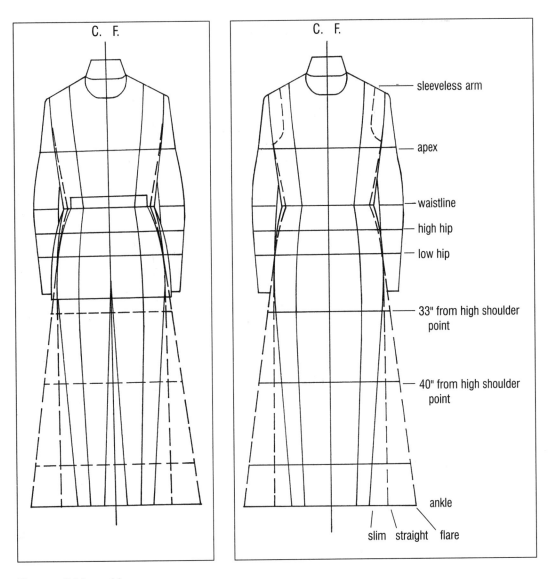

C. F.

C. F.

— sleeveless arm

— apex

— waistline
— high hip
— low hip

— 33" from high shoulder
   point

— 40" from high shoulder
   point

ankle

slim   straight   flare

Figure   6.11a and b
Dress Silhouette Created from the Flat Silhouette
The dress silhouette is slightly smaller at the hips so that a jacket can be worn over it. The
same guiding principles that apply to the skirt flats are used here as well. Arm position is
optional, depending on your personal preference. Should the dress have an "action"
sleeve, such as a dolman or kimono, follow the same procedure for transforming a set-in
sleeve into an action sleeve. With a sleeveless dress you can style the armhole as on this
silhouette, or more cut-away or covered as desired. Be aware of the apex placement on
the silhouette with regard to armholes and necklines for adequate coverage.

**Figure 6.12a and b
Coat Silhouette**

The dress silhouette can be used for creating a coat silhouette. Outer garments are generally drawn with a wider shoulder line, since jackets are often worn under them. You can extend the silhouette from this widened shoulder line to any desired length. This line should be parallel to the center front line. If you want a tent shape, angle out the silhouette as you would in the flat silhouette. Fig. 6.12a shows the coat silhouette in a dotted-line over the dress silhouette. Fig. 6.12b represents the final coat silhouette.

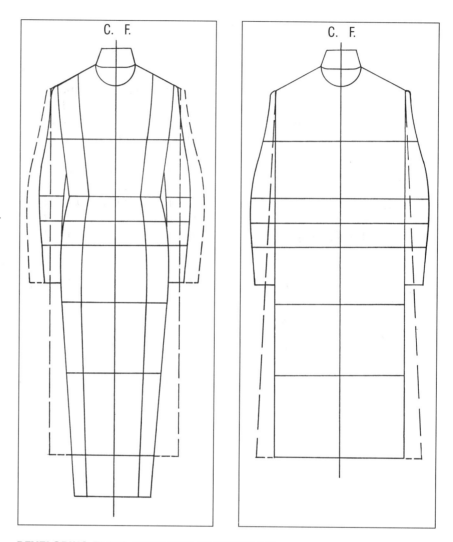

DEVELOPING FLATS FROM THE SILHOUETTES

Draw garments on any transparent or semitransparent paper, such as tracing paper or copy paper, respectively. Many designers prefer copy paper because of its body, whiteness, transparency and readiness to go into a fax machine. Although some designers render their flats in pencil, the majority use marker pens for finished presentation flats and specs. This technique gives the garment a more dimensional look and has great contrast on white paper.

A light-box is helpful to see the garment silhouette more clearly through copy paper. After enlarging to the desired size, place the silhouette directly on the light-box with a clean piece of copy paper over it. Then trace the silhouette and style lines that are relevant to your design. Use the style lines on the flat silhouette to symmetrize garment and details such as seams, pockets, buttons, etc. You may need to modify the silhouette and other style details to create your own design.

To finish your sketch, use a bold marker for drawing the outline or garment silhouette. Although a garment outline can be bold or thin, note that bold outlines shrink in reproduction and become thinner. Most flat techniques involve working larger and reducing, rather than the other way around. This is because reduction cleans up line quality and consolidates details. Generally, a bolder outline has more "pop" and stands out on a page.

Use fine-line markers for garment details such as seams, darts, top-stitching, etc. Use a ruler, french curve or template for accuracy and neatness. A combination of both bold and thin lines in finished flat sketches add dimension.

You can create back views without a back-view croquis simply by tracing the front-view flat and altering the neckline and detail (Fig. 6.13a, b, c and d). Use this method with any of the flat drawing techniques once the front view has been established. In certain presentations, showing a front and back view together can be helpful in understanding the total look of the garment, especially in the absence of a sample. Back views are generally shown when special details exist in the back of the garment that would otherwise not be seen. Consistency is crucial: collar direction, waistline and seam placement at shoulder should correspond to the front of the garment. Variations in length should be shown in both front and back views.

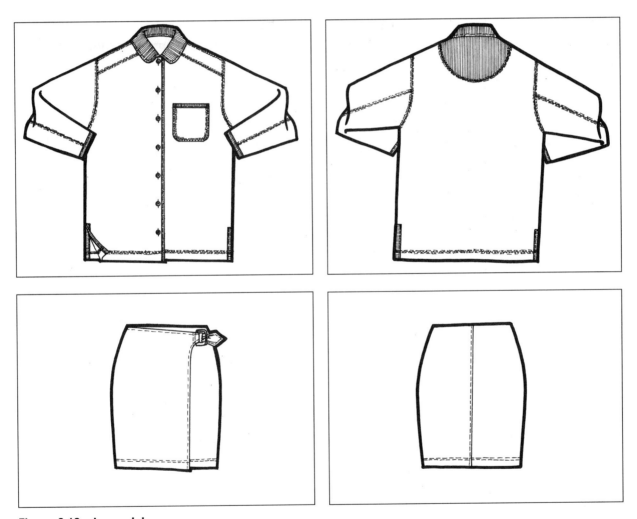

Figure 6.13a, b, c and d
Back view created from front-view silhouettes.

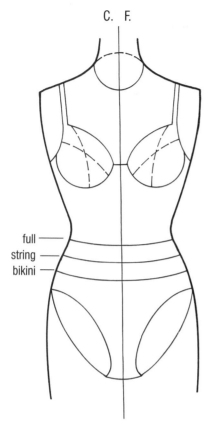

Figure   6.14a
Intimate apparel silhouette.

INTIMATE APPAREL SILHOUETTE

The intimate apparel silhouette is specifically developed for illustrating undergarments/foundations (Fig. 6.14a). It is curvier than the flat silhouettes discussed earlier and has a more accentuated waistline. The lower torso has been extended to allow for the panty gusset in front or back views. Note that the basic bra and panty shapes are indicated directly on the form to facilitate the design process. General style lines and seams for the bra cup are indicated. The lower torso contains three rises for panty silhouettes. The leg opening can be raised or lowered accordingly. In addition, you may alter the seam lines to create design variation if appropriate to the garment construction. The form can also be lengthened for sleepwear, nightgowns and pajamas as needed.

The garments illustrated here were created from the intimate apparel silhouette. These five garments represent the basic shapes used in intimate apparel design (Fig. 6.14b). In addition, other silhouettes can be created using the form, such as corsets, long-line bras, body-shapers, camisoles, boxers/shorts and slips. For best results, all garments should be drawn in pencil initially. The general approach is the same as described earlier in this chapter.

Intimate apparel garments require a more delicate rendering technique than other types of flats. Note that the outline is not as bold as the illustrated flat bodies preceding this section. A Micron Pigma marker .05 has been used for the outline. The stitching detail, an important feature of these garments, has been rendered with a .02. Special sewing techniques used in intimate apparel are indicated in the stitching detail. For example, the zigzag dotted line represents the two-step or three-step sewing processes. Single-needle top stitching has also been indicated. With intimate apparel, garment finishes can vary and may include other finishes such as double-needle top stitching, turn-back edge or overlock.

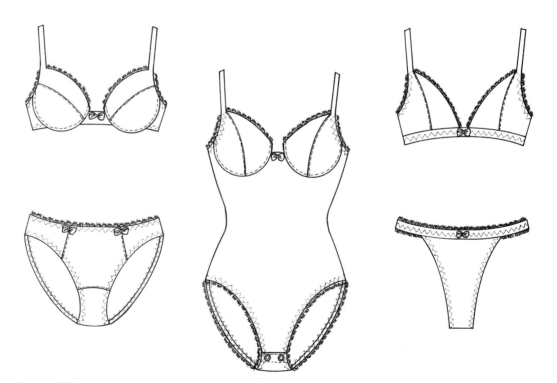

Figure   6.14b
Basic intimate apparel garments.

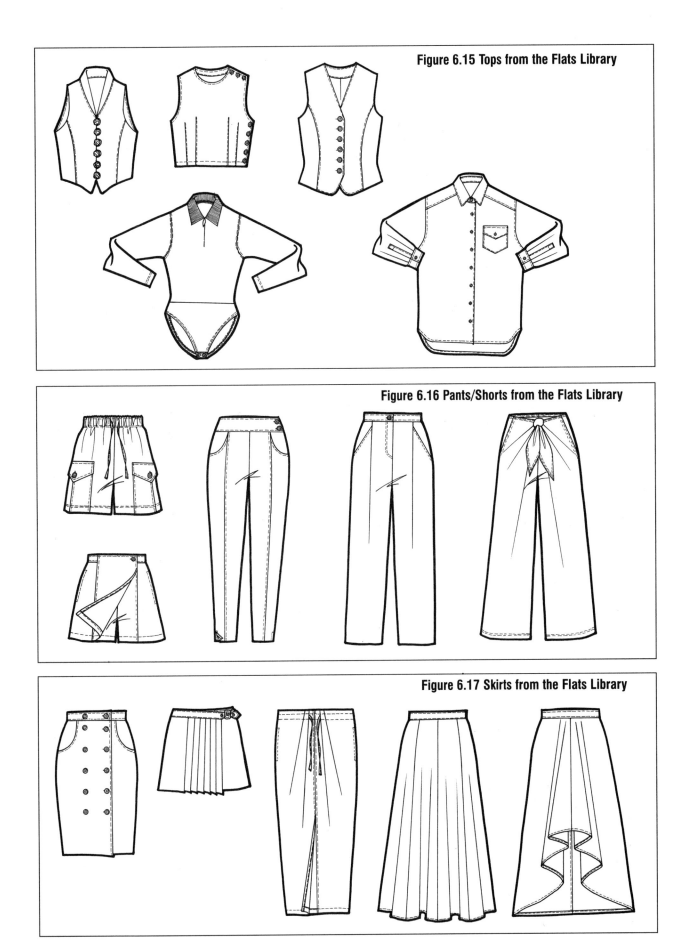

Figure 6.15 Tops from the Flats Library

Figure 6.16 Pants/Shorts from the Flats Library

Figure 6.17 Skirts from the Flats Library

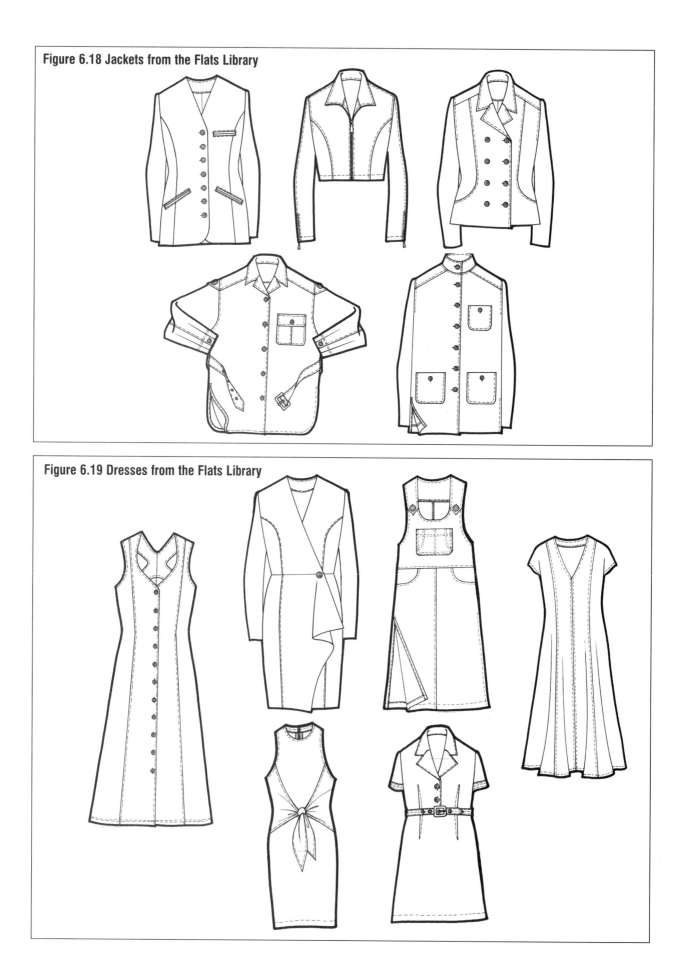

Figure 6.18 Jackets from the Flats Library

Figure 6.19 Dresses from the Flats Library

Figure 6.20 Outerwear from the Flats Library

Figure 6.21 Activewear from the Flats Library

DEVELOPING FLATS FROM A LIBRARY

Over time, a designer creates a collection of silhouettes, or "bodies," that he or she can continually utilize. Each designer customizes the library to his own needs and breaks it down accordingly. The following examples of tops, pants/shorts, skirts, jackets, dresses, coats/jackets/outerwear and activewear are organized according to their common link.

You may find you need to revise a "body" such as a jacket or shirt that you have previously sketched. Your library of flats can be valuable for this purpose. Once you've chosen a body or silhouette from your library of flats that closely resembles the final flat you want to achieve, place a clean sheet of copy paper over the sketch and trace the underdrawing using an H-series pencil. Use as many lines as necessary to achieve realism. Trace the parts that are the same as your new design—such as silhouette, neckline and pockets—and add the new details that alter the design from the original (Fig. 6.22a, b and c and Fig. 6.23a, b and c).

When you feel the lines are more or less correct, go over your pencil lines with a thick marker to create the outline silhouette, and fine markers for the inside construction details. Use a ruler, especially for center front lines, long seams, sleeves, etc. Small hip-curve rulers are also good for refining and cleaning up curves. Some designers find stenciling templates handy for curved details, as well as for buttons and pockets.

Erase pencil lines once you've completed drawing the thick and thin marker lines. If the flat still looks messy from erasures, photocopy it for

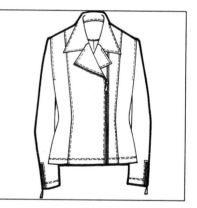

Figure 6.22a, b and c
Jacket developed from an existing flat.

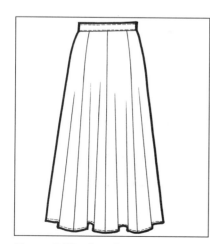
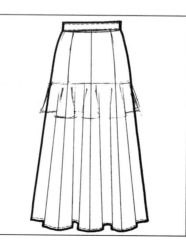
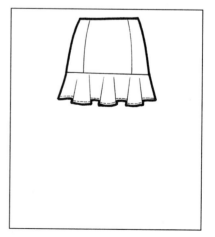

Figure 6.23a, b and c
Skirt developed from an existing flat.

an instant "clean-up." Use liquid white-out or correction tape to correct mistakes before making the copies.

When you need a sketch even faster, make a photocopy of a flat that most resembles the final flat you want to achieve. White-out or tape-out all unnecessary lines. Add new details by either drawing directly onto the existing surface or by making a clean copy and altering it. The latter method works well if excess corrections have made the original surface too rough to draw on.

Some designers pen in the details directly, without penciling-in the garment first. This can result in lackluster flats, loss of symmetry, shaky lines and disproportionate garments.

FREEHAND FLAT SKETCHING

This method is most often used by designers with a considerable amount of experience in rendering flats. It requires an eye for seeing garment proportion and a confident hand that can work with speed and accuracy. Designers of this level evolve their own method of freehand flat sketching, which may vary considerably from designer to designer.

Block-in the silhouette of the garment using as many pencil strokes as necessary, working from top to bottom and side to side. Check to see that the garment is symmetrical and in correct proportion. This method is somewhat parallel to life drawing, in that you are exploring and evaluating as you draw to get the most realistic proportion possible. After the silhouette is created to your satisfaction, add details such as pockets, seams, buttons, necklines, etc. If you are doing a series of flats for a related separates project (i.e., coordinated tops and bottoms), use the first garment you sketch as a basis for sizing and proportioning the rest. Translate the same "attitude" of the first sketch to the subsequent sketches to ensure consistency within the group. This also applies to the garment pull-lines, shading techniques, patterning, outline and generally the total technique used for finishing the flats.

Using a Sharpie or thick-line marker, draw in the garment silhouette. Use a ruler, french curve or template for any internal lines such as seams, pockets, collars, buttons, etc. These tools give your flats a precise, polished look. Try the Sakura Micron Pigma marker .08 or .05 for rendering these details, and a Sakura .03 or .02 for top-stitching and other very fine detailing. Experiment with a variety of markers to create fold lines within the garment and to add a lively dimension.

Because this is a freehand technique, there are no hard and fast rules of execution. You just have to learn to trust your "eye" with regard to flow, symmetry, proportion and detail. It takes confidence, experience and lots of repetition to achieve professional results with this method. You can combine different techniques to create your unique look. Being open to new materials and techniques is an essential part of the process of growing and developing your style. Shown here are four garments sketched in the freehand technique (Fig. 6.24a, b, c and d).

PRESENTATION OR ILLUSTRATIVE FLATS

Used in portfolio presentations, board presentations and designing on the flat (without the figure), these flats need to be treated as lifelike as possible, since the garment is often sold via the sketch. This is the crème de la crème of flat sketching techniques. Artistic license may be used here, giving the designer more freedom in his or her approach to drawing the garments. These sketches can be done in either black and white or color, depending on what is needed. Make certain to vary the line quality so the sketches really pop-out and sparkle. Shadowing and fold lines can be achieved with a grey marker, adding depth and realism to the drape of the garment.

Figure 6.24a, b, c and d
Flats developed using free-hand technique.

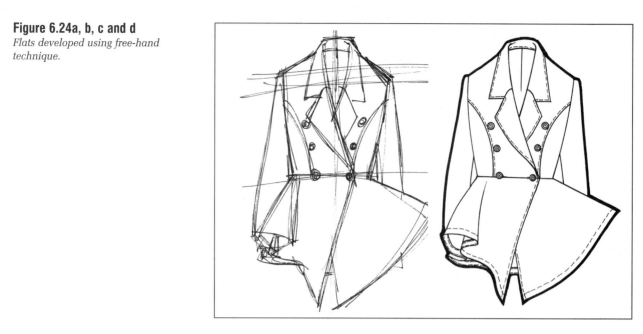

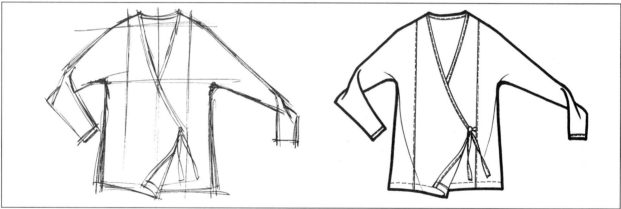

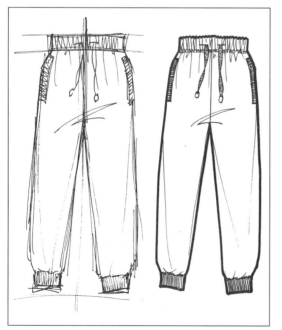

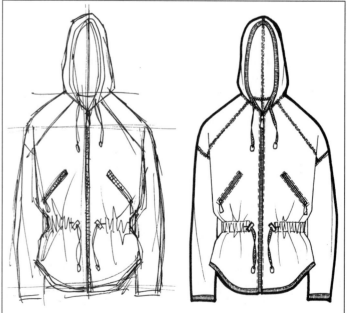

Patterns are often applied to show fabric grain and proportion to garment; some designers add computer-generated patterns for consistency (Fig. 6.25). In sportswear, it is essential the pieces be sized in relationship to one another to show how the pieces work together.

These sketches are extremely important and essential when garments are being produced off-shore. Production flats, sent with a spec sheet to the manufacturer, require the same accurate proportion and clear, consistent line quality as presentation or illustrative flats. Garment details must be exact, leaving nothing to the imagination or interpretation. The "attitude" or look intended by the designer must also be communicated through the sketch, since the designer is thousands of miles away. Although specs accompany these sketches, ultimately the sketch is the stronger voice. Because these sketches are translated literally by the production staff, the amount of fold lines to express softness or drape, as well as any embellishments, should be minimized.

At one time, using graphs to execute production flats was common. But this method often proves to be more problematic than not, since you must count boxes to achieve symmetry. Designers are often so preoccupied with the mechanics of this method that important techniques and drawing principles are neglected. In the long run, other methods will enhance your skills and techniques.

The techniques used to create all three flat types depend mainly on the designer's deftness and skill. Everything can be drawn freehand or with the aid of different types of rulers and stencils. Most frequently, designers use a combination of both. No matter what your level of skill, familiarize yourself with all the fundamental techniques of drawing flats, as each technique feeds and enhances the other.

PRODUCTION FLATS

Figure   6.25
Computer-generated patterns applied to flat bodies.

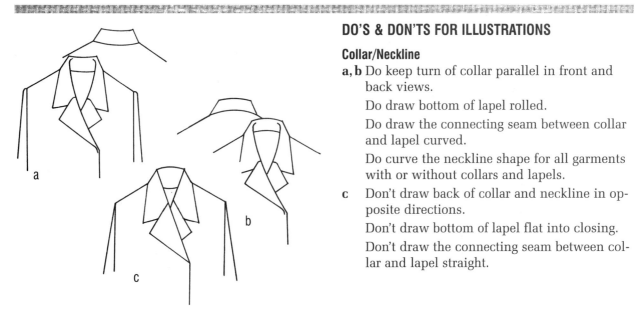

DO'S & DON'TS FOR ILLUSTRATIONS

Collar/Neckline

a, b Do keep turn of collar parallel in front and back views.

Do draw bottom of lapel rolled.

Do draw the connecting seam between collar and lapel curved.

Do curve the neckline shape for all garments with or without collars and lapels.

c Don't draw back of collar and neckline in opposite directions.

Don't draw bottom of lapel flat into closing.

Don't draw the connecting seam between collar and lapel straight.

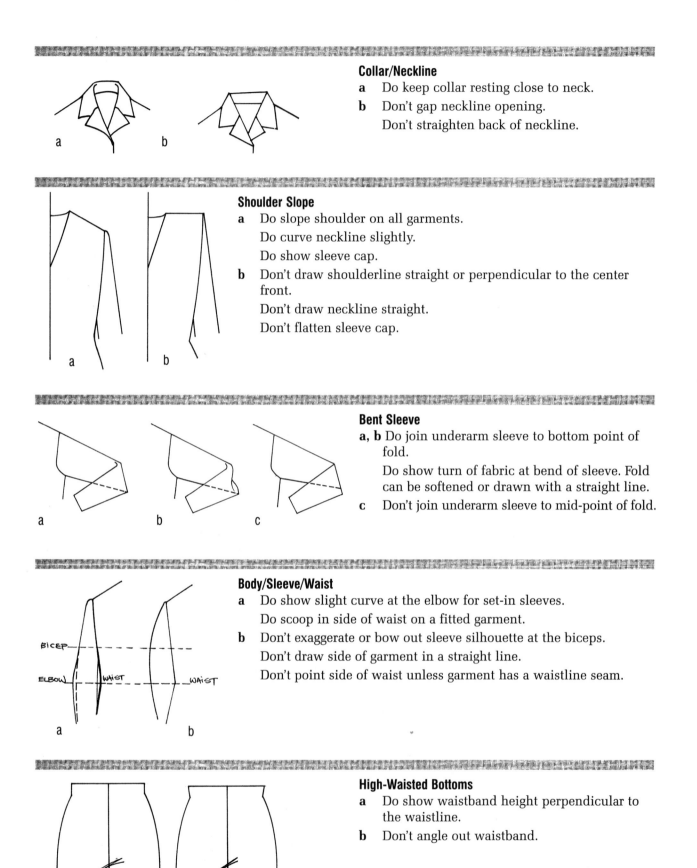

Collar/Neckline

a Do keep collar resting close to neck.

b Don't gap neckline opening.

Don't straighten back of neckline.

Shoulder Slope

a Do slope shoulder on all garments.

Do curve neckline slightly.

Do show sleeve cap.

b Don't draw shoulderline straight or perpendicular to the center front.

Don't draw neckline straight.

Don't flatten sleeve cap.

Bent Sleeve

a, b Do join underarm sleeve to bottom point of fold.

Do show turn of fabric at bend of sleeve. Fold can be softened or drawn with a straight line.

c Don't join underarm sleeve to mid-point of fold.

Body/Sleeve/Waist

a Do show slight curve at the elbow for set-in sleeves.

Do scoop in side of waist on a fitted garment.

b Don't exaggerate or bow out sleeve silhouette at the biceps.

Don't draw side of garment in a straight line.

Don't point side of waist unless garment has a waistline seam.

High-Waisted Bottoms

a Do show waistband height perpendicular to the waistline.

b Don't angle out waistband.

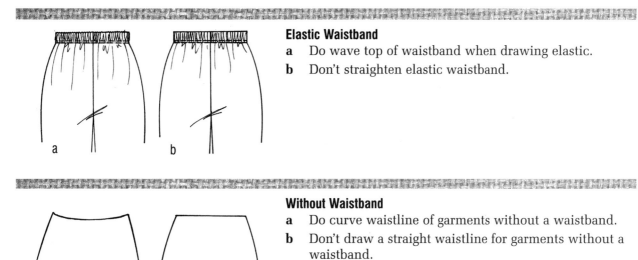

Elastic Waistband
a Do wave top of waistband when drawing elastic.

b Don't straighten elastic waistband.

Without Waistband
a Do curve waistline of garments without a waistband.

b Don't draw a straight waistline for garments without a waistband.

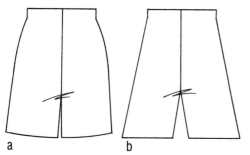

Pants/Shorts
a Do show legs approximately shoulder width apart.

Do curve hems slightly upward at side seams for A-line or flared silhouettes.

Do show the curvature of the hip at side seam.

b Don't show legs with too much space in between.

Don't show hemlines straight across from inseam to outseam on A-line or flared garments.

Don't draw the outseam straight from waistline to hem.

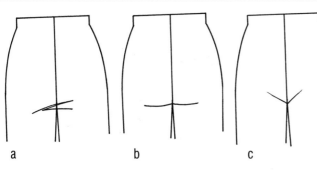

Tight Pants/Shorts
a Do show "break" at crotch for the front of all pants styles.

b Do show shape of buttocks only in the back view of tight fitting pants or leggings. For loose fitting pants show "break" the same as in front view.

c Don't show V-shape for crotch in the front view.

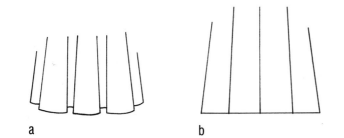

Hemlines
a Do turn end of hemline on a flared garment.

Do show dimension of folds at hemline (in and out).

b Don't show skirts with folds with a straight hemline.

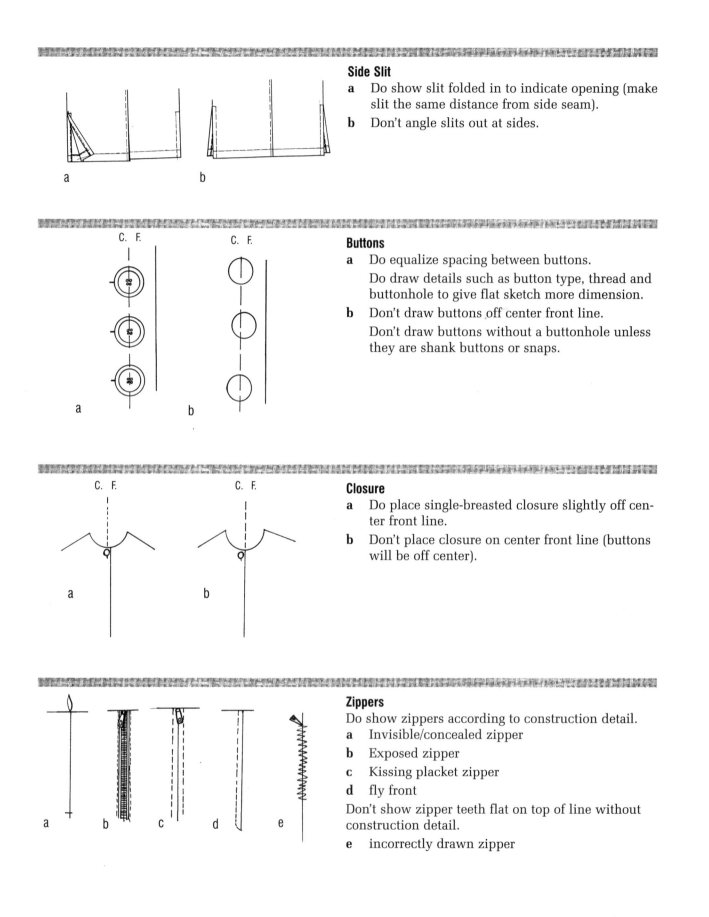

Side Slit

a Do show slit folded in to indicate opening (make slit the same distance from side seam).

b Don't angle slits out at sides.

Buttons

a Do equalize spacing between buttons.

Do draw details such as button type, thread and buttonhole to give flat sketch more dimension.

b Don't draw buttons off center front line.

Don't draw buttons without a buttonhole unless they are shank buttons or snaps.

Closure

a Do place single-breasted closure slightly off center front line.

b Don't place closure on center front line (buttons will be off center).

Zippers

Do show zippers according to construction detail.

a Invisible/concealed zipper

b Exposed zipper

c Kissing placket zipper

d fly front

Don't show zipper teeth flat on top of line without construction detail.

e incorrectly drawn zipper

Learning the fundamental principles in measuring garment specifications is extremely important in today's industry. Essentially, measurements, or "specs" as they are commonly called, are the designer's way of communicating his intention to those producing the garment. Measurements need to be as complete and accurate as possible if the production sample is to be correct.

Either the designer or a "technical" designer is responsible for specing garments. While the method of measuring can vary from individual to individual and from company to company, consistency from garment to garment is very important. Achieve consistency by indicating measuring points on the spec sheet or sketch itself.

Although the designer may have a clear view of what he wants, translating it into numbers is a different matter altogether. Often designers will shop the stores to find a similar body to what they want to spec. Or they might go through the company's library of garments or previous production-development specs to use as a reference. With practice, you will become proficient at visualizing the correct numbers/specs that will create the desired result for various silhouettes and size categories.

Learning the principles of specing is less of a mystery than some people may think. Using the spec sheet repeatedly eliminates the need to memorize, as methods of measurement and what needs to be measured are clearly indicated. The following points should be kept in mind as a basis for measuring or specing garments:

MEASURING SPECIFICATIONS

GENERAL METHOD

Garment Position: All measurements are taken with garment flat on a smooth surface.

Measurements: All measurements are generally taken as width (not as a circumference).

High Point of Garment with Shoulder Seam (HPS): With garment flat, the high point of the shoulder is the highest point where the front and back shoulder seams meet at neck edge or collar joining seam.

High Point of Garment without Shoulder Seam: With garment flat and underarms pinned together, smooth garment to shoulder. The high point of the shoulder is the highest point at the neck edge or collar joining seam.

Imaginary Line (IL): With garment flat, the imaginary line runs straight from high point of shoulder left to high point of shoulder right.

Garment's Left Side: For consistency between different measurers, always measure the garment's left side. At front, right side (garment's left side); at back, left side (garment's left side).

Note: Letters correspond to the position of measurements on sketches. Some measurements are left out intentionally to allow for variances in garment design and category. These are determined by individual company standards.

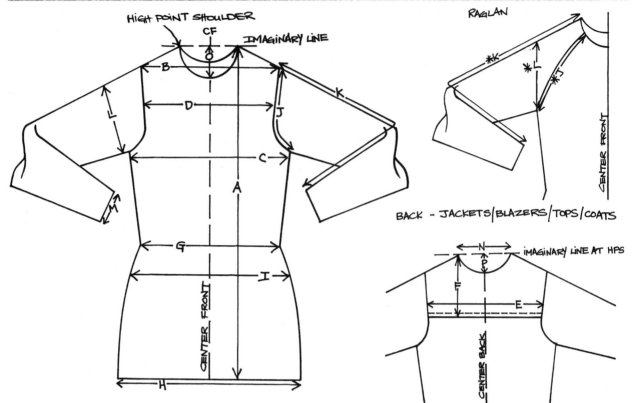

Measuring for Tops/Jackets/Blazers/Coats

A *Body length:* Measure at front from high point of shoulder to bottom edge of hem, parallel to center front.

B *Across shoulder of garment with yoke:* Measure across <u>back</u> of garment from armhole seam to armhole seam at natural shoulder line.

B *Across shoulder of garment without yoke:* Measure across <u>back</u> of garment from armhole seam to armhole seam at shoulder seam.

C *Chest width:* With all fullness spread, measure 1″ below bottom of armhole from garment edge to edge. *With dolman sleeve:* Measure ____″ from high point of shoulder, then straight across from garment edge to edge.

D *Across chest:* Measure ____″ from high point of shoulder, then straight across from armhole seam to armhole seam at front.

E *Across back:* Measure ____″ from high point of shoulder, then straight across from armhole seam to armhole seam at back.

F *Back yoke height:* Measure from high point of shoulder to yoke seam at back.

G *Waist width:* Find narrowest point of waist and measure ____″ down from high point of shoulder. Measure straight across from edge to edge.

H *Bottom opening:* Measure straight across bottom from edge to edge; *Shirt tails or side slits:*

Measure at top of shirt tail curve or slit straight across from edge to edge.

I *High hip:* Measure ____″ down from high point of shoulder; measure across from edge to edge.

J *Armhole, set-in sleeve:* Measure along curve of armhole joining seam from shoulder edge to side seam edge. Back armhole seam should be under the front armhole seam.

J* *Armhole, raglan/saddle:* Measure diagonally from center back seam to underarm seam edge.

K *Sleeve length from armhole:* Measure from sleeve opening edge to armhole, joining seam along top edge following slope of sleeve.

K* *Sleeve length from HPS:* Measure from sleeve opening edge to high point of shoulder along top edge following the slope of sleeve and shoulder.

L *Muscle width:* Measure 1″ from bottom of armhole, edge to edge, parallel to sleeve opening.

L* *Muscle width, dolman sleeve:* Measure ____″ from high point of shoulder along shoulder line. From this point, turn approximately 90 degrees from shoulder edge straight and parallel to sleeve opening.

M *Sleeve opening:* Measure along opening edge of sleeve from sleeve fold edge to underarm edge.

N *Neck width:* Shoulder seam to shoulder seam: at garment back, measure straight from high point of shoulder at left to high point of shoulder at right.

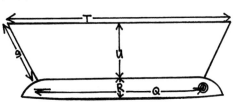

Two-Piece Collar

Q *Neckband opening:* With neckband unbuttoned and flat, measure along center of neckband from outside end of buttonhole to center of button following contour of band.

R *Neckband height:* Measure from neck joining seam to collar joining seam at center back.

S *Collar point:* Measure from collar joining seam to outer edge of collar along collar point edge.

T *Collar length:* Measure from one end of the collar to the other along collar joining seam.

U *Collar height:* Measure from neck joining seam to upper edge of collar at center back.

LAPEL WIDTH - SHAWL COLLAR

LAPEL WIDTH - NOTCH COLLAR

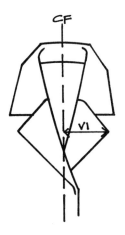

Lapel Width

V1 *Lapel width, garment with notched collar:* Measure from point of lower notch to collar fold perpendicular to garment center front.

V2 *Lapel width, garment with collar without notch:* Measure widest point of collar from collar fold to collar edge perpendicular to garment center front.

CUFF & SLEEVE PLACKET

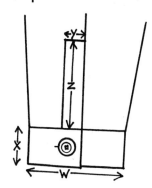

Cuff and Sleeve Placket

W *Cuff opening:* With cuff unbuttoned and flat, measure along center of cuff from outside end of buttonhole to center of button.

X *Cuff height:* Measure from cuff joining seam to bottom edge of cuff.

Y *Placket width:* Measure horizontally from edge of opening to stitching or placket edge.

Z *Placket length:* Measure from top of placket to bottom joining seam.

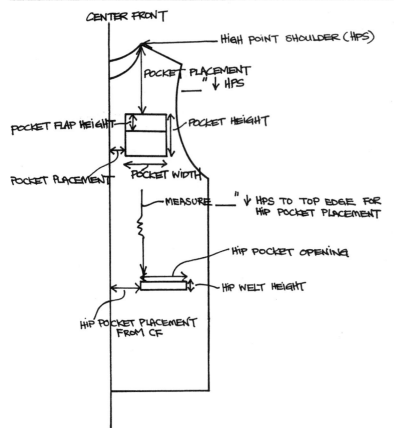

Pocket Placement for Jackets/Blazers/Tops/Coats

Pocket placement: Measure from high point of shoulder to top edge of pocket, from center front to edge of pocket.

Pocket height: Measure vertically from top edge to bottom edge at center of pocket.

Pocket width: Measure horizontally from edge to edge at top.

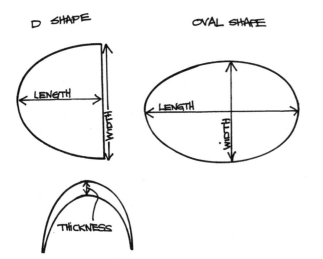

Shoulder Pad Placement

Shoulder pad length: Measure along top of pad following curve from edge to edge, including cover.

Shoulder pad width: On top surface of pad, measure across the widest portion from edge to edge, including cover.

Shoulder pad thickness: Measure vertically from top to bottom at thickest portion. If necessary, cut pad at widest portion.

Shoulder pad placement: Measure from neck edge or seam to edge of pad or pad cover.

Measuring for Skirts

A *Skirt length: garment with waistband (w/ wb):* Measure from waistband joining seam to bottom edge at <u>center back</u>.

(Styles with waistbands are measured at center back only.)

B *Skirt length: garment without waistband (w/o wb):* Measure from top edge to bottom edge at center front.

(Styles without waistbands are measured at center front only.)

C *Waist width relaxed, garment with waistband* (*rigid and elastic waist*): Measure through center of closed waistband under belt loops from edge to edge, relaxed.

C* *Waist width extended, garment with waistband-elastic waist:* Measure through center of closed waistband, fully extended, from edge to edge.

D *Waist width, garment without waistband:* Measure along top edge with front and back waistline edges together.

E *Waist width elastic, garment with section of elastic at waistband:* Measure through the center of the elastic relaxed from seam to seam.

F *Waistband height:* Measure from upper edge of waistband to waistband joining seam.

G *High hip, garment with waistband:* Use the three-point measure technique by marking 3″ below waist seam at center front and 3″ below waist seam at each edge of garment. Measure from edge to edge with pleats closed using the three points as guidelines.

High hip, garment without waistband: Use the three-point measure technique by marking ____″ from top edge at center front and ____″ from top edge at each edge of garment. Measure from edge to edge with <u>pleats closed</u> using the three points as guidelines.

H *Low hip, garment with waistband:* Use the three-point measure technique by marking <u>8″</u> below waist seam at center front and <u>8″ below waist</u> seam at each edge of garment. Measure from edge to edge, with <u>all fullness spread</u>, using the three points as guidelines. (<u>For petite sizes, measure 7″ below waist.</u>)

Low hip, garment without waistband: Use the three-point measure technique by marking ____″

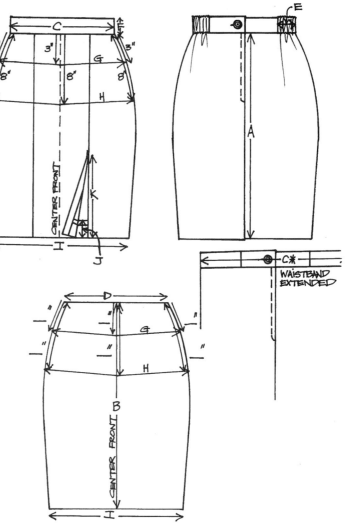

from top edge at center front and ____″ from top edge at each edge of garment. Measure from edge to edge, with <u>all fullness spread,</u> using the three points as guidelines.

I *Bottom opening, slim skirt:* Measure straight along bottom edge of hemline with vent/slit in place.

Bottom opening, full skirt: Measure along bottom edge following contour of hem with bottom edges together and all fullness spread.

Bottom opening, pleated skirt: Measure with pleats in place along bottom edge of hemline. Record number, width and depth of pleats.

J *Hem height:* Measure from hem edge to bottom edge (including hem tape).

K *Vent/slit height:* Measure length of actual opening at highest point.

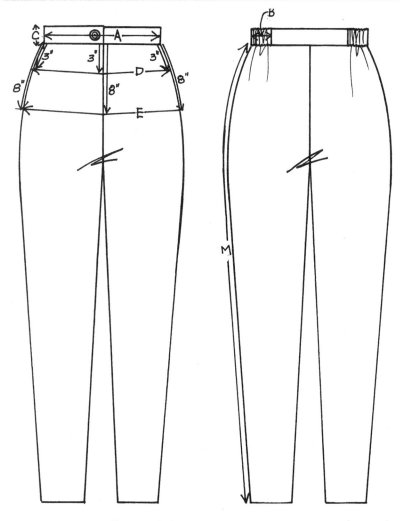

Measuring for Pants/Shorts: Waist

A *Waist width relaxed, garment with waistband (rigid and elastic waist):* Measure through center of closed waistband under belt loops from edge to edge, relaxed.

B *Waist width elastic, garment with section of elastic at waistband:* Measure through the center of the elastic relaxed from seam to seam.

C *Waistband height:* Measure from upper edge of waistband to waistband joining seam.

D *High hip, garment with waistband:* Use the three-point measure technique by marking <u>3″ below waist seam </u> at center front and <u>3″ below waist seam</u> at each edge of garment. Measure

from edge to edge with <u>pleats closed</u> using the three points as guidelines.

High hip, garment without waistband: (See Skirt Section, High Hip G).

E *Low hip, garment with waistband:* Use the three-point measure technique by marking <u>8″ below waist seam</u> at center front and <u>8″ below waist seam</u> at each edge of garment. Measure from edge to edge, with <u>all fullness spread,</u> using the three points as guidelines. (<u>For petite size, measure 7″ below waist.</u>)

Low Hip, garment without waistband: (See Skirt Section Low-Hip H).

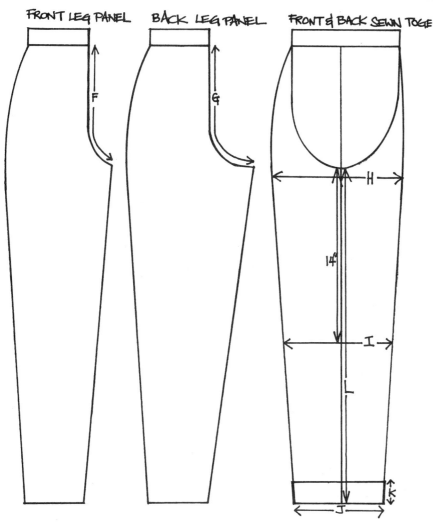

FRONT LEG PANEL   BACK LEG PANEL   FRONT & BACK SEWN TOGE

Measuring for Pants/Shorts: Rise and Leg

F *Front rise, garment with waistband:* Lay garment flat so that the rise seam is flat from waistband seam to crotch joining seam. Measure from crotch to waistband seam with rise seam flat. (Be careful not to stretch the seam.)

Front rise, garment without waistband: Lay garment flat so that rise seam is flat from top edge of waist to crotch joining seam. Measure from crotch to top edge of waist with rise seam flat. (Be careful not to stretch the seam.)

G *Back rise, garment with waistband:* Lay garment flat so that rise seam is flat from waistband seam to crotch joining seam. Measure from crotch to waistband seam with rise seam flat. (Be careful not to stretch the seam.)

Back rise, garment without waistband: Lay garment flat so that rise seam is flat from top edge of waist to crotch joining seam. Measure from

crotch to top edge of waist with rise seam flat. (Be careful not to stretch seam.)

H *Thigh:* Measure with pant leg inseam and outseam together. Measure 1″ below crotch, parallel to leg opening from edge to edge.

I *Knee:* Measure with pants leg inseam and outseam together. For Missy: Measure 14″ from crotch seam; for petite: Measure 13″ from crotch seam. Then, measure from edge to edge.

J *Leg opening:* Measure along bottom edge with inseam and outseam together.

K *Cuff height:* Measure from top edge of cuff to bottom edge of cuff.

L *Inseam:* Measure from crotch seam to bottom edge on inside leg seam.

M *Outseam, garment with waistband:* Place front and back panels together. Measure from waistband joining seam to bottom edge following the curve of the seam. (See previous

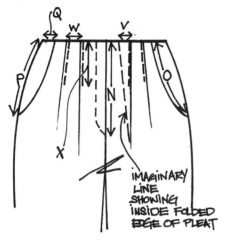

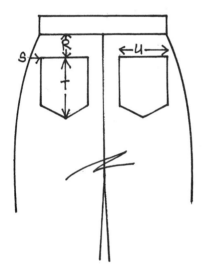

Measuring for Pants/Shorts: Pockets and Pleats

Outseam, garment without waistband: Place front and back panels together. Measure from top edge to bottom edge following the curve of the seam.

(Measure only inseam <u>or</u> outseam. Do not measure both.)

N   *Opening, front/back/side:* Measure length of actual opening.

O   *Front pocket opening:* Measure length of actual opening.

P   *Front pocket placement from waist:* Measure from waist edge or seam to top or bottom of pocket opening depending on pocket style.

Q   *Front pocket placement from side seam:* Measure parallel with waist edge or seam from side seam to pocket opening.

R   *Back pocket placement from waist:* Measure from waist edge or seam to top of pocket opening. For pockets on angle, measure to top lowest point.

S   *Back pocket placement from side seam:* Measure parallel with waist edge or seam to top edge of pocket.

T   *Pocket height:* Measure vertically from top to bottom at center of pocket.

U   *Pocket width:* Measure horizontally from edge to edge at top.

V   *Pleat depth:* Placing tape measure into pleat fold, measure from folded edge of pleat on outside to inside folded edge of pleat.

W   *Pleat width:* Measure from first pleat fold to second pleat fold.

X   *Stitchdown:* Measure from waist seam to end of stitching.

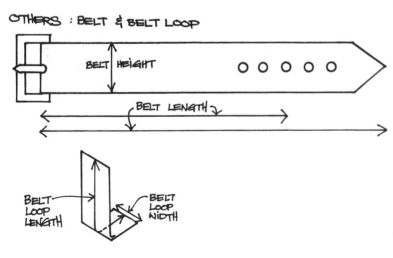

Belts & Belt Loops

Belt loop length: Measure vertically end to end <u>including</u> overlap.

Belt loop width: Measure horizontally from edge to edge at widest point.

Belt length: **1.** Measure from end (excluding buckle) to middle hole; **2.** Measure from end to end (excluding buckle).

Belt height: Measure from top edge to bottom edge of belt.

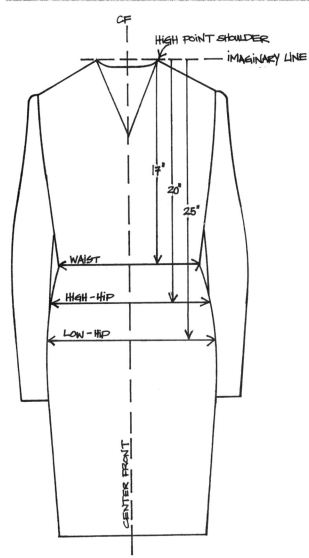

Measurements for Dresses

Dress measurements are essentially the same as those for the tops except for reference points such as waist, high hip and low hip. These measurements are taken from the high point shoulder. Length of garments are also taken from the high point shoulder.

Reference points for dresses change for petite, junior and large sizes according to size categories. The same is true for tops and jackets. Measurements and sketches included with this section refer to the missy size category.

CHAPTER 7

Presentation boards are an important tool in the fashion industry for selling and communicating ideas. Design applicants who know how to create boards have a definite edge in the job market.

Presentation Boards

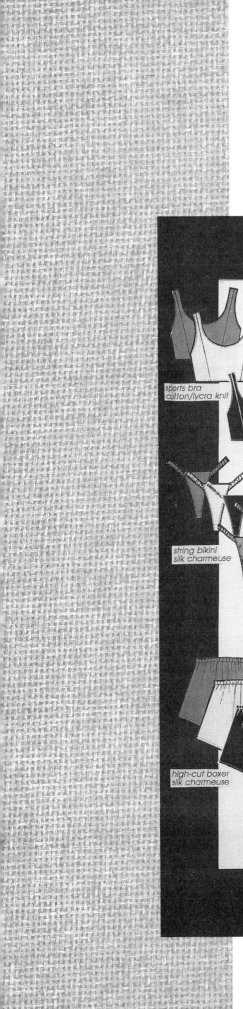

Presentation board by Jenifer Angilello and Daynanna Mendoza.

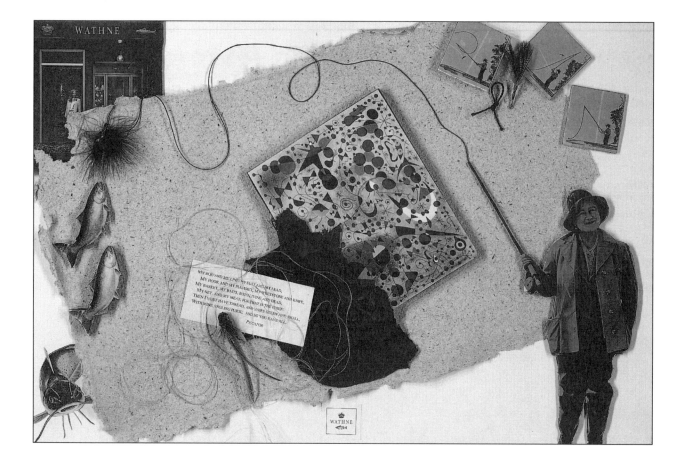

Presentation boards are an important tool in the fashion industry for selling and communicating ideas. Because most companies sell to many different vendors, they need a means to effectively demonstrate concept and fabric options. Presentation boards are extremely cost effective, since collections can be elaborately worked out and visualized without the expense of producing a single garment.

Using boards also allows for flexibility when a company is developing a product for a particular store. Buyers preview fabrics and discuss "bodies" with the manufacturer's design team via boards. This way, when a formal presentation is made to the buyers, they know pretty much what to expect, though changes can still be made if necessary.

Design applicants who know how to create boards have a definite edge in the job market. Featuring presentation boards in your portfolio communicates the sense of organization and neatness required for this kind of work. The skills needed to create these boards can vary according to their type and purpose. Generally, presentation boards are composed of materials or elements with a common theme or fabrication. Some are mainly comprised of photos and fabrics, while others include sketches of designs on the figure or on the flat.

Excellent drawing skills are essential for original design presentations. However, because there are such diverse skill requirements and purposes for creating board presentations, fashion design or merchandising applicants might be considered for jobs that include some or all of these skills. The presentation board is so widely used in the industry that some companies seek applicants who will do this exclusively.

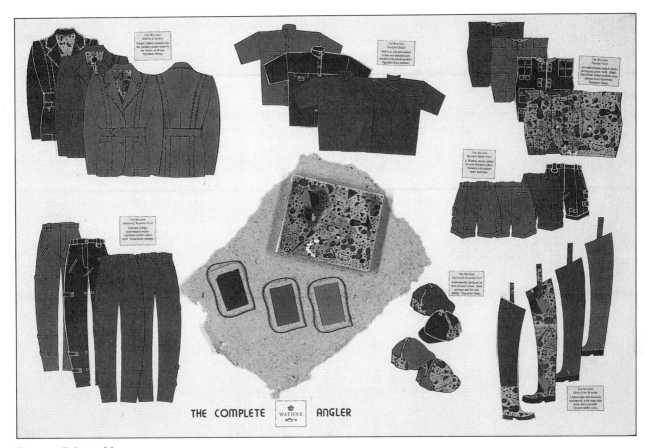

Figure   7.1a and b

Companion boards such as these "theme" and design boards suggest design direction for a given season. Inspired by a painting by Miro, they are rich in visual elements and texture.

Theme and design boards by Koko Lance.

CONCEPT BOARDS

Most companies today use some form of presentation boards in both developing and selling their design product. Once the research for design inspiration and fabric sourcing has been completed, the designer can zero-in on the main themes or concepts to be developed for that season's collection. Companies create concept and fabric boards to suggest the design direction for that season (Fig. 7.1a). In addition, some companies supplement these with design boards featuring either color or black-and-white sketches showing garment silhouette and detail. While flats are a popular method of illustrating style development (Fig. 7.1b), many companies show garments on a figure for emphasis.

Companies can create concept, fabric/color, design or customer boards, or a combination of these. The least common are customer boards, because the image of the customer is often incorporated within the other board types. Companies will use these, however, when they are creating new divisions and want to establish a new customer identity.

During the early design process, designers may develop idea boards—"comps"—that are used for gathering and organizing material related to a concept or theme. These boards are less polished than final presentation boards, tending to be more informal in technique and design.

TYPES OF BOARDS

The ultimate presentation board must be visually exciting, informative and flawlessly executed to be a convincing selling tool. The viewer must "get" its message immediately, which can be achieved with clear, attractive visuals. A good eye for placement and layout and a penchant for neatness produce the best results.

PRODUCT DEVELOPMENT

Another basic category of boards are those used for product development. By definition, product development is the process of adapting the elements of an existing product to meet the needs of a different customer base. Key concepts to consider are changing parts versus pure design, and using merchandise at a different price point. Presentation boards are widely used by manufacturers and retailers to facilitate product development.

In-house designers, freelancers or companies specializing in product development create these particular boards. It takes multi-skilled individuals to handle all facets of development. They are usually designers with a minimum of three to five years' experience in the industry and have a thorough knowledge of fabric/trim sources. They are also good researchers with an eye for trends, excellent color coordination abilities, good taste and exceptional drawing skills. Their presentation techniques are dramatic and flawless. These designers may be asked to create programs for a few items or a whole collection, based either on client-generated ideas or their own. They then work up each design concept on a board with images relating to the theme, and provide additional boards showing garments designed in that same theme.

FORECAST AND FIBER SERVICES

Another important type of boards are those created by forecast and fiber services for their clients. These boards suggest both silhouette and style trends, as well as seasonal color and fabric trends, projected one to two years in advance. Some services are fiber-specific and are supported by companies that produce the same fiber.

Figure 7.2

Each season, forecast and fiber services produce boards such as this one, which help the designer zero in on color and theme in the early stages of research.

Forecast color/fiber board courtesy of Cotton Incorporated.

Depending on their needs, companies can purchase all or a portion of the materials a service has to offer. Products include both style and color books as well as visual slide presentations. As a supplement or as a portion of the slide format, forecast services create "theme" boards and fabric/color story boards that are extremely rich in carefully chosen visuals (Fig. 7.2). The boards reinforce the visual presentation and help the designer sort out and focus on design direction. Appendix A, Fashion Information Resources, contains a list of forecast and fiber services.

No matter how complex or simple the project, careful planning is the key to creating professional presentation boards. Many designers make a "working" list that they adjust to suit each project. The list below is generally sufficient and applicable to most projects, in that each stage of development enables you to gain momentum and move ahead with a minimum of backtracking. Each of the following stages will be discussed in sequence:

PLANNING THE PRESENTATION

- Purpose
- Focus
- Quantity of boards
- Art supplies
- Visual materials (photographs and photocopies, fabric/trim, sketches)
- Layout
- Techniques and technologies (labeling, computer design, color copier, handwork, creating dimension, velcro, reproducing the board)

PURPOSE

Knowing the purpose of your presentation board can answer many questions in the planning stage. Will it be used for a formal presentation? Is it a "comp" board used for gathering material in preparation for a more formal presentation? Will it have sketches? If so, will they be figures, flats or a combination of both? Do you need to show your designs in colorways? These are just some of the questions you might ask yourself before forging ahead.

FOCUS

The focus of a board can refer to two distinct and different areas: customer/market and visual focus. Because of the importance of focusing all portfolio work on a customer/market, read Chapter 3 thoroughly. Ideally, presentation boards, as well as portfolio pieces, should have the same concentration. Because they are part of a whole, they need to interrelate both visually and conceptually. This is important to the unity of the entire portfolio and demonstrates professional awareness. Visual focus will be discussed later in this chapter.

QUANTITY

Presentations can range in breadth from a single board to multiple-board presentations. A single board might be used to highlight one garment or several, and may incorporate elements such as visuals, fabric/trim and sketches (Fig. 7.3). Because not everyone in the fashion industry is visually oriented, requests to see specific pieces that have been recolored from your original presentation are quite common. A single-board presentation can satisfy this need and reassure a buyer who wants to actually see the garment in a different color.

Multiple-board presentations are generally used for large-scale design development programs and may consist of a mood/theme board, fabric/color board (these are often combined to relate the color story to the visuals) and sketch boards (Fig. 7.4a and b). The size of the program, the number of designs and fabric selection determines the quantity of boards required for a given presentation. Companies will invest a lot of time and creative energy into these, as their objective is to "wow" the buyers and generate larger sale figures.

ART SUPPLIES

Making presentation boards is a specialized activity that requires the right materials. Before you begin, make sure you have everything you need to facilitate your work. A basic list of supplies used for creating board presentations might include the following:

- foam core board or Bainbridge board
- decorative papers in various colors and textures
- a heavy duty mat knife suitable for cutting boards
- scissors and pinking shears for cutting paper and fabric swatches
- transferable lettering and borders
- various adhesives

Figure   7.3
A single board can incorporate several elements such as visuals, fabric/trim, sketches and colorways. Often, the process of creating boards is a team effort.

Presentation board by Alyssa Bibart and Mi Kim.

Because making presentation boards involves a great deal of cutting and pasting, you will need a wide assortment of adhesive products, such as rubber cement, repositionable spray adhesive, rubber cement transfer tape, adhesive transfer sheets, double-sided adhesive film, velcro tape, and/or a wax coater. A detailed overview of art supplies appropriate for making presentation boards is provided in Appendix B, Art Supplies for Fashion Designers.

VISUAL ELEMENTS

The elements, or visuals, that make up a professional board presentation fall into three basic categories: photographs/photocopies, fabric/trims and figure/flat sketches.

Photos/Photocopies

Selecting the right visuals for boards containing mood/theme components is extremely important. These elements communicate what you are trying to say and need to be clear in order to capture the spirit of your designs. A knowledge of basic design principles, such as spatial relationships, color, form, dramatic size contrast and proportion, are useful in the selection and placement of visuals.

Choosing photographs to coordinate with your fabric/color story creates a more aesthetic result and adds to the "flow" of your presentation. Because boards are meant to be viewed from several feet away, the images need to be large enough to be seen and dramatic enough to make an impact. Here you can let your creativity and imagination soar.

Fabrics/Trims

Fabrics are a crucial part of the design process and must be appropriately showcased. Organizing swatches in a logical way can add to a presentation and help clarify your intention. For example, some designers like to group fabrics by type and fiber content. Others prefer to arrange fabrics by color. Whichever way you choose, be consistent throughout your presentation. Place fabrics that coordinate together as they would appear in a design. Fabrics that are overlapped in a design should be shown on the board in this manner, as well.

Whenever possible, trim fabric swatches to be the same size, with the exception of prints, which usually need to be larger to show the repeat of a pattern. Although "pinked" edges are preferred because they prevent fraying, some fabrics look best with a blunt edge, such as those with a pile. Fabrics that have a tendency to "roll," such as knits or jerseys, can be placed under a window-mount to conceal the edge. An alternative method for these fabrics is gluing them to an adhesive-backed paper.

Trims, including braid, ribbon, buttons and any decorative element, need to be organized and grouped with the swatches. Often, showing the trim as it would appear on the actual design lends reality to a presentation. Sewing buttons on the fabric, rather than gluing or taping them to a board, always looks neat and professional. If you wish to include a design of your own trim, display a reference along with your hand-painted sample to show its source of inspiration.

Sketches

Boards containing sketches are often part of a product development presentation. A designer includes sketches when he or she needs to accurately show various styles. Because buyers actually buy from these presentations, the sketches need to visually describe the garment perfectly. No amount of written explanation can substitute for a good sketch. Like the old adage says, "a picture is worth a thousand words."

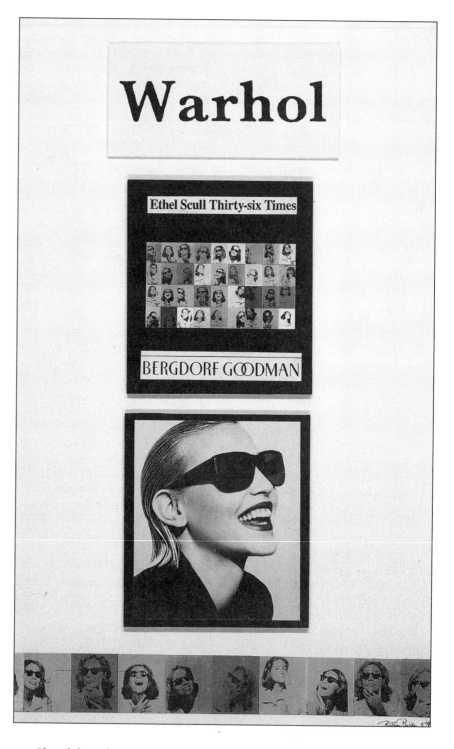

Sketch boards are usually separate from the mood/theme boards that sometimes accompany them. Flat sketches are most frequently used in these presentations and are especially popular in the sportswear market for showing coordination and colorways (Fig. 7.5). Chapter 6 discusses several techniques for creating and rendering flats.

You can show figure sketches along with flats in order to feature a particular garment. A beautiful drawing is very captivating and can "romance" a presentation. Figure sketches, used frequently in the bridge and designer markets (Fig. 7.6), are good when you need to communicate a "look." These presentations also showcase a strong drawing ability.

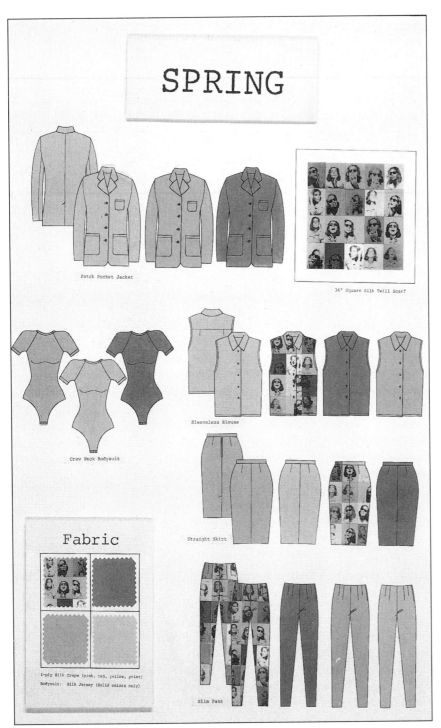

Figure 7.4a and b
Multiple-board presentations are often used for large-scale design development programs. This one targets a specific store and customer.

Presentation board by Bettina Bierly.

LAYOUT

Layout is crucial to the final result of a presentation and an important part of the planning stage. Simply, the layout is the arrangement of all the elements that will be part of the presentation. The arrangement you choose should be both logical and aesthetically pleasing. Haphazard or random arrangements can be confusing, unintelligible and even unsettling. Permanently gluing any elements without first planning your layout is extremely risky and can jeopardize a potentially good presentation. It can be costly, as well.

You are ready to lay out your board only after you've purchased your supplies, chosen your visuals and completed your sketches. Whether

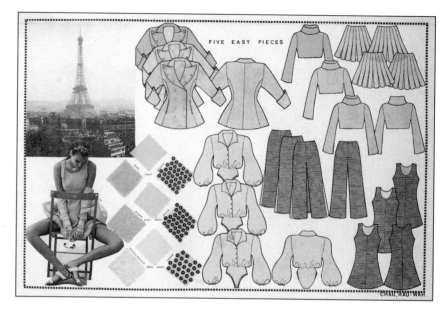

Figure 7.5

Flat sketches are most frequently used in the sportswear market for showing coordination and colorways. This example emphasizes a pastel color story in wool crepe, mohair and sequins.

Presentation board by Hau-Wah Chau.

you are creating a single- or multiple-board presentation, place your loose elements on the board to establish balance and flow. You can also lightly tape these to secure their positioning. This initial positioning helps you make decisions about size, quantity of pieces ("Do I have enough, too little?"), balance and general "flow" of the board. Once you are satisfied with the layout, mark each element's position in pencil at the corners so you know where to place it permanently with adhesive. Relying on your memory for placement can lead to errors and extra work. Thorough planning helps you do it right the first time and achieve a more satisfying result.

Most boards are "read" from left to right, as in reading a book. Since this is the way the eye naturally travels, professional board designers like to use the upper left side of the board to place the most important element. Consider this focal point when you are planning your board layout.

TECHNIQUES AND TECHNOLOGIES

The techniques and technologies used for creating presentation boards can vary based on two factors: time and the accessibility of equipment. Techniques can vary from cutting and pasting, hand-work/sketching and rendering, color copying or computer-aided graphics.

Most presentations consist of not one, but rather a combination of techniques. This is usually for a variety of reasons, one being that presentation boards are often created by more than one individual. A second reason for combining techniques is time constraints. Sometimes several methods are used in conjunction because they are most expedient within a given time frame. And finally, the type of equipment available to you can have impact on your presentation board end-product.

Labeling

To achieve a professional result, mechanically generate any form of titling or labeling, no matter how small. Hand-lettering looks amateurish and gives the impression of a "school project," rather than a professional one. Selecting the right size and font is an important part of designing the board. The art supply list in Appendix B lists several lettering choices used by professionals.

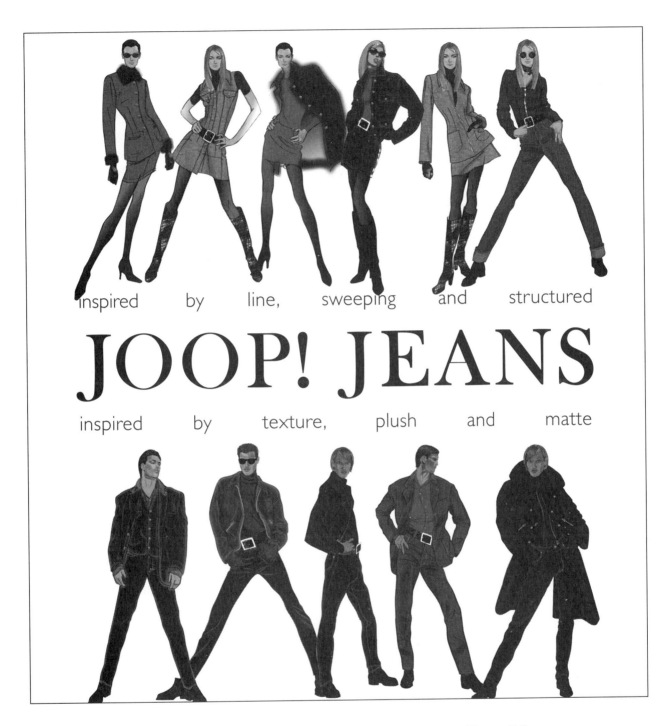

inspired by line, sweeping and structured

JOOP! JEANS

inspired by texture, plush and matte

Computer Design

Companies that have expensive computer equipment will most definitely utilize it in their board presentations. Garments can be scanned in or even created on the computer itself. Fabrics can also be scanned in, as well as resized, recolored, balanced and, in effect, re-designed. Refer to Chapter 8 for a more in-depth discussion of the uses and technical capabilities of computers.

Color Copier

More often used as a supplement to the computer—or to generate a computer-like effect—is the color copier. Since it is an expensive piece of equipment, companies that cannot afford their own use copying ser-

Figure 7.6

Figure sketches are more often used when a fashion "look" needs to be communicated and are frequently used in the bridge and designer markets. A strong drawing ability is showcased through these presentations.

Presentation board with figures by Geoffry Gertz.

vices such as Kinkos. Speed is the specific advantage of using either a computer or a color copier for producing sketches with fabric for boards. It is fast and saves rendering time. The suggested exercises included with this chapter will explain techniques involving the color copier that can generate impressive results.

Handwork

Some designers still do hand-work to sketch and render fabric, often in combination with the techniques described above. A particular color or pattern may not copy well and requires the human touch. Time constraints can also impact decisions on what and what not to hand render. Although there is a strong tendency to favor the time-saving technologies, there are those who prefer the less "mechanical" look of the hand-rendered sketch. This choice involves both personal preference, as well as an evaluation of the presentation requirements.

Creating Dimension

When specific areas of a board need to be highlighted, many designers like to mount an additional layer or layers of foam core on the main board. Use a re-positionable adhesive or adhesive-backed transfer sheet to achieve a smooth result. A ruler and utility knife are essential to create a perfect shape for straight-edge visuals.

The shaped visual presents a bit more of a challenge. Once glued to the projected layer of foam core, it is cut by following all its curves. Cutting through foam core is a practiced and acquired skill. To get the best results, cut halfway into the board (known as scoring), then go back over it a second time. Once the visual chosen to be projected is cut, glue it to the main board.

Velcro®

Many professionals use Velcro® strips or dots to facilitate changes on any pieces that might have to be changed, which is often the case with garment sketches or fabric swatches. These can be pre-mounted to a sturdy paper or thin layer of foam core, then repositioned or mounted as frequently as necessary.

Reproducing the Board

Because presentation boards are both fragile and cumbersome to take on an interview, many professionals prefer to have copies made for their portfolios, rather than risk damaging their originals. The cost of reproducing boards varies, depending on the method. An expensive method (approximately $60 per print) requires an actual photograph, which is then scanned to ensure a quality print. The advantage is that the reproduction quality is excellent and the board is shot in one piece.

The less expensive method of color copying the board is done in two sections and pieced together. This technique is satisfactory for those who are just starting out and may not be able to afford better. Another inexpensive method with good results is to make a slide transparency, which runs about $8 per slide. Once the slide is created, you can then make an enlarged color copy from it, usually 8 ½" x 11" or 11" x 17". These prints have good color and clarity and are suitable for portfolio presentation.

"FIVE EASY PIECES"—SINGLE-BOARD PRESENTATION

This single board exercise is designed to incorporate many of the components and techniques professionally used in presentation boards, including fashion design, determining customer focus, sketching and mastery of the color copier or computer graphics (Fig. 7.7). The cost of materials ranges from $25–40, including the cost of color copies. A knowledge of drawing flats is required for the design component. This exercise makes an excellent portfolio piece, as it highlights several skills. The board direction you choose should complement the orientation of your other portfolio formats (i.e., horizontal or vertical).

Select a location that would be accessible for a long weekend and design five coordinated sportswear pieces. Your designs should focus on a particular customer and market and be suitable to go from day to night with a change of jewelry or accessories. To assist with customer focus and identity, you may identify a store and use its logo within the board presentation. Select fabrics appropriate for the climate. Include appropriate trims, buttons or fashion details and coordinate these with the fabric in the final presentation.

STAGES OF DEVELOPMENT

1. Select a Vacation Spot

The place you choose must be accessible for a weekend. China and Fiji are out!

Figure 7.7

"Five Easy Pieces"—Single-board presentation

This board is designed to incorporate components and techniques used professionally in presentation boards, including designing for a specific geographic locale, determining customer focus, flat sketching/layout, and mastery of the color copier or computer graphics. It contains the following elements: visuals of vacation spot, flats (front and back view), colorways (print plus three coordinating colors), and fabrics labeled for content and season.

Presentation board by Jing Chao.

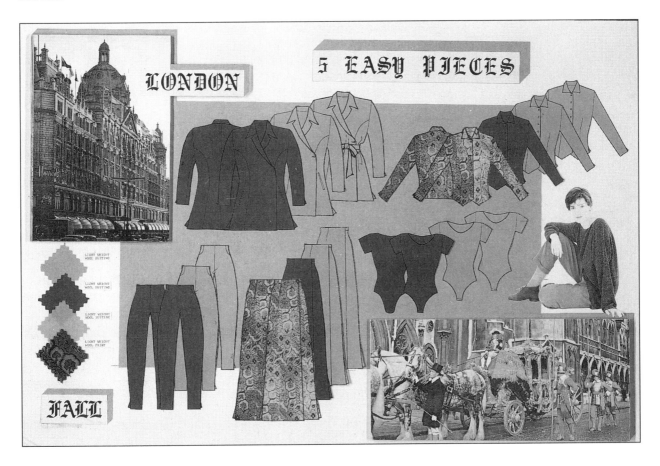

2. Fabrics and Trims

Appropriate color and fabric weight are important considerations when planning your designs. For example, vibrant colors work well for a tropical climate. Although neutrals and darks are always considered fashionable, remember color creates a more alluring presentation. Choose either a print or texture, then coordinate solids extracted from the print. This will automatically create a natural coordination for your group and help you develop colorways.

You will be showing each garment in front and back view (same size) in your print plus two to four colorways. Show the back view in one colorway only, and arrange it with the same color in front view. Not every garment need be shown in every colorway. What determines each garment's colorway is analyzing how it will be worn and coordinated with the other garments. Some customers prefer a jacket that matches a bottom weight, while others will wear contrasting pieces. In designing, you want to satisfy as large a customer base as possible. By developing a design group in colorways, you create a range of choices for different customer preferences.

3. Designing the Flats

Designing a sportswear group most often starts with the jacket, since the proportion of the other pieces and the necklines of the tops are based on it. Begin with 20 to 30 thumbnail flats, then edit those down to five: one jacket, one skirt, one pants and two tops (blouses and bodysuits fall into this category). To help you coordinate the pieces, draw the flats by category in pencil on tracing paper, i.e., all jackets together, with shirts, pants, tops, etc., on their own pages. This approach makes it easy to compare proportion and detail. By trying different placements of jackets over bottom weights as well as blouses, you will be able to determine how well your designs "work" together.

Optional pieces such as a vest, dress or coat may be added to your group once the five main pieces are selected. A pareo or scarf may be counted as an accessory rather than one of the items. Keep in mind that all pieces must work together, coordinate easily to span the weekend and be climate-appropriate. (Refer to Chapter 6 for the techniques for sketching flats.)

4. Polishing the Flats

Once you have edited your thumbnails down to five pieces and possibly one or two optional garments, you are ready to select a technique for finishing your flats. An instructor or professional can help you edit your designs. Generally, the most preferred method is the contrast technique, which emphasizes a strong garment outline and a fine line for inside detail. This helps the garments to "pop," or standout, in the presentation. However, technique is a preference that can vary from individual to individual and company to company. (Refer to Chapter 6 for appropriate techniques for board presentation.)

5. Reproducing the Fabric

Make acetate copies of your flats (any copy shop carries these special sheets) in preparation for the fabric-reproduction stage. Then place the acetate copy over a photocopy of your print or solid fabric (colored paper may be substituted). You now have a copy of your garment in your chosen fabric (Fig. 7.8). Reduce print fabrics from as large an actual piece of fabric as possible; most prints need at least three reductions to become the correct scale for your flats. However, print reduction should be evaluated on an individual basis. Sometimes true scale must be sacrificed for a legible reproduction of the print.

The photocopying process can, however, change the color of certain fabrics so they no longer match the actual swatches. When this occurs, use color copies of your fabrics so the garments and fabric match. Many professionals prefer to color copy all the visuals for board presentations to achieve a polished, even look. It also gives them various options for displaying the fabrics, since they do not have to contend with gluing problems or frayed edges.

6. Choosing Visuals

You need to find just the right visuals to coordinate with your color story. Select one or two really strong pictures that are universally representative of your vacation spot. For instance, New York is famous for its skyline, Paris for the Eiffel Tower and Miami Beach for flamingoes and palm trees. Visuals must instantly communicate the intended message. Small photos can get lost on a 20″ × 30″ board, so select a good sized photo that coordinates well with your fabric/color story to add to the drama of your presentation.

Include an image of your customer as one of the visuals. The viewer should be able to see the appropriateness of the designs to the target customer. Your visual might be a head shot emphasizing the customer type, or a full-length photo of the customer wearing clothes in a category or feeling related to your designs. If you select a photo of a clothed figure, make sure the clothes are vague so as not to compete with your designs. If the photo has a similar color and feeling to your designs, so much the better. One important customer image is sufficient and less confusing than several examples.

7. Planning the Layout

Once all the visuals are board-ready, you can plan the layout of your presentation. You want to create a flow so that the eye travels around the board. Some professionals like to use the left side of their presentations as a focal point because the eye naturally "reads" the board from left to right, like a book. This is a good spot to place one of the important visuals.

8. Flats

Follow a definite format for placing flats. The front and back view of each garment (shown in the same color) can slightly overlap one another. Similarly overlap the colorways corresponding to each garment. Garments can be positioned in either a horizontal or diagonal arrangement. Whenever possible, place tops above bottoms. Avoid positioning pieces haphazardly, as this will draw the eye away from the designs and create unnecessary visual movement on the board.

9. Showing Vignettes

When a garment has a special detail or treatment, it often enhances a presentation to show that detail in a small sketch called a vignette. The vignette is usually done in black and white so as not to compete with the

Figure 7.8

In preparation for fabric reproduction, an acetate copy of the flats is laid over a photocopy of fabric. Using a photocopy or computer-generated reduction of your fabric results in a flawless and even presentation.

Flats by Alan Paul Harris.

Exercise I (continued)

design of the garments. A popular way of highlighting this feature so it does not "float" on the board is to put a light border around it with one of the Letraline-style tapes. Place the vignette near the garment or garments to which it relates.

You can also make vignettes out of actual muslin or fabric and sew or glue them to a presentation board. Although this can be extremely effective and add both dimension and realism, it is rarely done due to time constraints. For those who sew well, however, it creates an opportunity to show off your special skills.

10. Fabrics

Fabrics and trims should be "packaged" together so the fabric and color coordination can be seen. Avoid scattering your swatches around the board in a haphazard manner. Cut or trim fabrics with scissors or pinking shears. Some professionals tape fabrics to a surface before cutting to ensure a perfect shape. You can also mat fabrics to the back of a piece of foam core, with windows for viewing. This method is extremely effective for concealing edges and especially good when using varied or pile fabrics. Place fabrics importantly in a presentation. Treating them dimensionally is an excellent way of showcasing them.

11. Title/Labeling

Once all the elements are in place, decide on title placement and labels. Mechanically generate all lettering. Unless you are an experienced calligrapher, hand lettering looks unprofessional and unpolished. Generally ½″ or ¾″ lettering is adequate for titles. Labels should be smaller; 10- or 12-point is appropriate. The art supply list in Appendix B includes several lettering options for boards. Those who prefer to use Letra-set lettering often photocopy their titles and labels to prevent peeling, rather than applying the lettering directly to the board.

12. Adhesives

Mark the position of all the elements with pencil before gluing to ensure accurate placement. Leaving this to chance is risky business and could jeopardize hours of hard work. Consider the density of materials before selecting any adhesives. Fragile papers and fabrics should be glued with products that will not bleed through and mar your presentation. Spray Mount™ and rubber cement tape are good choices. Spray Mount, peel-off adhesive sheets and hot wax are excellent for covering large surfaces

"ART INSPIRES DESIGN"—DOUBLE-BOARD PRESENTATION

Almost every season, designers zero-in on an art reference for both color and fabric inspiration for their collections (Fig. 7.9a and b). Some painters whose works of art have successfully become fashion trends are Matisse, Dali, Klee and Mondrian. However, the possibilities are infinite for creating designs inspired by art.

This exercise encourages individual creativity through selecting an artist's work as a fabrication and developing colorways from it for a coordinated design group. Museums and libraries are an excellent place to identify works of art that are visually appealing and will lend themselves to textile conversion. When choosing a work of art, consider its appropriateness to a customer and market for design interpretation.

Use 20″ × 30″ foam core for this presentation. Make both boards the same orientation so they will be compatible for viewing.

Board I—Inspiration/Customer

As an inspiration board, this contains the visuals that show your design point of reference (see Fig. 7.9a). Include the following elements:

- painting or fine art piece (color copy)
- name of artist
- image of customer
- target store

Figure 7.9a

This double-board presentation is an example of how art inspires design. The first board contains the visuals that show your design reference and includes the following elements: painting or fine art piece, name of artist, image of customer and target store.

Presentation boards by Yukie Takisawa.

Exercise II (continued)

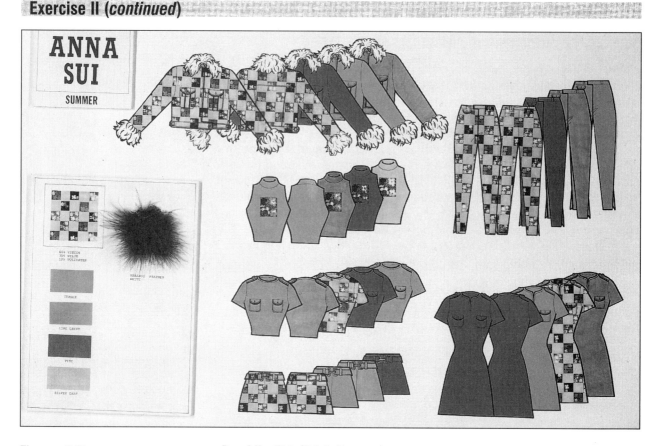

Figure 7.9b

The second board shows a coordinated sportswear group and includes the following elements: flats (front and back view), colorways (print plus three coordinating colors) and fabrics labeled for content and season.

Presentation boards by Yukie Takisawa.

Board II—Flats/Fabric/Season

A design board showing a coordinated sportswear group consisting of five to seven pieces (see Fig. 7.9b). Show each item in front and back view and developed in colorways. Items do not necessarily have to be shown in all colorways; evaluate them on an individual basis. This is usually determined by how the items are worn together. Generally, the jacket and bottom weights (skirt or pants) are designed in the same colorways to satisfy the customer who wants a matching top and bottom. Those customers who do not prefer a matched set also have options. Although prints might not be used as frequently in pants as in tops, the trend of a current season might determine this. In other words, what was considered "out" one season might be the "hot" trend in the next. Include the following elements:

- flats (front and back view)
- colorways (print plus three coordinating colors)
- fabrics labeled for content
- season (without specific date)

Review the previous exercise for flat technique, reproducing the fine art print and glueing methods. Add labeling with brief garment descriptions, if desired. You can use decorative papers to enhance your presentation and reinforce the design theme. No element on the board should compete with your designs. Plan the arrangement of all visuals carefully for best results.

CHAPTER **8**

Just as a hammer or wrench is a powerful extension of the hand, think of the computer as an extension of the designer's hand. The computer is simply another exciting tool to enhance creativity and efficiently execute the designer's ideas.

The Computer
as a Design Tool

ILLUSTRATIONS BY GEOFFRY GERTZ

"Will it hinder my creativity?"
"Do I need to relearn how to design?"
"Will I really save that much time?"
"Can I adapt to the computer if I am technically challenged?"
"Technology changes so quickly. Is computer design just a trend that I can bypass?"

These are some of the questions commonly asked when confronted with the task of incorporating computer design into the apparel design process. First, let's demystify this challenge. In the most basic terms, a computer is simply a tool. Just as a hammer or wrench is a powerful extension of the hand, think of the computer as an extension of the designer's hand, as well as his or her creativity. The physical presence of the computer and its peripheral devices (hardware) and the many available design applications (software) are used in combination, as with any other design medium. Remember when you first learned how to draw with a pencil? How many unsure strokes did it take until you were able create an acceptable image? To be honest, all of us have at least once blamed a poor drawing on a bad pencil or an uncooperative drawing tablet. Trite, but true, practice did make perfect.

Now think of your transition to pastels, markers or even gouache as a rendering medium. Although the first attempts may have been difficult, each successive transition simplified your acquisition of skills and broadened your knowledge of design principles and elements. Think of the computer, with its design applications, as that next new medium that needs to be mastered and included in your design repertoire. The computer is simply another exciting tool to enhance creativity and efficiently execute the designer's ideas.

Line, shape or silhouette, color and texture are all elements of design that must be communicated effectively throughout the apparel design process. From concept to illustration, to production drawings and presentations, the designer's manipulation of these elements can range from simple (Fig. 8.1) to complex (Fig. 8.2).

The designer may choose to use the computer in any or all of the stages in the design process. While computers have long been a mainstay in the areas of textile design and apparel production, i.e., pattern-making, grading, machine knitting, marker placement, cutting and inventory control, this discussion will focus on the use of the computer in the design process, from concept to presentation.

DEVELOPING CONCEPTS/STORING INFORMATION

Designers communicate visually. During the initial stages of concept development you can use the computer to collect, manipulate, assemble and store or archive images. For instance, any two-dimensional image—a drawing, photograph or shallow object such as a fabric swatch, yarn sample or trim—can be placed on a scanner and input to the computer. Any three-dimensional object can be input as well through the use of a digital camera or video camera. Some designers even use the mouse or graphic tablet with pressure-sensitive pen to create original images directly on the computer. Regardless of the input method, the designer can store his or her concept images for use any time, in any combination.

Just as a computer can be used to edit words, it is also a powerful image-editing tool. For example, your concept for a particular design may be based on a specific texture or pattern, but your sample is a color contradictory to your intent. Rather than confuse the viewer by saying "imagine it this way," use the computer to remove the color or manipu-

Figure 8.1

The computer can be used to create a loose, free-hand sketch, as in this example.

Figure 8.2

Computer drawing programs can also be used to create complex illustrations. This example includes scanned fabric samples, as well as photographic images of a golf club and shoes.

late it to the exact hue, value and saturation level desired. You can also manipulate patterns by adjusting scale, eliminating elements and changing colorways (Fig. 8.3). For surface designers, these functions are an efficient, cost-effective alternative to time consuming paintings. Some graphics applications even assist in placing a motif in repeat.

Remember that great vacation photo of the Grand Canyon that is amazingly appropriate for your Southwestern Collection? The only problem is your amazingly unfashionable Aunt Edith in the foreground. Luckily, there are many photo-manipulation applications to assist you in relocating or removing Aunt Edith and replacing her with a top fashion model. Layout-design applications are used to collage images created or stored in various software applications. Each image may be recolored, scaled, cropped or edited in almost any variety of ways.

The greatest advantage of using the computer to create concept boards (Fig. 8.4) is the ability for the message that the concept board communicates to change and grow with the evolution of the design project. For each phase of the project, the designer may return to the con-

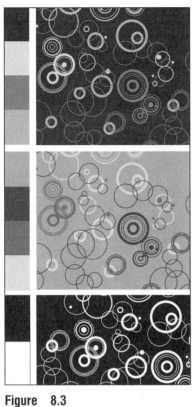

Figure 8.3
Computer design programs enable the designer to easily recreate patterns in various colorways.

Figure 8.4
This concept board combines elements produced by several different programs to achieve a unified page format.

cept board to refine the statement. No more trying to peel off glued, often one-of-a-kind images. Information is stored on the computer's hard drive, CD-ROM and portable disks and tapes of various storage capacity. Throughout the design process, the designer has the ability to quickly send artwork and technical drawings via modem, a device that allows computers to communicate with each other over phone lines. Large files may be sent to graphics service bureaus, domestic and overseas manufacturers and even clients. This method saves the designer the time and expense of transport and travel.

Presentations need not be in board format. A screen-image slide show or video presentation could be equally effective. Every day, more individuals are accessing the Internet to shop on-line catalogs or catch up on the latest fashion trends via on-line magazines such as *Elle*. Likewise, designers can market their skills to potential clients through their own home-page portfolios on the World Wide Web. Furthermore, the designer, in conjunction with manufacturers, can approach retail buyers with on-line fashion shows and line sheets.

Look to the future for advancements in interactive presentations; they're not just arcade games for kids anymore! Wouldn't carrying information stored on a pocket-size disk or CD-ROM beat lugging around a large presentation board any day?

For the beginner to computer design, raster-pixel paint programs are the most intuitive. (Examples of these programs can be seen in Fig. 8.6, which shows a screen from Photoshop 3.01, and Fig. 8.8, a screen from Fractal Design Painter.) Once you become familiar with the computer's hardware components, operating system software and method of navigation of the command menus, you can easily learn pixel paint programs because the software application relates directly to natural drawing media. Color transparency, line qualities and textures are simulated and programmed to be pressure sensitive utilizing a graphics tablet and pen. As soon as the artist begins to recognize and associate the program's icon commands with natural drawing media, the steps are as immediate and intuitive as illustrating by hand.

The computer is designed to recognize continuous tone images by pixels. A pixel is the smallest unit from the raster, or grid, that displays and records the digital data of a scanned photograph or computer-generated illustration. Each tint, tone and shade in a composition is separated to be represented by one pixel on a grid. The smoothness, sharpness or jagged edges of a composition are controlled by the image's resolution, which is dependent on the number of pixels per square inch in an image. Low-resolution images display blurred, jagged edges (Fig. 8.5a). High-resolution images display sharp detail and smooth edges (Fig. 8.5b). Smooth shapes are displayed by many pixel values of a hue to create soft edges (Fig. 8.6). These are referred to as anti-aliased edges.

In addition to image resolution describing linear detail, pixels are also measured by the color depth, or bit resolution. This describes the amount of color information each pixel contains. The greater the bit depth each pixel provides, the more available colors to accurately display an image. One-bit images are black and white, eight-bit images describe 256 colors, and 24-bit images describe 16 million possible values.

RASTER/PIXEL PAINT PROGRAMS

Figure   8.5a

Figure   8.5b
Low-resolution (8.5a) and high-resolution (8.5b) illustrations of the same image show the difference in clarity achieved by changing the number of pixels, or dots, per square inch.

Figure   8.6
This magnified drawing shows how the blurred image consists of many small squares of different values.

Figure   8.7

This illustration was created by using scanned images of leather and yarn texture.

You can create computer-generated illustrations entirely on the computer, or start with a scanned line drawing and fabric textures for rendering the illustration (Fig. 8.7). A scanner is an input device that captures images by shining light onto the artwork to be scanned. The light bounces back and is captured by a strip of light-sensitive cells called a charge-coupled device (CCD). The CCD converts the light waves into digital information called bits. The scanning software reconstructs the information into a computer image file. The raster software program opens the scanned file so the data can be used for the composition. All flat objects or shallow objects can be scanned, including croquis sketches, buttons, fabric, yarn samples, logo patches, etc. Scanning software, such as Adobe Photoshop, allows the designer to input the image as line art, gray scale or color.

Rasterized or pixelated computer-fashion illustrations have two distinct advantages over traditional rendering techniques. One is the flexibility of accessing simulations of every possible natural drawing material to render the fashion figure. Second is the opportunity for unlimited styling of the fashion figure. Paint programs such as Fractal Design Painter and Fractal Design Dabbler provide the designer with the greatest possible variety of drawing textures and drawing tools (Fig. 8.8) These programs are designed to be used with a graphics tablet and pressure-sensitive pen for maximum effect. The designer can select a paper texture of any color and choose a drawing tool such as a pen, pencil or charcoal to rough-out the croquis. With a click of the pen, you can lay down broad washes with the water color brush.

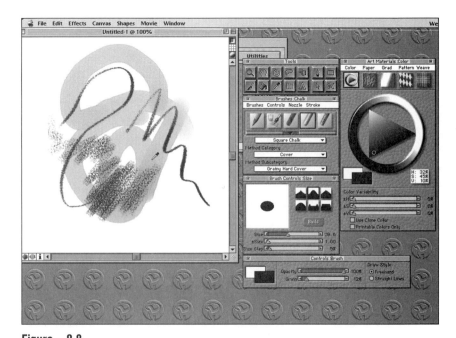

Figure   8.8

A raster-pixel paint program such as Fractal Design Painter enables the artist to recreate the effects of different media such as pencil, watercolor, chalk and airbrush.

Figure   8.9a and b
The same face can be reused in numerous variations by altering details such as hairstyles and accessories.

Next, use pastel tools to render the fabrication. Save these stages of figure illustration in separate files so you can create variations without starting from scratch. The freedom of creating and saving separate stages allows the designer to experiment much more than when using traditional methods.

As an alternative to free-hand sketching on a tablet, scan a croquis line drawing into the computer to create the proper figure proportion on the monitor. In the beginning, it is difficult to judge proportion on the monitor until you become familiar with the technical interface. Saving fashion heads as separate files can be very useful. Because of the small details, the face can be rendered twice: the final finished size, and then reduced or scaled to be composited to the figure. The same face can also be rendered and saved many times with different hairstyles, make-up color palettes and accessories, depending on the theme of the collection (Fig. 8.9a and b). This archive, once created, can be used for many projects requiring consistency. Since the focus of the illustration is the garment design, having a "template" of the face in different styles increases the speed of rendering and directs more emphasis on the design.

Rendering the fashion figure with digitized textures and garment details is another powerful feature of computer-generated fashion illustration. This method enables the designer to realistically communicate his vision before sample garments are created. Using scanned textures and motifs also increases rendering speed. Consistent fabric rendering unifies and

Figure   8.10
Scanned denim, buttons, belt buckle, logo patch and alligator texture add realism to this illustration.

polishes the final composition, especially when a figure line-up is created to illustrate a fabrication group. Scanned buttons, zippers, logo patches or any other detail enhance the realism of the garment illustration (Fig. 8.10). Especially useful are the program functions that allow the designer to rescale details, rotate objects and cut and paste seamlessly. Rendering these details using traditional methods can be time-consuming, thus inhibiting experimentation.

COLOR MANIPULATION

As mentioned earlier, color can be manipulated on the computer quite simply throughout every stage of the design process. The designer can interpret, create or manipulate color based on three models of color: hue, saturation and value (HSV); red, green and blue (RGB); and cyan, magenta and yellow (CMY). The designer may use the HSV model just as he or she would mix paint pigments. Start with the hue, then manipulate the saturation and value with quantities of black, white or grey. Although a bit more complex than the HSV color model, the RGB model is the interpretation of color—the combinations of red, green and blue—as light transmitted by the monitor. Finally, the CMY model, or CMYK (with the addition of K for black) allows the designer to envision how the printed image could appear.

The color that the designer sees as transmitted light, however, does not necessarily indicate the color that will print as pigment. For accurate color matching, designers may refer to printed color recipe books that disclose the quantities of cyan, magenta, yellow and black (these are the color inks a color printer uses). Some graphics applications allow the designer to access established color systems, such as the Pantone Matching System (PMS), which is already a familiar tool in the fashion industry. With this universal color system, a designer working in New York can link-up with a production facility off-shore and accurately transmit or change colors.

Aside from color accuracy in rendering the fashion figure, you can change colors independently from changes in silhouette. This permits the designer to view and present many colorways without reconstructing the entire drawing. Each color variation of a drawing can be saved as an independent file. Not only can you save an image in many color variations, but you can develop and document seasonal color palettes so designers working in teams can design with a consistent palette.

VECTOR/ OBJECT-ORIENTED PROGRAMS

The most familiar and obvious form of computer illustration is drafting technical flats. Here, the designer is able to achieve pure symmetry, smooth line quality and duplicate the same flat to be rendered in many fabrications. Paint programs for fashion illustration use pixels to describe, record and print the digital information (Fig. 8.11a); programs for flat illustration use object-oriented vectors to the same end (Fig. 8.11b). Vectors describe shapes mathematically and are resolution independent. When the file is saved to disk, it is comparable to a word processing document in the amount of memory required, which is measured in megabytes (MB). Approximately one megabyte is required to store a 175,000-word document.

Vector programs rely on the PostScript language developed by Adobe Systems, Inc., to interpret and transmit the virtual page from the computer to the printer. This type of illustration is extremely flexible because the drawing can always be edited and requires very little memory. For the most accurate printed image, the printer used must have a PostScript language interpreter.

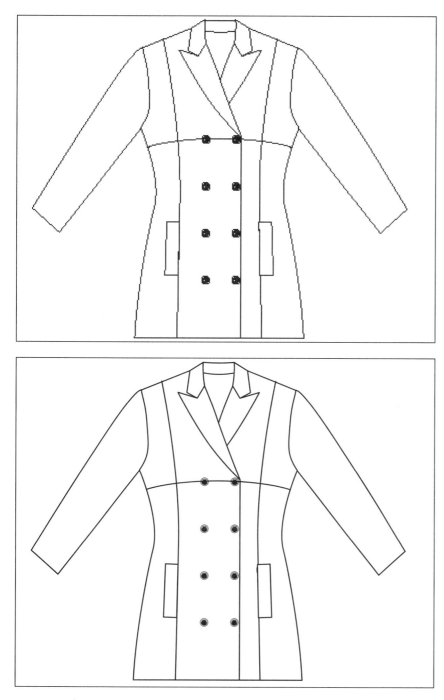

Figure 8.11a
Images created with pixel paint programs result in a jagged line effect.

Figure 8.11b
With vector programs, curves and angled lines are defined mathematically for a smoother image.

To begin drawing flat garment shapes using a vector program, create a grid to represent figure proportion. Initially, it is difficult to accurately judge figure proportion on the monitor. Depending on the monitor's size, you will need to zoom in to draw detail and zoom out to critique proportion. The grid assists the designer in maintaining consistent proportion for pieces and parts of the flat illustration.

This type of computer illustration employs the Bezier curve pen tool. Draw programs such as Macromedia FreeHand, Adobe Illustrator, and CorelDraw utilize this tool to create a continuous flowing line quality. To use the mouse instead of the traditional marker and ruler, use the pointer to select the desired pen tool icon. Define a starting point on the virtual page with a click of the mouse; click again and drag the mouse to create the curve or direction of the line. Once the curve is established, create "handles" to re-edit the curve. Using the pointer, click and drag the handles to manipulate the shape or direction of the curve. After the shapes are created and connected, the enclosed shapes can be selected to be filled with color, texture or pattern.

With practice, the experienced computer designer can begin to save a library of flat shapes or garment details for future collections. These images can be reused in many different ways, for example by dropping them into spec sheets (Fig. 8.12). Since vector drawings are never finished until they are printed, the designer can always edit line, detail, color or size. Vector illustrations can be resized without the concern of changing file resolution, since the drawing's resolution is determined by the printer's output resolution. This technique of computer illustration is more technical than raster paint programs, but allows for greater freedom of editing.

PRESENTATION DRAWINGS

The final stage for the computer-generated presentation is the page layout. Before output, the designer can digitally cut and paste graphics and design illustrations onto one page. QuarkXPress and Adobe PageMaker are page-layout software applications that software fashion designers can use to achieve slick magazine-quality layouts and prints.

Create concept and presentation boards with these programs. The designer can import the fashion figure illustrations from the raster paint program and place the images into a page-layout program to create a figure line-up. You can freely place and resize the figures. Scanned photographs from raster paint programs can also be imported to create backgrounds for the fashion figure lineups.

For merchandising purposes, place the technical flat drawings next to the figures to demonstrate additional colorways. In the fashion industry, expressive words and names are as important as the fashion figures to convey the mood of the collection. With computer typography, fonts, or typefaces, can be selected and filled with textures and colors to create headings for the fashion figure lineup. Newer versions of graphics applications, traditionally thought of as either paint programs or object-oriented programs, are introducing combined raster and vector aspects in order to facilitate page layout. Files are usually printed from page-layout programs because all of the illustrations and graphics are created in separate programs and then assembled into the page-layout program.

APPLICATIONS AND EQUIPMENT

Compared to basic computer word processing, specific system requirements for computer graphics applications are demanding. Necessary elements include processing speed, memory upgrades, additional graphic accelerator boards, storage space and sharp color displays. When purchasing any off-the-shelf graphics applications, read the list of system requirements on the side of the box.

Increased resolution implies a greater number of pixels and the need for greater processing speed and information storage. This exceeds the capacity of the standard 1.44 megabyte floppy disk used for word processing. Often, designers must invest in additional hardware, such as portable removable hard drives, to increase information storage capacity. Because of the ability to capture photorealistic digital textures and patterns in combination with gestural illustrations, designers can render fashion drawings to closely resemble the final sewn garment. This method of visualization enables designers to edit and revise their designs without the construction expense of sample garments, which in turn rationalizes the expense of ad-

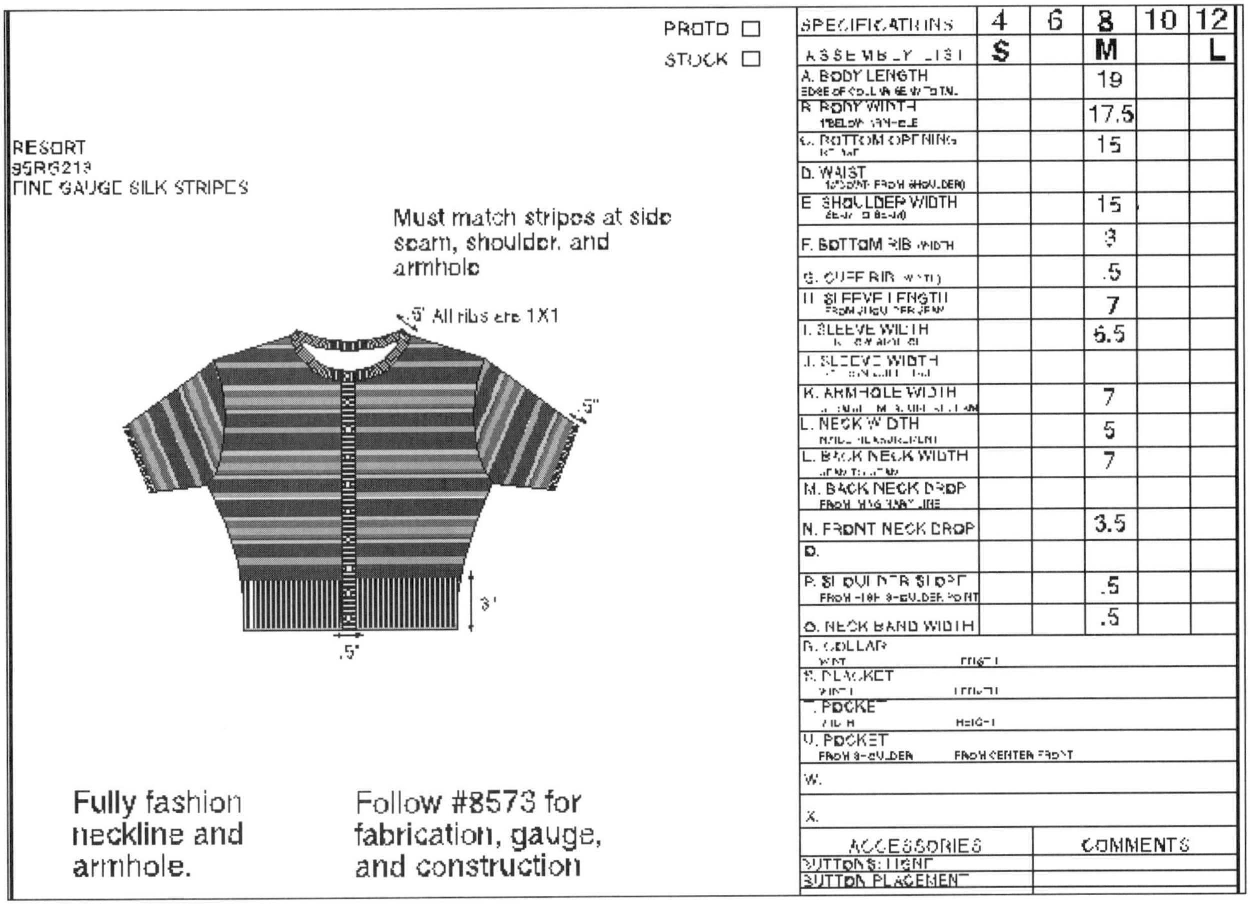

Figure spec sheet text:

| | | PROTO □ | | | | | |
| | | STOCK □ | | | | | |

RESORT
95RG219
FINE GAUGE SILK STRIPES

Must match stripes at side seam, shoulder, and armhole

.5" All ribs are 1X1

Fully fashion neckline and armhole.

Follow #8573 for fabrication, gauge, and construction

SPECIFICATIONS	4	6	8	10	12
ASSEMBLY LIST	S		M		L
A. BODY LENGTH (EDGE OF COLLAR SEW WIDTH)			19		
B. BODY WIDTH (1 BELOW ARMHOLE)			17.5		
C. BOTTOM OPENING			15		
D. WAIST (12 DOWN FROM SHOULDER)					
E. SHOULDER WIDTH (SEAM TO SEAM)			15		
F. BOTTOM RIB WIDTH			3		
G. CUFF RIB WIDTH			.5		
H. SLEEVE LENGTH (FROM HIGH SHOULDER)			7		
I. SLEEVE WIDTH (1 BY ARMHOLE)			6.5		
J. SLEEVE WIDTH					
K. ARMHOLE WIDTH			7		
L. NECK WIDTH (INSIDE MEASUREMENT)			5		
L. BACK NECK WIDTH			7		
M. BACK NECK DROP (FROM HIGH BODY LINE)					
N. FRONT NECK DROP			3.5		
O.					
P. SHOULDER SLOPE (FROM HIGH SHOULDER POINT)			.5		
Q. NECK BAND WIDTH			.5		
R. COLLAR					
S. PLACKET					
T. POCKET					
U. POCKET					
W.					
X.					

ACCESSORIES	COMMENTS
BUTTONS: LIGHT	
BUTTON PLACEMENT	

ditional sophisticated equipment. The future of fashion marketing will move toward designers creating their own catalog to convey their message to the customer. By creating digital illustrations, the figures and flats can be composited with photographic material without having to recreate the original artwork. This allows the fashion designer greater control from concept to presentation and even sales.

When purchasing a computer and its various peripheral devices, you must do your homework. First, specifically define your needs for graphics applications. Before buying the hardware, determine the software you'll want to run on it. The side panel of software packaging explains not only its key features, but more important, a detailed list of system requirements, including minimums for processing speed, application memory (random access memory, or RAM) and storage memory. Often, you'll realize an initial investment in additional RAM will be necessary to operate most graphics programs.

Before making your purchase, survey design professionals to see what they are using, what they like or don't and why. Then compare features and prices in computer trade publications. Finally, if you are a student, take advantage of academic pricing, which is usually available through your college bookstore or specialized catalogs.

The software and graphics applications previously mentioned (Painter, Dabbler, Photoshop, Illustrator, FreeHand, CorelDraw, QuarkXPress and PageMaker) are commonly used in a variety of combinations by many design industries. The popularity and competitive pricing of these off-the-shelf graphics applications afford the fashion designer ease of communication with other designers, publishers and service bureaus, as well as a cost-effective means of keeping current with software version updates.

Figure 8.12

Vector drawings can be cut and pasted into a spread sheet to create a garment spec sheet. The same drawing can also be used for other purposes, such as line sheets and presentation boards.

Many high-volume apparel producers use software developed specifically for the design-to-production tasks of the industry. Although this software is cost prohibitive to most freelance designers and small design houses, companies that develop apparel-design and production-specific software offer personalized technical support and employee training. Currently, there is a move to develop computer graphics applications that are specific to the needs of fashion designers, which are used in combination with or are alterations of familiar and affordable off-the-shelf products.

From 1990 to the present, software developers have been designing and manufacturing software applications to realistically simulate natural drawing media. In addition, hardware developments, such as the graphics tablet with pressure-sensitive pen, combined with newer paint package software, allow technology to meet the criteria of flexibility and spontaneity of the artist. With an intuitive graphical user interface (GUI) or a user-friendly environment, the designer can focus his or her energy on orchestrating colors, patterns, figures and technical drawings, combining these with text, then bringing together all of the elements of a collection. Be it a raster/pixel paint application, a vector/object-oriented application or a layout application combining both, the fashion designer or illustrator has many tools to communicate visually.

Generally, computer technology is readily embraced by creative industries and individuals who are accustomed to interacting with technical devices used to perform repetitive tasks. In contrast to the fashion-design aspect of the apparel industry, the computer is the mainstay for textile design and garment production. But the newest area of growth and change for the acceptance of digital technology is its use as a tool for creative design and development by the fashion designer and illustrator. As a new generation of design professionals have entered the industry, their familiarity with computers, operating systems and software has elevated the popularity of this creative new medium.

The computer is fast becoming a cost-effective tool of choice for fashion designers. The ability to experiment with silhouette, color and texture; save multiple versions; reduce repetitive tasks; and bring together all of the inspiration for a collection is an incredible advancement in the fashion industry.

Geoffry Gertz, the artist who created all of the illustrations shown in this chapter, has found computer illustration to be a remarkably flexible and useful tool:

> *As a fashion designer and fashion educator, I have been able to combine fashion design theory and practice with computer technology. Using the computer to design and present my collections, I am able to control, better and faster, the design process from concept to customer. In my new cyber environment, I am able to sketch croquis, develop surface patterns, recolor groups for merchandising and assemble super slick presentation boards. There is nothing that is more exciting than using today's cutting edge technology to educate future fashion designers and illustrators. — Geoffry Gertz*

A Glossary of Computer Components

CPU: Central Processing Unit. This is the central component of the computer and includes the powerful processing chip and its circuitry. The chip performs high-speed mathematical or logical operations that assemble, store, correlate or process information. The system box in which it is stored is also referred to as the CPU.

Drive: A storage device installed in, or portable to, the CPU or system box to read, save and transfer files to disks.

- The **hard disk drive** reads and writes to a disk sealed in the CPU, or system box.
- A **floppy disk drive** reads and writes to insertable floppy disks.
- A **magnetic optical (MO) disk drive** reads and writes to a special high-capacity storage disk in which the mode of reading is optical and the mode of writing is magnetic.
- A **removable cartridge hard disk drive** reads and writes to a high-capacity portable external hard drive.
- A **CD-ROM drive** reads compact discs. This read-only technology is used to access pre-recorded software applications, large size digital images and multimedia presentations.

Graphics Tablet with Pressure-Sensitive Pen: An input device that is a mapped representation of the monitor's screen. The tablet is scaled to represent the entire screen; the pen is positioned on the tablet to correspond to the cursor position on screen. This tool simulates the natural drawing media for the artist when used with appropriate graphics applications.

Keyboard: An input device that is programmed by the software to communicate commands and information to the CPU using a set of keys.

Monitor: A device that accepts video signals from a computer and displays information on a screen.

Mouse: A hand-held, button-activated input device that, when rolled along a flat surface, directs an indicator to move correspondingly about a computer screen, allowing the operator to move the indicator freely to select operations or manipulate text or graphics.

Printer: An output device that processes digital information sent from the CPU to reproduce the objects and text created in the software application onto paper and related materials.

Scanner: An input device that moves a finely focused beam of light, or electrons, in a systematic pattern over a surface in order to reproduce or sense objects and subsequently transmit an image to the CPU.

Suggested Readings

Haynes, Barry and Crumpler, Wendy. *Photoshop Artistry, A Master Class for Photographers and Artists.* SYBEX, Inc., 1995.

Meehan, Tim. *Great Photoshop Techniques.* MIS:Press, a subsidiary of Henry Holt and Company, Inc., 1994.

Rich, Jim and Bozek, Sandy. *Photoshop In Black and White.* Peachpit Press, Inc., 1994.

Williams, Robin. *How to Boss Your Fonts Around.* Peachpit Press, Inc., 1994.

Williams, Robin. *The Little Mac Book.* Fourth Edition. Peachpit Press, Inc., 1994.

Williams, Robin. *The Mac is Not a Typewriter.* Peachpit Press, Inc., 1990.

Williams, Robin, with Sikpra, Barbara and Calkins, Vicki. *PageMaker 5 Companion.* Peachpit Press, Inc., 1994.

And, of course, the user manuals and tutorials that are packaged with the specific software applications and updates.

CHAPTER 9

More functionally designed, versatile clothing, rather than that which is fashion driven, seems to be directing men's wear into the 21st century. In following this trend, men's wear will have greater versatility and individuality.

Men's Wear Presentations

Presentation Board by Alan Paul Harris.

The evolution of men's wear design has always continued along a subtle path. In comparison, women's fashion has been more chameleon-like, as well as more obvious. The men's wear designer understands this important distinction. The difference in the way each gender approaches fashion drives each industry independently: Women's wear demands constant change of silhouette and proportion; men's wear resists the radical for the assurance of the reliable and classic. This response is evident in fabrics with more traditional patterns and weaves, as well as fewer changes in silhouette. Despite the slow design evolution, men's wear designers have emerged as celebrities in the last 50 years, some achieving mega-star status.

From its inception, men's wear design has always had an influence on women's clothing. Military uniforms have and continue to be a constant source of inspiration. Nehru and Mao jackets, newsworthy fashions of the Sixties, continue to reappear. The safari suit, cowboy and southwestern influences have become signatures for Ralph Lauren. "Le Smoking," Yves Saint Laurent's version of the tuxedo for women, has become a staple for tailored evening wear. Giorgio Armani, revolutionary designer of men's wear in the Eighties, established a sexier, less conservative image via Richard Gere in "American Gigolo." Credited with the "Power Suit" for women, he helped bring equality to the boardroom. Probably more fashion trends have been influenced by men's wear than almost any other. Men's wear continues to reinvent itself, literally touching every design market.

Unlike women's wear, the men's wear industry is generally characterized by lifestyle, rather than customer type. Traditionally geared toward suits and tailored clothing, this was for the most part the mainstay of the men's wear industry until the mid-1960s, when more casual lifestyles and relaxed attitudes came upon the scene. With the fashion revolution emerged the need for clothes that served both business and leisure activities—clothes that could address the same customer with expanding needs, money to pay for it and a penchant for designer names. Although brand names such as Arrow or Hathaway were well established in the industry, designer brand names were not. These "names" lent credibility and confidence to a design and became the "stamp of approval" the customer needed and wanted. New designer images were advertised to sell and promote the product. Men's wear became more relaxed and diversified, offering options that previously were nonexistent.

Many looks now coexist with one another, providing for men's multiple lifestyle needs. They range from the casually tailored sportswear of Perry Ellis (Fig. 9.1), to the modern, athletic weekend wear of Courreges (Fig. 9.2). Less formal evening clothes, such as the example by Dominique Morlotti (Fig. 9.3), create an option for club-wear. One thing seems certain: More functionally designed, versatile clothing, rather than that which is fashion driven, seems to be directing men's wear into the 21st century. As men learn to de-uniform tailored clothing, they open up more creative dimensions in dressing. For some, this translates to an expansion of Friday Wear. The men's wear customer will need to adjust from the simplicity of suit dressing to the more complex concept of coordinates. In following this trend, men's wear will have greater versatility and individuality.

The men's wear industry is divided into several specialty areas. Most companies produce more than one specific category of garment, such as Tailored Classics for men, as well as Boys. Larger companies usually have several divisions that manufacture a variety of specialties

COTTON BASKET
WEAVE SWEATER

'GRANDPA' PULL-OVER
SHIRT IN WASHED
LINEN

STRIPE PANTS

Figure 9.1

*In the 1990s men's wear has become more relaxed and diversified than ever before, as
seen in this design sketch for Perry Ellis.*

Illustration for Perry Ellis, courtesy of Fairchild Publications.

Figure 9.2

Many different looks coexist with one another, each created for a man's multiple lifestyle needs. This design by Courreges is one example of modern, athletic weekend wear.

Illustration by Courreges, courtesy of Fairchild Publications.

Figure 9.3

As men learn to expand on the traditional "uniform" of tailored clothing, more creative opportunities in dressing become possible. This example by Dominique Morlotti might be an option for club-wear.

Illustration by Dominique Morlotti, courtesy of Fairchild Publications.

and employ several designers or design teams, each responsible for one or more of the divisions. In addition, companies often make licensee agreements that may include designing for other areas, such as home furnishings, jewelry, sunglasses and even car interiors.

The following are some of the specialty areas in the men's wear industry:

- Young Men's
- Boys
- Traditional/Tailored Classics
- Contemporary Sportswear/Separates
- Activewear
- Black Tie

Men's wear items are generally organized in terms of classification or category, which can be sold as individual items or as part of an entire collection. Although not confined to a particular price point, the term "collection" is generally associated with a more sophisticated, higher priced product. "Main Floor" merchandise of large department stores consists of moderately priced classifications that are merchandised and displayed separately—often on easily accessed tables located off the main aisles—in categories such as ties, shirts, underwear, etc. These items are mostly traditional in styling, their appeal coming from the hype and image bought by big advertising dollars. An example of this is the successful advertising campaign featuring the incomparable Markie Mark in Calvin Klein underwear. Because of the generic sameness of these items, advertisers must compete for sales by promoting their image. Men's wear has joined the competitive arena.

Several men's wear classifications found in main floor merchandise or collections are:

- Knits/Tops (cut and sew)
- Woven Shirts
- Bottoms
- Outerwear
- Sweaters

Figure   9.4a, b, c and d
Professional men's wear portfolios often focus on a specialty area such as Contemporary Sportswear/Separates. It is not uncommon to include a related area, as in this Activewear example formatted in a horizontal, or landscape, orientation.

Portfolio format by Jason Neil Rovnak.

Private labeling is an important segment of all industries today, including men's wear. See Chapter 3 for information regarding the growth and importance of the private label trend in the fashion business. One of the main reasons for this increasing trend is that private label generates a larger profit for retailers, and brands are considered to hold their market share. Private label is considered by many industry professionals to be the wave of the future.

THE MEN'S WEAR PORTFOLIO

Putting together the men's wear portfolio requires very much the same approach as any other fashion design specialty, yet these portfolios do feature specific qualities related to industry needs and requirements. A professional men's wear portfolio is generally focused on a specialty area such as Traditional/Tailored Classics or Contemporary Sportswear/Separates. The introductory page included here, and the design format following it, illustrate this approach (Fig. 9.4a, b, c and d). See Chapter 4

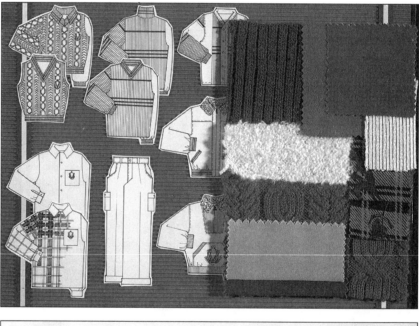

Figure 9.5a and b

Designers can create distinctive palettes by combining color forecast information with their own unique color sense. "Color stories" should not stand alone, but should be part of a portfolio format.

Portfolio format by Jason Neil Rovnak.

Figure 9.6a and b

Presentation boards are used extensively in product development, as well as private-label manufacture, and can range from a single-board presentation to an infinite number depending on the size of the collection. This example shows a theme and design board with flats in colorways.

Presentation boards by Alan Paul Harris.

for additional examples of introductory pages. Notice that a horizontal or landscape orientation has been used to format this portfolio. Focusing your portfolio to a specific area and formatting your spreads in a single orientation help you maintain continuity and demonstrate professional awareness.

COLOR SENSE/PALETTE

Because "bodies" or silhouettes in men's wear generally change very little from design season to season, men's wear designers demonstrate their creativity through color and fabrication. Designers create distinctive palettes by combining color forecast information with their own unique color sense. These "color stories" can be developed as part of a format for the portfolio (Fig. 9.5a and b), or in the form of board presentations. Express color flow and balance by showing designs on a figure or in flats. Show garments in colorways in either type of format, usually two to four colorways that work within the color palette of the group.

PRESENTATION BOARDS

The ability to create design concepts through board presentations is as essential in men's wear design as any other area. Presentation boards are used extensively in product development, as well as private-label manufacture (Fig. 9.6a and b). Created to generate sales, they can range from

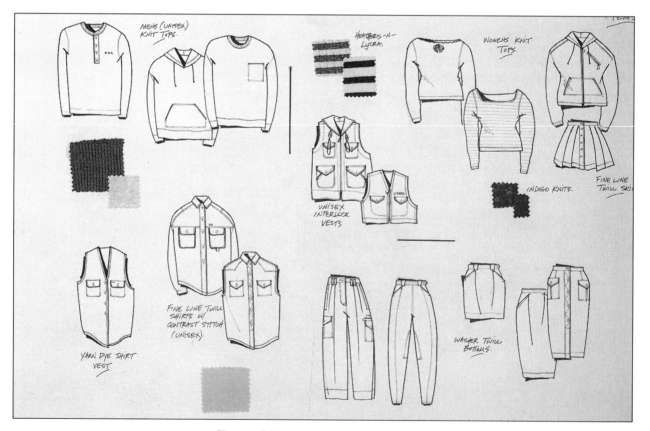

Figure 9.7

Unisex idea board. Often designers create preliminary "idea" boards, which are presented to buyers for selecting design direction.

Presentation board by Alan Paul Harris.

a single-board presentation, such as this idea board (Fig. 9.7), to an indefinite number depending on the size of a particular collection. This example is a two-board presentation consisting of a theme board and design board with flats in colorways. Board presentations can be reproduced to fit any portfolio.

Fabric facsimiles are usually computer-generated or created on a color copying machine. (See Chapter 7 for techniques related to fabric reproduction.) Labeling is important because it identifies each garment and often is accompanied by a brief description. Notice how the theme board visuals correspond to the design and fabric board. The approach is straightforward and direct. No guesswork involved here.

FLATS

The greater part of design work in the men's wear industry is represented in the form of flat sketches. Easily read and practical for showing colorways, styles of flat sketching can vary greatly from designer to designer. Most important, make them proportionally accurate and technically correct. At the same time, flats should not be boring. They should have their own personality, which inspires the patternmaker or draper creating a finished sample.

Use flats for both portfolio format presentations, as well as board presentations. These free-hand flats or "floats" (Fig. 9.8a and b) are part

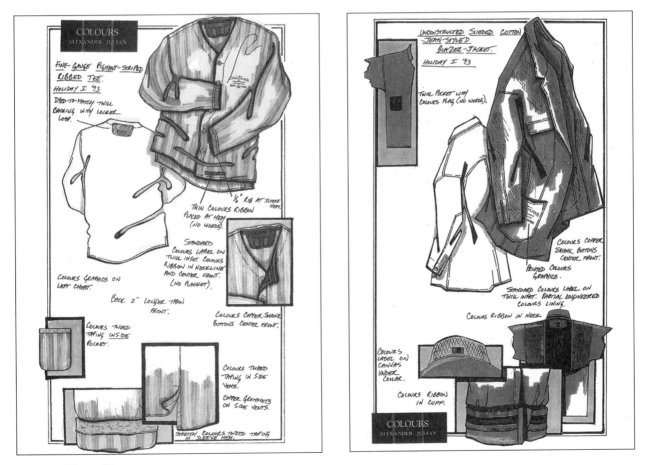

Figure   9.8a and b
These free-hand flats or "floats" in full color include vignetted garment sketches and details that could later be applied to a spec sheet. Their aesthetic appeal and practical value make for an excellent portfolio format.

Flat vignettes by Andre Croteau.

Figure   9.9

This presentation board illustrating knit tops shows subtle changes of styling detail, found mostly in necklines and fabrication. The almost draftsman-like quality of the style and presentation creates a flawless and well-organized impression.

Presentation board by Alan Paul Harris.

of a portfolio format and show each garment in color, in both front and back view. Notice details are in color as well, and vignetted and labeled for further clarity. This format uses a vertical orientation. The drawing style has a unique and engaging quality. Another example is Fig. 9.5a, which uses a horizontal portfolio format. The flats are simply rendered in black and white to show fabric pattern and texture. Fabrics are placed with Velcro on top of the acetate sleeve to invite handling. This page is part of a larger format where the garments are illustrated on figures as well (Fig. 9.5b).

This single board illustrating knit tops (Fig. 9.9) shows subtle changes of styling detail, found mostly in necklines and fabrication. Style and presentation has an almost draftsman-like quality, creating a flawless and well-organized impression.

Creating well-proportioned flats is extremely important for clear communication from workroom to production. Read Chapter 6 carefully for a basic understanding of the approach and technique for drawing flats. Select a technique for drawing flats that is right for your level and experience. Fig. 9.10a illustrates the natural proportion of a men's wear croquis. As in the previous examples illustrated in Chapter 6, the flat silhouette is obtained from the men's wear croquis (Fig. 9.10b). When you superimpose the flat silhouette over this, you will see the flat silhouette has been expanded (Fig. 9.10c). The larger silhouette allows more room for drawing garment details. And, visually, the broader silhouette is more dynamic, especially for board presentations.

The all-in-one flat silhouette may be used for individual garments. The top part of the silhouette is suitable for jackets; the slightly curved

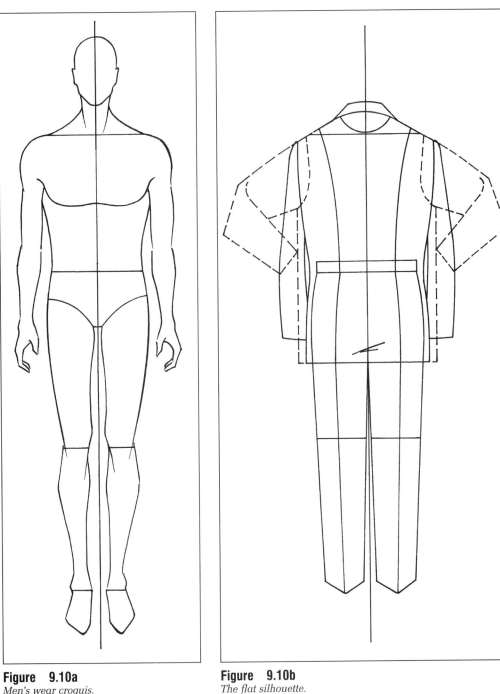

Figure 9.10a
Men's wear croquis.

Figure 9.10b
The flat silhouette.

Men's wear croquis and flat silhouette by
Hong Tan.

arm indicates the position for a two-part or tailored sleeve. An example of
a jacket developed from the flat silhouette utilizing the curved arm position
is shown in Fig. 9.11a. The action sleeve (drawn with the arms bent), is appropriate for shirts, knit tops, soft jackets, etc. The shirt in Fig. 9.11b was
developed using the action-sleeve arm position. See Chapter 6 for appropriate use of sleeve positions. Notice that the closures for these garments
move from left to right, which is traditional in men's wear garments.

The lower part of the flat silhouette is suitable for pants and shorts
and can accommodate these garments in a variety of lengths. Fig. 9.11c

Figure   9.11a

Jacket developed from the flat silhouette utilizing the curved arm position.

Figure   9.11b

Shirt developed from the flat silhouette using the action-sleeve arm position.

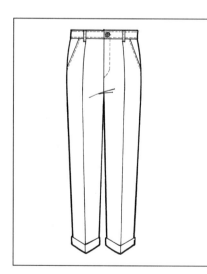

Figure   9.11c

Pant developed from the flat silhouette.

Flat sketches of jacket, shirt and pants by Hong Tan.

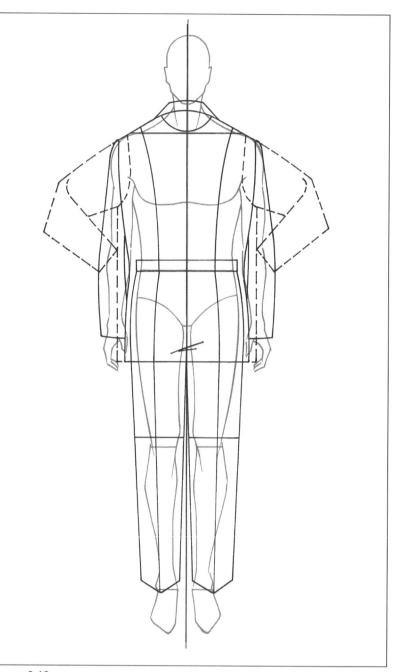

Figure   9.10c

The flat silhouette superimposed with the men's wear croquis.

Illustrations by Hong Tan.

is an example of pants developed from the flat silhouette. The silhouettes included here should be used as a basis for drawing your flats and never traced completely. This allows you the freedom to develop the garment less rigidly, more naturally. This technique simulates free-hand drawing, yet there is security in working with the forms, as you would an under-drawing. Once you have mastered this technique, move on to drawing flats using the free-hand method described in Chapter 6. Drawing free-hand is faster, and most professionals adopt this method out of necessity. An understanding of proportion is essential before tackling the free-hand technique of drawing flats.

Although flats can be drawn in a variety of materials depending on a designer's needs and preferences, marker technique is generally preferred as a finishing technique. This is especially true with regard to flats used for board presentations. Black markers that have contrast in line "weight" make garment silhouettes pop and details stand out with clarity. See Chapter 6 for suggested materials and a detailed description of techniques for rendering flats.

Frequently, fold-out presentations are used to supplement a men's wear portfolio to demonstrate a unique style of design thinking, a different specialty not included in the portfolio, or a customized presentation format. This award-winning example (Fig. 9.12a, b, and c) was created for the CFDA Scholarship Design Portfolio Competition. It represents excellence in men's wear design and presentation technique.

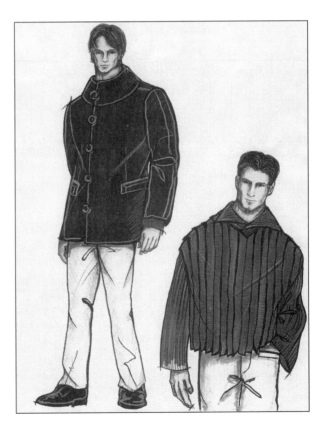

Figure   9.12a, b and c
This award-winning portfolio was created for the CFDA Scholarship Design Competition and represents excellence in men's wear design and presentation. The original spreads were color-copied throughout, creating an even and flawless impression.

CFDA 1996 Scholarship Design Competition portfolio by Masataka Suemitsu.

CHAPTER 10

Children's wear designers repond uniquely to scale, color, dimension and texture. Utilizing physical elements, their designs must stimulate and excite their small customers, and very often teach them something about their physical world.

Children's Wear Presentations

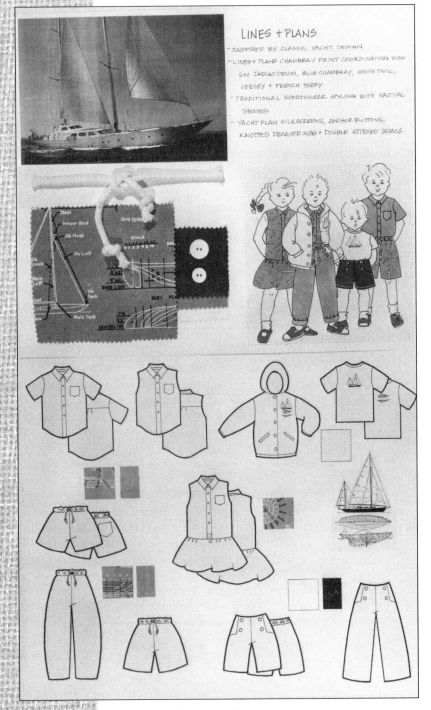

Illustration by Susan Cohan.

Children's wear designers are generally fun-loving and very much in touch with their childlike selves. Imaginative and whimsical, they can relate to the child's world, seeing things through their eyes and from their perspective. All of us can remember a time when we were small and the adult world seemed so large. Perhaps the appreciation of small-scale detail is evoked by this memory. The children's wear designer responds uniquely to scale, color, dimension and texture. Utilizing physical elements, their designs must stimulate and excite their small customers, and very often teach them something about their physical world.

An ability to recapture the child's impressions and fantasies are genuine assets in designing children's clothes. The design product is a synthesis of these early impressions and ultimately becomes the designer's vision. Yet, it must go even further. The children's wear designer must be able to recreate these concepts and interpret them into functional, wearable, durable clothes—clothes that are comfortable and appealing and assist the child through various stages of development. When practicality and fantasy are combined, the result is a successful design product that satisfies both the physical and emotional needs of the child. Most designers aspire to achieve this special blend.

DEFINING AGE AND GENDER

The children's wear designer must be aware of various age groups and their special requirements. From newborns to early teens, each group has specific needs determined by the developmental growth of the child and his physical abilities. For portfolio purposes, it is important to define these age groups visually by pose and attitude, which demonstrate the child's capabilities. For example, portfolio formats for the infant or newborn will differ greatly from those of a four-to-six year old (Fig. 10.1 and 10.2). Because infants don't walk or even crawl, they are shown seated or lying down. But a four-to-six year old has greater physical abilities and can be shown in a variety of ways. In addition, gender characteristics become more defined as the child gets older. It is important to show gender differences since designers usually specialize in one or the other. Creating distinctions in hairstyle, stance and props can help to further communicate and define age and gender.

Children's sizes usually correspond to their ages. Each size range consists of a group of sizes for children of similar body proportions and developmental needs. Because children's growth patterns vary so much in height and weight, the size they wear might not be exactly the same as their age. For example, a four year old might still wear a size 3T.

The following is a breakdown of the different age groups and their characteristic features. Included are the sizes that correspond to each general group; variations according to gender are indicated.

INFANTS

Generally, an infant's age range is from birth to the early walking stages (usually at about one year). The infant's head is approximately one-quarter of his total height. Since infants do not walk or crawl, they are typically shown either propped up or lying down. Sizes are 3, 6, 9, 12 and 18 months; or Small, Medium, Large and Extra Large.

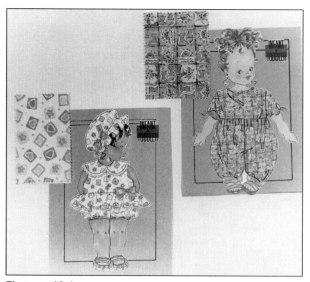

Figure 10.1

A portfolio format for infants' wear. Because infants do not walk or crawl, they are shown seated or lying down.

Illustration by Linda M. Small.

Figure   10.2

Because 4 to 6 year olds have greater physical abilities, they can be posed in a variety of ways. At this age, gender differences become more distinct.

Illustration by Hyun-Ju Kang.

TODDLERS

This age range begins with the early walking stages, approximately one year, and continues to about age three. The child's head is still large in relationship to the rest of the body; the proportion just slightly smaller than an infant. Because children at the early end of this stage are still having difficulty walking, they are often shown lying down, crawling or sitting. Sizes are 2T, 3T and 4T. The "T" stands for toddler and is used to distinguish this size range from the next.

CHILDREN

A popular range for designers, children's ages range from preschool (three years old) to the age of six. Boys and girls in this range begin to look noticeably different and clothing styles reflect this change. Children are posed standing and characterized in stance by a slight protruding belly. Sizes range are 4, 5 and 6X. Boy's sizes are 4 to 7 (no size 6X for boys). Other size distinctions are slim, regular and husky. After this stage, boy's wear becomes incorporated with men's wear because they share similar styling and production considerations.

GIRLS

This range encompasses grade-school children from the ages of seven to ten. As muscle replaces baby fat, the limbs and torso slim and lengthen. Poses often have an awkward "colt-like" appearance; the body has not yet developed the feminine curves of adolescence. Sizes are 7, 8, 10, 12 and 14. Some standard items, such as shirts and jeans, are sized 7 through 16 to accommodate a greater customer base. In addition, there is a 7 to 14 Chubby range representing a limited market.

PRE-TEENS

Adolescence is characterized by maturation and body growth. The torso becomes elongated and the waistline more defined. For girls, curves begin to take shape in the hipline and breasts. A boy's waistline elongates and tapers to a narrow hipline. This is the transitional stage between childhood and adulthood; however, poses take on decidedly grown-up qualities. Sizes are 6, 8, 10, 12 and 14.

JUNIORS

This range is worn by the teenager or late adolescent who requires a new size range to accommodate her almost-adult body. The teenage girl with slim, shapely hips has a newly defined waist and high, rounded breasts. The teenage boy continues to develop increased definition in the chest, arms and legs. Poses are generally animated and have a young-adult quality. A slightly larger head usually distinguishes this age group from the adult. Sizes are 3, 5, 7, 9, 11 and 13. This range is often not considered part of the children's wear industry, as young adults prefer to buy from women's wear manufacturers.

TRENDS AND INSPIRATION

As in every area of the fashion industry, a constant flow of ideas and inspiration is necessary for creating design collections each season. Both creative and critical thinking are essential to the design process. The children's wear designer has many options from which to draw upon for inspiration. An awareness of both domestic and international events is helpful in maintaining a sense of reality and modernity within the creative context (as opposed to relying solely on fantasy themes).

A current style, fashion detail or concept can influence the children's wear market. Sometimes this is a general trend considered "hot" at the moment, or it might be a specific designer's influence in the present season. Children's wear designers become aware of current trends through presentations and materials generated by fashion forecast services. This information can be purchased by a company or freelance designer. Costs vary according to the types of materials and services. Some services provide overviews of both European and American designer shows, highlighting important style and color/fabric trends. Forecast services will also prepare custom presentations for specialty areas such as children's wear or juniors upon request. In addition, *Colleziones,* available in two formats—infants and children—are great for trend awareness. These volumes cover both European and American designer collections and encapsulate the important trends for each.

Children's wear manufacturers often look to the junior market for design direction for the 7-to-14 and 8-to-20 size categories. Because many younger children want to look like their big brothers or sisters, the designer must learn to translate these looks in an appropriate way for their younger customer. Scale, proportion and detail are important considerations. Their intention is not to duplicate a style, but rather to capture its essence or feeling.

Shopping the stores can help designers gain awareness of trends in different fashion categories and markets. Explore department and specialty stores, which offer a variety of merchandise at different price points. Every category, regardless of how seemingly unrelated, holds the potential to provide inspiration for the children's wear designer. Visiting stores regularly creates greater fashion awareness, which can ultimately become integrated into the designer's thinking.

Trade publications and current fashion magazines can supplement store visits. *Earnshaws* and *Children's Business* are trade publications specifically for the children's wear market. European publications include *Divos, Vogue Bambini, Moda Bimbi, Colleziones Baby* and *Studio Bambini. Glamour, Mademoiselle* and *Seventeen* are also excellent idea resources for the junior market.

HISTORICAL INSPIRATION

Historical inspiration can be an unending resource for the children's wear designer. Each season, fashion trends may reflect a decade or historical period sweeping the design scene. Movies and theater are often the vehicles for this inspiration. A constant in children's wear is the inspiration of the 19th- and early 20th-century styles, characterized by Victorian dresses and sailor suits. The details from the past add freshness and charm to modern clothing. The designer's task is to interpret the historical into modern terms, creating designs that are practical and wearable.

Costume collections are an excellent source for historical research. The Costume Institute of the Metropolitan Museum of Art and The Museum at FIT–Design Laboratory are but a few of the hands-on collections utilized by designers. When these are unavailable, substitute paintings, sculpture and illustrated books. Picture collections, such as those in the New York Public Library, contain plates and photographs on costume ranging from antique to current styles.

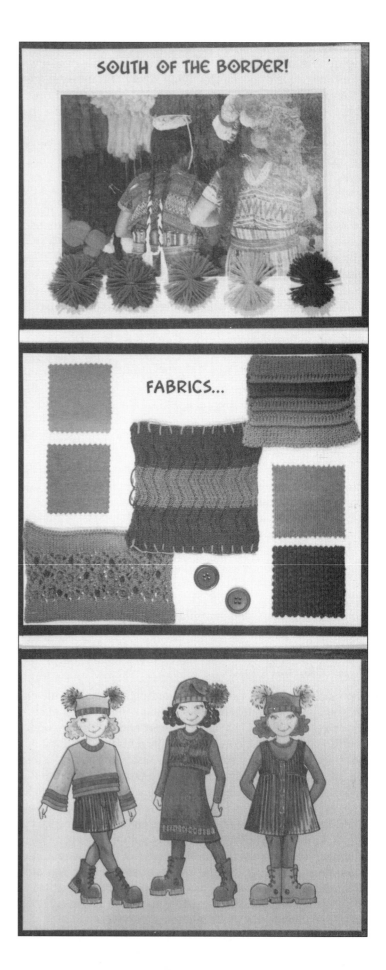

Figure 10.3

Ethnic clothing can provide a rich source of inspiration for the children's wear designer. Often, countries in the news inspire current trends. This portfolio format of a knitwear group in sizes 4–6X, consisting of a mood, fabric and design page, is inspired by Mexican colors and textiles.

Illustration by Crista Boyajian.

Television channels specializing in movie classics can help young designers familiarize themselves with several decades of the 20th century. Designers consistently revive and reinterpret styles from the 1930s to the 1970s. Children's shows and family shows can be great resources for styling, as well.

ETHNIC INSPIRATION

Ethnic clothing can provide a rich source of inspiration for the children's wear designer (Fig. 10.3). Countries in the news often inspire current trends. Children enjoy the color and fantasy that culturally inspired clothing can provide. The special crafts of each culture, such as beadwork, appliqué, weaving, dying and printing give the clothing a unique and imaginative quality. Native American, Eskimo, Mexican and Central American, Asian, African, Slavic, Swiss and Scandinavian cultures are popular design sources. In addition, the cowboy has been a perpetual inspiration for designers of children's wear. Museums, costume collections and travel can lead the designer to new cultural discoveries applicable to design.

CHILDREN'S LITERATURE

Popular children's stories and nursery rhymes have long been a source of inspiration for the children's wear designer. Children enjoy the association with their favorite characters. Classic fairy tales such as Cinderella and Snow White have been interpreted many times over for party dresses. Modern classics have also had an impact. Who could forget the charm of Eloise at the Plaza, in her white dress and blue sash? Or, Madeleine and her friends in their coachmen's coats and wide brimmed Halo hats? Children's literature brings fantasy and fun to dressing.

CHARACTER LICENSING

The popularity of a favorite TV show, cartoon, movie or storybook character can inspire a children's wear design. If a children's apparel manufacturer wishes to use that character in a design, they are required to buy the rights to do so. The design can appear in various forms, usually a logo, appliqué or print. Disney, for one, has licensed many of its characters, including Mickey Mouse (Fig. 10.4), The Little Mermaid and Pocahontas. Timing is a very important factor in licensing arrangements. Manufacturers must be able to make production arrangements quickly and meet quantity demands before the "hot" character loses popularity.

FABRIC AND TRIM

The designer views new fabric lines every season. Textile companies provide color cards, as well as "headers" showing fabrics in several color ways, to designers. Innovative fabrics with new performance features that make children's garments more durable and comfortable spark interest. Whether traditional or high-tech, the designer uses fabric to create fresh design interpretation.

One of the problems children's wear designers encounter concerning fabric is that very few companies currently specialize in children's wear fabric. Consequently, textile companies that serve the women's wear market are patronized for appropriate prints and textures.

CHARACTER LICENSING IN A SPECIALTY AREA

Because character licensing is a popular area in the children's wear industry, it is important to include a least one spread in your portfolio. A character-licensing project in your portfolio shows your creative ability to develop a potential character for this area of the industry. This exercise can be equally effective for either a portfolio format or board presentation.

Select a character from either a favorite TV show, movie or storybook. Try to choose a character that has not been used or saturated within the market. This promotes more originality and creative thinking and prevents you from being too influenced by what has already been done.

Select a specialty area, size and gender, then design a group based on your chosen character. Specialty areas are outlined below following this exercise. Be aware of how the image of the character will be translated into the design or fabrication, such as in a silk-screen print, heat transfer, appliqué or embroidery, emblem, etc. Take into account that character designs are usually mass marketed, therefore don't over-complicate designs. Include the fabric with the presentation of the designs, as well as visuals to reinforce the image of the character. Designs may be represented on a figure or flat and should be rendered in color. Color is extremely important to the overall presentation, because many characters are identified by specific colors as well as image. Would Mickey Mouse be immediately recognized if he were not wearing his usual red-and-white outfit? Your choice of character and interpretation demonstrates both your selective and creative ability. Perhaps your new character design will be the next "hot" item in the children's wear market.

Trims are an important component of children's wear garments. Embroideries, ribbons, laces, braids and buttons are inspiration for new designs each season.

The activities of children and their developmental needs are important considerations for the children's wear designer. Lightweight, fast-drying materials are essential for outdoor activities. Warmth, comfort, stretchability and washability are also important in the designer's selection of fabric. Give special consideration to federal government regulations regarding fabric used in sleepwear, which must pass testing requirements before it is allowed to be sold and made up into garments. Disney, for example, tests paints and trims for acidity. Other safety considerations include avoiding the use of drawstrings, trims that can be swallowed easily, glitter fabric, etc.

SPECIALTY AREAS

The children's wear industry is divided into many specialties. Certain manufacturers create garments for a specific age group, such as Infants. Other companies produce one specific category of garment, such as dresses, for more than one age group. Many larger companies have several divisions and manufacture a variety of specialties. They often employ several designers, each designing for one or more of the divisions.

The following are some of the specialty areas in the children's wear industry:

Infants' Wear
- Layettes: shirts, wrappers, gowns, buntings
- Christening gowns/dressy whites
- Stretch coveralls/onesies/rompers
- Diaper pants
- Dresses and suits
- Outerwear, snowsuits, snow sacks
- Knitwear: sweaters and cardigans, booties and hats
- Separates: cotton knit polo shirts, leggings, onesies, shorts, pants, T-shirts, henleys, kimono wraps and cardigans

Toddlers/Boys and Girls
- Brother/sister sets: shorts, skirts, overalls, shirts
- Rompers
- Other sets/T-shirts and leggings

Sportswear
- Slacks/shorts/leggings
- Skirts and jumpers
- Blouses and shirts
- Jackets and vests

Figure   10.4

The popularity of a favorite TV show, cartoon, movie or storybook character can inspire a children's wear design. Disney has licensed many of its characters, including Mickey Mouse, The Little Mermaid and Pocahontas. In licensing arrangements, Disney has final approval on all design aspects, including garment design and character representation.

Illustration courtesy of Mickey & Co. by Donnkenny. Disney characters © Disney Enterprises, Inc. Used by permission from Disney Enterprises, Inc.

- Sweaters
- Swimsuits
- Sweatsuits
- T-shirts

Dresses

- Tailored and party dresses
- First-communion dresses, dressy whites
- Ensembles
- Jumpers and blouses
- Casual dresses

Sleepwear and Lingerie

- Robes
- Nightgowns and pajamas
- Slips and petticoats
- Shirts and panties
- Hosiery

Outerwear

- Coats: dressy and casual
- Jackets and parkas
- Ski and snowsuits
- Raincoats/slickers/ponchos

THE CHILDREN'S WEAR PORTFOLIO

SIZE AND ORIENTATION

Many professionals in the children's wear industry prefer a 14″ × 17″ size to accommodate the many and varied elements they wish to show in their portfolios. However, the creative children's wear portfolio is versatile, and size and orientation are a personal choice. Many design professionals like the horizontal orientation because it works best with the smaller scale of the child's figure. The horizontal orientation also allows for comfortably displaying several designs per page while still having adequate room for the other design elements.

CONTENTS AND ORGANIZATION

Designers first entering the industry should have a range of age groups and design categories represented in the portfolio. Although children's wear companies usually specialize in a size area and possibly a gender, newcomers to the industry cannot anticipate the area in which they will eventually specialize. By contrast, experienced designers usually specialize in a specific segment of design and, consequently, their portfolios are more focused on a size, gender and design category. Designers rarely design for both boys and girls, except in the Infants and Toddlers groups.

Specific skills are important, if not inherent, in designing children's clothes and should be evident in the children's wear designer's portfolio. These elements can set you apart from your competitors and help you land the job you want. The following design elements are most often included in children's wear presentations:

- Croquis designs
- Mood/Theme Visuals
- Fabric/Hardware/Trim
- Flats
- Colorways

PORTFOLIO FORMATS AND PRESENTATION BOARDS

The number of pages to include can vary according to the breadth and scope of each portfolio. Most professionals agree that less is best. Having a body of work to select from for each interview allows you to customize your presentations for each company and market. Generally, four to six concepts with approximately two to four pages each is sufficient for one interview. Develop several design ideas; work in groups and avoid single-figure designs per page. Solitary designs waste space and show a lack of professionalism. Show only your very best work. Each spread should be consistent with the next. Uneven design thinking and concepts are telltale signs of an amateur.

The children's wear designer needs to show an ability to create design concepts through board presentations (Fig. 10.5). These include the same elements of design used in portfolio formats but are usually in a larger scale. The advantage of this expanded presentation is to show each garment in several colorways, or to show multiple deliveries in one presentation.

FLATS

Approximately 80 percent of the design work in the children's wear industry is represented in the form of flat sketches. Flat sketches must show children's proportional differences and be clear and technically correct. Because there are many different age groups within the children's wear market, it is necessary to develop a croquis and flat form specific to the age group you are designing for. The Child's Fashion

Figure 10.5

This presentation board features a Girls 7–14 group inspired by a "blanket" theme. Boards enable you to expand your presentation to include designs on figures, flats, fabric samples, even visuals. Presentation boards have become an important tool in selling design concepts.

Illustration by Hyun-Ju Kang.

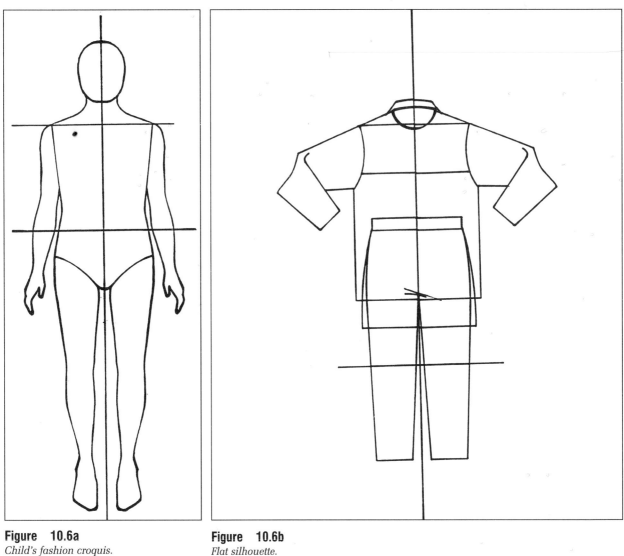

Figure 10.6a
Child's fashion croquis.

Croquis and flat silhouette by Hong Tan

Figure 10.6b
Flat silhouette.

Croquis (Fig. 10.6a) illustrates the correct proportions for a six or seven year old. A mid-range age was chosen to simplify the approach.

The Flat Silhouette (Fig. 10.6b) was developed from the Child's Fashion Croquis. As in the men's and women's chapters, the silhouette is purposely generic to encourage creative designing. The Flat Silhouette, superimposed over the Child's Fashion Croquis (Fig. 10.6c), indicates the general fit of garments over the figure and should be used as a guide, never traced. Since children's garments tend to be less tailored, the arm position here illustrates the "action sleeve." However, the positioning of sleeves can vary according to the construction and the "look" desired and should complement the garment silhouette. The lower half of the flat silhouette may be used for pants, shorts or skirts. Dresses and jumpers may be created by using the entire silhouette as a general guide for proportion.

Illustrated here are three garments developed from the flat silhouette: a jumper (Fig. 10.6d), drawstring pants (Fig. 10.6e) and zip pullover (Fig. 10.6f). All flats are finished in a marker technique using a varied line quality. Refer to Chapter 6 for technical information regarding flats and their execution.

Figure 10.6c
Comparison of flat silhouette to child's fashion croquis.

Figure 10.6d

Figure 10.6e

Figure 10.6f

These flats were created from the flat silhouette and finished using marker pens in three sizes. Notice the consistency in proportion from garment to garment, achieved by using the same flat silhouette for all three.

Flat illustrations by Hong Tan.

Flats are often part of portfolio format presentations, as well as board presentations. They demonstrate the designer's knowledge of construction, proportion and general technical skill. Often, flats show design while the children's croquis illustrates merchandising ideas and concepts. You must include flat presentations in the portfolio since the largest segment of sketching in children's wear is on the flat. Spec sheets with flat sketches may also be shown as a spread, mixed in with portfolio format presentations. Showing a spec sheet featuring one of your designs from a design group shows your ability to execute flats, as well as an understanding of their purpose. See Chapter 4 for general tips regarding positioning and flow of design units.

TRADITIONAL FABRICATIONS

The children's wear market has specific criteria regarding the use of appropriate color, pattern and fabric. Traditionally, black is used infrequently in children's wear garments, except for accessories, because mothers have an aversion to it. Good business dictates that items are geared toward those who have the purchasing power, so garments are often designed to appeal to mothers, grandmothers and aunts. Practicality is an important design consideration, consequently white garments are generally reserved for special occasions.

Traditional gender-based use of color is still maintained. A man might buy a pink shirt as an accent to a suit or sweater, but in children's

wear pink is still bought for girls, blue for boys. Yellow and mint green are considered appropriate for both. Although dress codes have relaxed to a degree, traditional colors and fabrications continue to reign in the children's wear market in terms of sales.

Pattern scale is an important element in designing garments for children. Designers usually avoid large patterns as they can appear overwhelming to a child's proportions. Because children's garments are generally smaller than those of adults, oversized patterns tend to look fragmented and out of place. Some traditional fabrics that are often used in the children's wear market are:

- Auto-stripes
- Printed knits
- Rib-knits
- Novelty knits (e.g., pointelle)
- Polo shirtings
- Dobbies and yarn-dyed woven stripes and plaids
- Florals (small-scale)
- Conversational prints (novelties, e.g, tea cups, fruit)
- Character licensing (Barbie, Yankees, Mickey Mouse)
- Silk-screen prints
- Embroideries
- Denim/chambray (all children's portfolios should have a group in this category, even dresses)

Figure 10.7

This unique example, featuring a butterfly theme for Girls size 7–14, is a CFDA scholarship award winner. The butterfly theme has also been incorporated in the packaging of the porfolio and adds charm and delight to the presentation. A preface and colorways further enhance the presentation.

CFDA scholarship portfolio by Crystal White.

THEME ORIENTATION

Children's wear is most often theme driven. Regardless of the specialty area, garments will have a print, color, design style or special detail in common. This helps to establish a group feeling and makes merchandising clothes on the selling floor much clearer. Garments with a common link look better when displayed, and grouped items generally attract more attention than single, isolated garments. Include four to six thematic spreads in your portfolio to demonstrate your creative ability to work with themes. The portfolio shown here presents a coordinated children's wear group focused on the theme of butterflies (Fig. 10.7).

SPORTSWEAR COORDINATION

Because separates are a large segment of the children's wear industry, you need to show your ability to coordinate garments in the portfolio. (Items included in the sportswear category are listed earlier in this chapter.) Often, sportswear is theme driven, by an idea, detail, color or fabrication. By illustrating a group of items from the same theme or fabrication on a child's croquis, the designer shows several possible ways that these items can be worn. So ultimately, when garments are merchandised in a store, the consumer is encouraged to buy several items to achieve "the look" rather than just one outfit. Sportswear items are also bought to coordinate with garments in a customer's existing wardrobe. This is the basic philosophy for sportswear design. Coordinated items give the customer more choices and flexibility. They expand a wardrobe.

STYLIZING THE SKETCH

The children's wear designer, probably more so than in any other design area, can exaggerate poses, attitude and even proportion of the child's figure (Fig. 10.8). These qualities enhance a children's wear presentation and capture the spirit and characteristics associated with children. Larger heads and feet, knocked-knees or freckles add a captivating charm to drawings of children. Those who can capture this essence have a true potential for designing in this market.

Figure   10.8
This fold-out presentation shows how exaggerated poses, attitude and even proportions of the child's figure can enhance a children's wear presentation and capture the right spirit.

Illustration by Hyun-Ju Kang.

CHAPTER 11

Accessories help us create entertainment for ourselves through our appearance. If we think of clothing as the leading actors and actresses, accessories are the supporting roles.

Fashion Accessories
Presentations

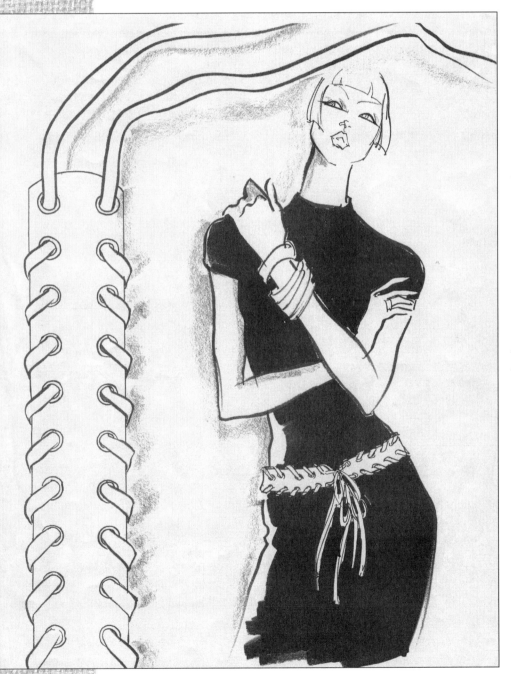

Illustration—Anne Klein & Company
Designer: Renaldo Barnette.

Accessories help us create entertainment for ourselves through our appearance. In the same manner that theatrical props reinforce the theme of a play, accessories do the same for clothing. If we think of clothing as the leading actors and actresses, accessories are the supporting roles. Handbags, belts and footwear might be considered the opening acts, as these items are must-haves and serve both practical and aesthetic needs. For most women, it would be unimaginable to think of spending a single day without shoes and a purse. By contrast, millinery and gloves might be considered the closing act. Although they serve a practical purpose at times, they are generally bought to complete or polish an outfit.

Accessory designers often find their way into the industry indirectly. Few begin with the goal of becoming an accessories designer. They are an eclectic group with diverse backgrounds. Although some come through traditional training, such as the unique Fashion Accessories Program at FIT, others become drawn to the industry via apparel design positions and internships. Similar to an apprenticeship, internships afford the opportunity of on-the-spot training in a "real life" situation. Optimally, the ideal training ground for a hopeful accessories designer is some technical training in a fashion-design, millinery or accessories program with an internship built-in.

Accessories lend an important balance to the clothing we wear. In selecting accessories for their fashion shows, designers are extremely careful in their choices. Selecting the right hat or shoe can add to the drama of a collection. Proportion and color are important considerations, as well. But most of all, the feeling or "look" must be right for the theme and style of the clothing (Fig 11.1). Designers will shop endlessly for just the right accessory to enhance their fashion message on the runway. The style of a fashion accessory can be classified in one or more of the following categories:

Figure   11.1

A fold-out presentation including accessories linked by the theme, "Auntie Mame's Oriental Evenings." The collection was inspired by Paul Poiret's fascination with Orientalism prior to World War I.

Fold-out presentation by Amy A. Gallo.

- Classic
- Sporty
- Minimal
- High Fashion
- Retro
- Ethnic

A love/hate relationship exists between the ready-to-wear garment and accessory industries. Independent accessories can be threatened by ready-to-wear garments that come with accessories such as hoods, belts, scarves, etc. However, as clothing becomes more minimal, accessories become more important, lending a bold excitement to apparel. Accessories can either serve as a contrast or complement to clothing. Even though black is the key color in both accessories and ready-to-wear, these areas are directly related in their seasonal color offerings. The consumer is more likely to open her pocketbook if she can match an accessory with a garment she recently purchased.

"Accessories help us express our individualism and visibly announce our personality," says Carry Adina, a well-established handbag designer. "The first thing retailers evaluate about customers is their accessories, because they tell a lot about their spending habits. Generally, they will look at a customer's handbag and shoes to determine their buying potential." Consequently, accessories can suggest our income level, communicate whether we are conservative or trendy, a purist or detail-oriented, and how we feel about ourselves and the image we wish to project to the world.

Accessories have long been a symbol of status or rank in society. In ancient times only the extremely wealthy could afford to own a pair of shoes. Not until the Industrial Revolution were shoes mass-marketed to the public. In the 20th century, the status shoe began to emerge in diverse categories. Roger Vivier created evening shoes treasured as works of art. Nike and Reebok took the lead in sneakers and sport shoes. Gucci immortalized the loafer. Chanel redefined classicism with her two-toned pump, and Manolo Blahnik reinvented glamour with his luxurious "slide" or mule.

Millinery is another means of communicating social position. Historically an outfit was not considered complete unless it had the right hat to go with it as a "crowning touch." It was not uncommon to have the same material used for a gown made into a hat to complete an ensemble. In the 1930s, 1940s and 1950s, matching hats were all the rage and were often complemented with gloves. Millinery designers such as Lily Dache, Mr. John and Halston helped to glamorize the wearing of hats. In the past, designers often began a fashion career as millinery designers. Chanel, Adolfo and Halston are prime examples.

An interesting phenomenon is experienced by those who wear hats, which Patricia Underwood refers to as the "hat check." While passing someone on the street, millinery aficionados report everything from a glance to a head turn. Whatever the reaction, they are definitely aware of being checked out because of their hat. A hat gets you noticed! And perhaps this might be one good reason for their popularity. Yet besides being functional, there is a mystery that veils the wearer, perhaps because hats partially conceal the face and, at the same time, transform the wearer. Wearing a hat is like playing dress up when you were a child except now you don't need an excuse. Millinery becomes the vehicle for self-expression.

CATEGORY SPECIFICS

The major areas of fashion accessories are:

- Handbags
- Footwear
- Gloves
- Millinery
- Small leather goods
- Belts
- Sunglasses
- Costume jewelry

The accessory designer uses many of the same research techniques and forecasting sources as the apparel designer. However, the fashion-accessories portfolio must reflect certain abilities in order for an interviewer to identify potential talent. Talent for designing accessories is not necessarily demonstrated by accessory designs alone or by strong drawing skills. Other clues that signal talent and interest in this area are a good color sense, choice of interesting materials and textures, an eye for detail, a strong imagination and creativity. Although these qualities are important in general for demonstrating design aptitude, they are essential in the entry-level fashion accessories portfolio.

Experienced accessory designers include swatches of materials, colors, finishes, novel stitching or quilting patterns, as well as photos or press of actual manufactured products in their portfolios. Whether you are a beginner or professional, demonstrate your knowledge and strengths and show what you do best. If you have some technical experience, you may want to supplement your portfolio with samples that demonstrate your knowledge of patternmaking and model making. Technical sketches are an excellent way to communicate this knowledge (Fig. 11.2a and b). These simple, black-and-white sketches are often preferred to more elaborate color samples because of their realism and clarity. For this reason, they are more suitable for production purposes and result in a more accurate model, according to Ulrich Grimm, Design Director for Anne Klein Accessories.

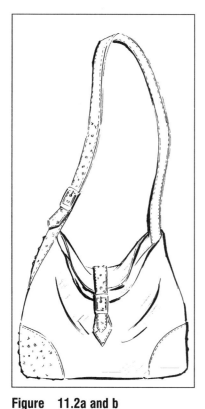

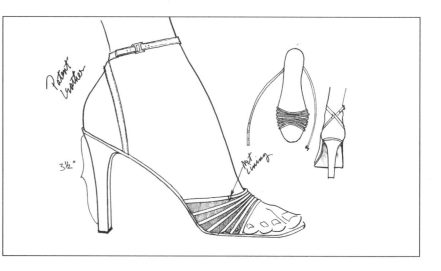

Figure   11.2a and b

These technical sketches are excellent supplements to a portfolio and demonstrate a knowledge of patternmaking and model making. Because of their realism and clarity they are often preferred for production purposes over more elaborate color samples.

Illustrations courtesy of Anne Klein & Company/Designer: Ulrich Grimm.

Figure 11.3a and b

Actual materials and technical notes supplement these dynamic illustrations, rendered in gouache. Notice how the materials create a rich, inviting, tactile quality that relates back to the visuals on the mood/theme page. This example was taken from a larger 30-page format, which also included a design for a perfume bottle and hang tags.

Portfolio format presentation by Susan-Jayne Foster.

Exercise

DESIGNING ACCESSORIES TO COORDINATE WITH APPAREL

An accessory company might ask you to do a project similar to this one to test your imagination and creative ability. Using magazine tearsheets of garments, design the accessories to go with the clothing. There are usually few or no restrictions with projects of this kind since they are a test of your creative ability. Keep the following in mind before diving in:

How many designs are required? They are looking for a prolific design ability. Don't be stingy!

Will this be an accessory collection or should the designs be in one category such as shoes or handbags? A safe bet is to base your designs on what the company offers. However, a more creative solution would be to give them a collection, as it inspires new ideas.

Should I use the same color story as in the tearsheets? Here is an opportunity to demonstrate your creative ability. Try for a less predictable result by adding a new element such as a print, material or texture.

What technique should I use to render my designs? Use a medium and technique you are comfortable with and that has given you good results.

Do they want a specific type of format for this presentation, i.e., board, fold-out, quick sketches, etc.? This is generally your creative decision.

Usually the turn-around time on the project indicates your interest in working for the company. If you receive the project Friday and you return it Monday, your chances will increase. Of course, the project should indicate by its flawless presentation, superb design and coordination, and creativity married with reality that your weekend was well spent.

If there are no restrictions on format, you may want to consider a fold-out presentation. This is a popular choice for return projects because it is extremely portable and can be recycled for other interviews.

Those who come from a fashion-design background can easily make the transition into the accessories market. Such was the case with Sue Seipel, a footwear designer currently with Unisa. While interviewing for an apparel design position, her potential talent for designing accessories was recognized through her ability to illustrate apparel and creative, coordinating accessories. Since many companies have accessory divisions, opportunities such as this are not unusual. Designing accessories increases your awareness of the relationship of accessories to apparel and can ultimately expand your marketability as a designer. This example (Fig. 11.3a and b) includes a mood/theme page, design page and coordinating accessory pages, and is part of a larger spread consisting of more than 30 design page components. Actual materials and technical notes supplement these dynamic illustrations, rendered in gouache. Notice how the materials create a rich, inviting, tactile quality that relates back to the visuals on the mood/theme page.

PRESENTATION BOARDS

Presentation boards are an excellent vehicle for displaying theme and design concepts in a portfolio. Read Chapter 7 for a general approach to designing and creating board presentations, as well as suggested techniques and materials and board reproduction.

A presentation board may include accessory designs in one category, or show different coordinating areas as in Fig. 11.4. Coordinated items are usually identified with the term "collection." In either case, use strong, clear visuals to reinforce the theme created by color and material samples. Fig. 11.5a, b and c are examples using a geographic locale as a design theme—Paris, Korea and Tokyo, respectively. These boards illustrate several areas of accessory design and also include colorways for each category. Colorways are offered to give the customer more options. Items shown in matching or coordinated colors encourage customers to purchase more than one. These renderings are in a variety of media, which include gouache/watercolor, marker and colored pencil. Many professionals choose to combine media for greater depth and detail in their presentation sketches.

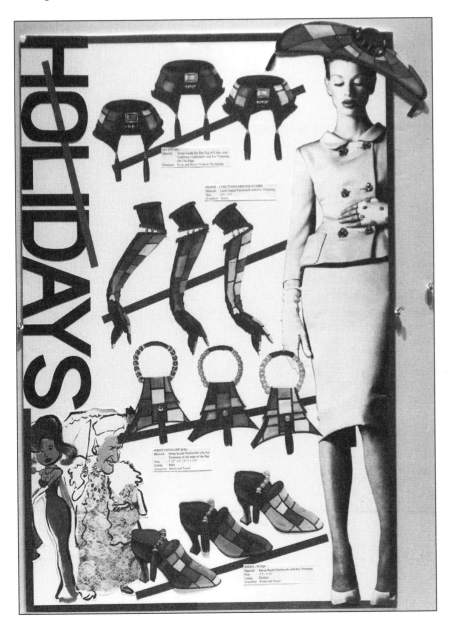

Figure   11.4

This presentation board shows a mini-collection of different coordinating areas of accessories. Notice that the items are offered in several colorways for greater customer appeal.

Presentation board by Kang Li-Wen.

Figure 11.5a Paris presentation board by Hyun A. Lim.

Figure 11.5b Korea presentation board by Bok-Hea Kim.

Figure 11.5a, b and c

These examples, rendered in mixed media, use a geographic locale as a design theme. Many professionals choose to combine media for greater depth and detail in their presentation sketches. Captions are included under each area to clarify detail, material, construction and finish.

Figure 11.5c Tokyo presentation board by Hyun A. Lim.

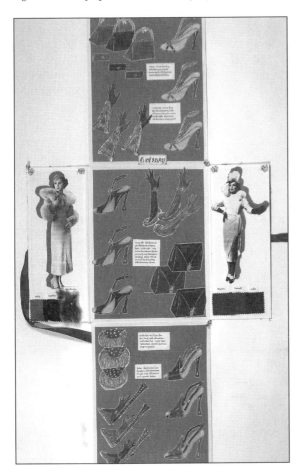

Figure   11.6a and b

The "surprise" of opening a specialized presentation at an interview is both dramatic and intriguing. This example, which looks like an unopened gift, unfolds in four directions to reveal a glamour-inspired accessory collection.

Fold-out presentation by Janel Bohling.

SPECIALIZED PRESENTATIONS

Fold-out presentations are frequently used alone or as supplements to a fashion accessories portfolio. The "surprise" of opening a specialized presentation at an interview is both dramatic and intriguing. The example, which looks like an unopened gift (Fig. 11.6a and b), opens up in four directions to reveal a glamour-inspired accessory collection. You can create a fold-out presentation for a variety of reasons: to show an ability to design in another price point or market, to demonstrate a unique design concept, or to customize a presentation format for a potential employer. Whatever the reason, a specialized presentation is an excellent supplement to a portfolio.

How creatively you format your fold-out presentation communicates your uniqueness as a designer. The design industry is always on the lookout for those with clever ideas that can be translated cost effectively. An unusual shape, eye-catching visuals or an alluring color story

Figure   11.7a and b
This three-leaf fold-out made of foam core opens up to showcase accessory designs mounted on a Florentine paper. Note the outer leaves of the foam core have been shaped asymmetrically.

Fold-out presentation by Kang Li-Wen.

are important elements to include in specialized presentations. Fig. 11.7a and b, a three-leaf fold-out made of foam core, opens up to showcase accessory designs mounted on a Florentine paper. Note the outer leaves of the foam core have been shaped asymmetrically. The four-leaf presentation in Fig. 11.8, created from illustration board, coordinates the box-like shape of the background paper with the accessories.

Accessories still carry the allure of status in a variety of fashion categories. For example: a Chanel bag with its quilted design and chain handle and the Chanel shoe with contrast toe; an Hermès "Kelly" bag; a Judith Lieber minaudiere; Gucci loafers; a Prada backpack; Armani glasses; Louis Vuitton accessories and luggage; or a Loro Piana cashmere shawl.

Each season the list expands. Why are accessories sought after with such passion? They are affordable, even at higher price points compared to a garment in the same category. Accessories are a way of instantly updating a wardrobe. They add newness without the hefty price tag of a whole outfit.

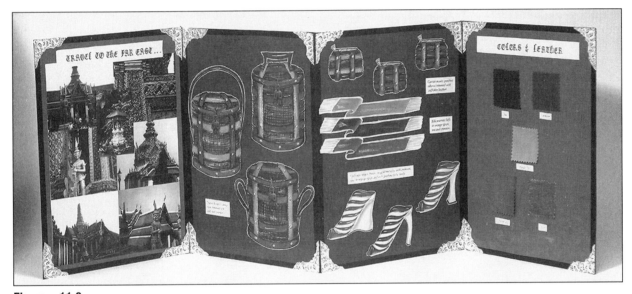

Figure   11.8
This four-leaf presentation, created from illustration board, coordinates its box-like shape with its hand bag accessories.

Fold-out presentation by Janel Bohling.

CHAPTER 12

Also known as a fashion diary, sketchbook or journal, the croquis book is an important accompaniment to the portfolio and can help you get an internship or entry-level position. Croquis books demonstrate drawing skills, sources of inspiration and color/fabric sensitivity.

The Croquis Book

Croquis book sketch courtesy of Anne Klein II.

Also known as a fashion diary, sketchbook or journal, the croquis book is an important accompaniment to the portfolio and can help you get an internship or entry-level position. Quick sketching techniques are vital for communicating ideas to the various areas of a fashion house. Thumbnails, or rough sketches, concept ideas and fabric suggestions help document your distinctive process of design. They demonstrate drawing skills, sources of inspiration and color/fabric sensitivity. The croquis book is a record of your creative process. It shows your ability to generate abundant ideas for a specific portion of a collection, leading up to the whole. It is a personal account of your ideas, and can consist of anything that captured your interest while working toward a design solution.

Looking at a finished portfolio from an employer's perspective, certain questions arise. Was the concept part of a class assignment? How long did it take to create the finished pieces? Will this designer be able to communicate ideas in the sample-room environment? Are these original sketches? How was the research done for each concept? The croquis book helps to answer these questions and demonstrates the scope of your ability.

SELECTING AND USING YOUR CROQUIS BOOKS

STYLE AND SIZE

Selecting a croquis book is a very personal decision. Some designers like to carry a small book with them at all times, on the chance they might see something they wish to record. Convenient sizes are 3″ × 5″, 5″ × 7″, 8 ½″ × 11″ and 11″ x 14″. Designers tend to use a book that is lightweight and easy to carry. If it fits into a pocket or satchel, so much the better. There are many styles from which to choose. Some are bound like a book

Figure   12.1

Because designing is often spontaneous, some designers will jot down their ideas on any available scrap of paper, such as this Michael Kors example. Notations about fabric, style, accessories and even the model who will wear the design are often included. These quick sketches can be used for various purposes, including a runway order, as indicated by the number 17.

Croquis book sketch by Michael Kors.

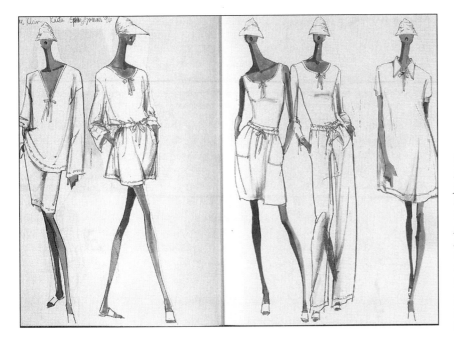

Figure 12.2

Some designers prefer to work in more formal design groups in their croquis books, developing an entire concept using the same color and fabric. The professional designer balances the group to include a variety of silhouettes of tops and bottoms. Consistency is maintained in his or her use of detail, trim and over-all design feeling.

Croquis book sketches courtesy of Anne Klein & Company/Designer: Renaldo Barnette.

and have perforated pages for easy removal. Others are spiral bound and lie flat for easy viewing. Still others are compact enough to be inserted into a portfolio with a loose-leaf binder and integrated into the portfolio presentation. Copy shops will bind 8 ½″ × 11″ copy paper in plastic, complete with a transparent front and back cover. This makes an inexpensive and practical croquis book. The croquis book shows another dimension of your abilities and adds variety to a portfolio presentation.

Figure 12.3

The most desirable poses for the fashion croquis are either frontal or three-quarter view, as these best show garment silhouettes and details.

Croquis book sketches by Renaldo Barnette.

THUMBNAIL SKETCHES

Because designing is fun and often spontaneous, some designers will jot down their ideas on any available scrap of paper. Later on, these sketches find their way into a croquis book, with the addition of notations on accessories, fabric and even the model who will wear the design (Fig. 12.1).

The contents of a croquis book are very personal, therefore it can take on various forms. Some designers spot sketch as they go along, taking ideas from anything and everything. These sketchbooks tend to be more informal, but no less valuable, because they are an excellent way of recording ideas that can later be developed into design concepts. The sketches do not necessarily relate to one another nor is this necessary or even desirable. In contrast, some designers like to work in more formal design groups, developing an entire concept with color and fabric (Fig. 12.2). This is an effective method for evolving several fabric/color groups for a given season. Designs are often drawn in multiples, with as few as two or as many as 20 per page, depending on the designer's preference. Seeing your related designs in a spread facilitates design development. You can easily go from one idea to another, creating design continuity by including similar style lines and details as you go from one design to the next. Working in this way eliminates the need to look back to previous pages to recall your earlier designs.

The most desirable poses for the croquis are either frontal or three-quarter views, as these best show garment silhouettes and details (Fig. 12.3). Since figures used in sketchbooks are generally

Figure   12.4

Professionals generally come to rely less on drawing over a croquis and more on direct drawing methods, since free-hand sketching is faster. Constant practice improves both drawing speed and accuracy.

Croquis book sketches by Renaldo Barnette.

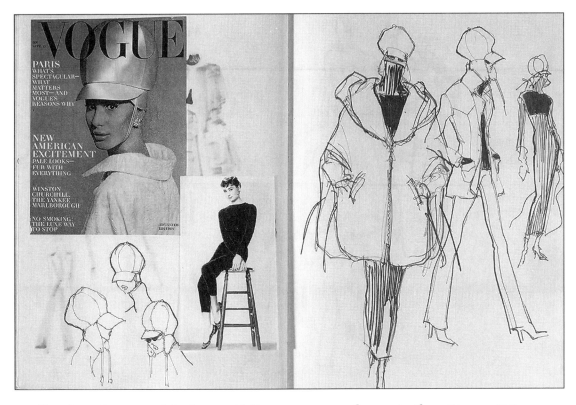

smaller than those used in the portfolio, you can easily create the smaller figures by reducing any one of your larger poses on a copying machine. Use a figure with correct proportion to get the best results.

USING A CROQUIS

To facilitate the sketching process, some designers prefer to use a small croquis. The smaller figure is an excellent tool in the quick sketching process, helping the designer work more quickly to generate ideas. Used as a base or underdrawing, it can be slipped under a page in the sketchbook and worked off of. Generally, the design is sketched in first, then the head, hands, legs and feet are added once the design is conceived. Designers often line up their croquis, completing one design and then moving the croquis over to begin a new one. This method has several advantages. First, the designer can watch his or her design process evolve as each idea is generated by the one before it. Second, the designer does not have to remember designs from previous pages, as all the designs can be viewed at once. For this reason, many designers choose to work on copy paper and glue in the pages they want to keep. Finally, using the croquis helps the designer create a more even presentation by regulating the size of the designs. This eliminates a "hit or miss" result when one design is larger than another. This is not to say that one design cannot have more emphasis, as long as it is intentional.

Constantly sketching in your croquis book improves your drawing ability, as well as your speed. The more you practice, the faster and more accurate your sketches will become. Professionals generally come to rely less on the croquis, and more on direct drawing methods. At first, direct drawing can be hit or miss, and your results uneven. However, if you stick with it, it will pay off with positive results (Fig. 12.4).

Figure   12.5

Designers are constantly clipping out references for design. These often become seeds of inspiration that begin to germinate in the croquis book. In this example, a photograph of Audrey Hepburn and a Vogue *cover from the 1960s become the springboard for the designer's imagination.*

Croquis book sketches by Renaldo Barnette.

Figure 12.6

Although some designers like to draw directly in their croquis books, others prefer to glue in pages of sketches. This latter method is useful for editing out unwanted sketches. Pages can also be attached to one another to create a fold-out.

Croquis book sketches by Paul Chan.

TECHNIQUE AND PRESENTATION

VISUALS

Designers are often excited and inspired by different kinds of images, colors and textures. These visuals can literally come from anywhere—a photo of a fabulous face or head (Fig. 12.5), a picture postcard, scraps of fabric or yarn, even materials not usually associated with fashion or clothing. Because designers are often avid readers, they are constantly clipping out references for design. These often become seeds of inspiration that begin to germinate in the croquis book. There is no set figure regarding the number of inspiring images needed for a specific design project. Design is everywhere. Each designer must react to visual stimuli in his or her own way. A photo image, a scrap of fabric or color, a button or trim glued into the croquis book become the springboard for imagination.

Croquis books come in a variety of papers and present several technique options, predicated on the designer's preference. Some like to draw directly in their books, while others prefer to glue in pages of sketches. This latter method is useful for editing out unwanted sketches. Alternately, you can attach pages to one another to create a fold-out presentation (Fig. 12.6). Copy paper is a favorite among designers for this purpose, the advantage being that the reviewer can see the relationship of each sketch without having to remember it from a previous page. The disadvantage is that too many pages can create a bulky croquis book. Streamline your presentation by editing the pages to include more designs per page.

Because the croquis book documents design development, some designers like to include their process sketches (Fig. 12.7), as well as the edited and more polished versions (Fig. 12.8a and b). This shows a versatile sketching ability that can impress an interviewer.

Include original sketches, not photocopies. Original sketches tend to be more credible and tactile. Most designers work in pencil or use a variety of marker pens for direct sketching. However, technique is a very personal choice and should be completely left to the designer's discretion. Do keep your handwritten notations, as they help the reviewer track your design process (Fig. 12.9). Remove all grades or evaluation comments.

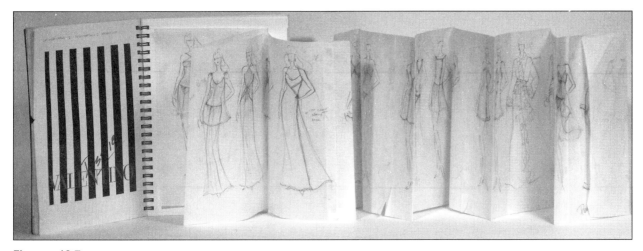

Figure   12.7
Because the croquis book documents design development, some designers like to include their process sketches as well as the edited and more polished versions.

Croquis book sketches by Paul Chan.

Some designers like to make a distinction between concepts by using divider sheets. Whatever your approach, make the sketchbook invite handling, with easy-to-turn pages and a binding that communicates your personal fashion savvy.

Place your croquis book in the back of your portfolio case for easy access. Present it after showing your portfolio to demonstrate your design process. Or refer to your croquis book after each design concept. Weaving it into the presentation shows how much value you place on

Figure   12.8a and b
This polished presentation format extracts designs from the sketches in Figure 12.7. Including both process and finished sketches in a presentation shows a versatile sketching ability that can impress an interviewer.

Presentation format by Paul Chan.

all
cashmere
pieces

Figure   12.9
Handwritten notations help the reviewer track your design process and have a spontaneous and informal quality.
Croquis book sketches by Renaldo Barnette.

Denim
Jacket
&
Shirt
Hip Hugger

Suede
Elbow
Patches

Denim
Hip Hugger
Shirt

Suede
Yoke
on
Denim
Vest

Suede
Gloves

Suede
Collar

the actual process of designing. For this latter method, some designers prefer a croquis book that inserts into the portfolio binder. Either approach engages the reviewer and alters the rhythm of a presentation. The temptation of a beautifully created croquis book is hard to resist. Most reviewers enjoy and welcome the change of pace a sketchbook brings to the interview. It also helps break the ice with questions that allow the reviewer to discover your unique approach.

CUSTOMIZING A PRESENTATION

Creating a specific presentation for an interview can make a favorable impression—and perhaps help you get the job you want. By researching a company beforehand, you become familiar with their look and price point. Some designers go to department or specialty stores to familiarize themselves with a clothing line. Looking at magazine or newspaper advertisements can also be enlightening. Once the research is complete, prepare one or several groupings for your interview geared specifically toward that company. Customizing a presentation for your interview shows your interest in working for that company and demonstrates your quick sketching ability.

Exercise

CUSTOMER VISION CROQUIS BOOK

For those who are new to croquis books, you may want to start with a small size, such as 30 3 50 or 40 3 60. These are perfect for developing a customer vision (you can even use yourself here). Include images of the customer, as well as other visuals that relate to the customer's lifestyle—where she lives, leisure activities, hobbies, favorite colors, verbal expressions, musical preferences, etc. (Fig. 12.10a and b). Refer to Chapter 3 for suggested customer types and profiles. These will help you distinguish and identify types of customers, one of which you can create in your croquis book.

Include your own sketches to tell the story of your customer. These may be spot sketches of your design ideas, or simply sketches of something that has caught your eye. This is an informal journal and does not have to follow a sequence. Sketches can be spontaneous, even rough, and drawn directly or glued into the book. Notes in hand lettering may be used to supplement the visuals and sketches. The finished product should be rich and visually specific to both you and your customer. It is about your reactions to everything surrounding the customer. All of this feeds the design process.

Suggested materials:

- croquis book
- copy paper
- pencils
- marker pens
- visuals (photos, color copies, fabrics, colors, trims)
- rubber cement
- glue stick
- letra-set press or computer-generated type

Figure   12.10a
Customer vision croquis books are perfect for those who are new to croquis books and helpful in developing a customer vision.

Figure   12.10b
This informal journal can include images of the customer, as well as clothing preferences. You can combine visuals with your own sketches and notations.

Customer vision croquis book by Eve Morse.

CHAPTER 13

To fully understand the designer's role in
an apparel manufacturing firm, one must
examine its organizational structure. This
chapter outlines the functions of a
manufacturing firm and includes the
personnel responsible for each function.

The Job Market:
Basic Organization
of Manufacturing Firms

To fully understand the designer's role in an apparel manufacturing firm, one must examine its organizational structure. This chapter outlines the functions of a manufacturing firm and includes the personnel responsible for each function. During the course of the design process, designers will interact with most, if not all, of these key areas. Design meetings, marketing strategies and production requirements facilitate the contact between the designer and the key areas of the firm. The more responsibility held by the designer, the greater his or her input will be in these key areas that create and promote the designer's product.

Manufacturers of both clothing and textiles are organized in a similar way and follow the same basic process. A large company may have a more intricate and specialized structure than a small company, but the same basic functions must be addressed.

COMPANY ORGANIZATION

MANAGEMENT

Management has four major functions within a company: planning, organizing, leading and controlling. The president or CEO (who also may be the owner) and all vice presidents, each of whom has an area of responsibility, are all top managers. Depending on the organizational structure, company vice presidents may be in charge of divisions by function (i.e., vice president of sales, vice president of merchandising), by product (i.e., vice president of men's wear, vice president of women's casual wear) or by region (vice president for Midwest, vice president for Southeast).

Top managers are responsible for setting long-range plans, deciding company policy, determining focus and direction and representing the company to the outside world. Generally, they may have one or more administrative assistants who support them in fulfilling their responsibilities.

There are usually three levels of management in a company: top, middle and first-line or front-line or supervisory. Middle and first-line managers usually work within a specific department and report to top management. For example, the director of design would be considered a middle manager reporting to the vice president of design. The director of design would have responsibilities over the designers. The designers (and assistant designers) would be considered first-line managers, with shared responsibilities over the sample hands or drapers.

MERCHANDISING

Merchandising usually works with all departments in a company—management, design, sourcing, production and sales—to make sure the finished product is executed correctly and on time. This includes determining the target population, researching the market for current trends, planning the overall direction for the coming season, giving direction to the design staff (i.e., types of items to be produced, colors and fabrics to be used), determining the product's price range and planning promotion strategies. Merchandising works with management and sales to develop a line plan and makes sales projections for each season. The merchandising department also supervises the creation of all selling aids (line lists, salesmen samples, swatch booklets, color cards, etc.). Another critical responsibility is giving presentations to the sales force to familiarize them with the concepts of the line to help them pitch it to retailers. In a large company, a merchandiser or design director will head up this area, with the help of one or more assistants. In a smaller company, the owner or designer will see to these responsibilities.

The design staff of a large company may have several designers, each with one or more assistants; in a small company, the designer may work alone to perform all the duties. Some companies do not have a designated designer, per se, this function instead being performed by the owner alone or in conjunction with a stylist who provides market research and general direction. The design staff ordinarily gets its direction from the merchandiser or design director and then generates a number of ideas through sketches. The best of these are chosen and samples are made to test the viability of the designs. The buyer chooses the final line from these samples. The principals of the company, the salespeople and the merchandising and design staff are all involved in this final selection process.

FABRIC RESEARCH AND RESOURCING

In a clothing manufactory, the fabric research and resourcing person researches the market for current trends and fiber and trim directions and brings them back for the merchandising and design staff. Or, he may purchase materials decided upon by the merchandising and design staff in consultation with the principals of the firm. In the latter case, the Piece Goods department would be responsible for researching the market to find the best possible goods available from a quality and price standpoint. There may be one or more assistants in the department to help the buyers. In a textile house, the title for this position would be the yarn buyer.

PRODUCTION

Production can occur either before or after the line is presented to retail buyers by the sales force, depending on the size of the company and the volume of their business. Most large, national brand manufacturers must buy stock fabric and start factory sewing before the line is shown in order to complete the garments and ship them on time to the stores. This is especially true if the manufacturer has a large number of sku's (stock keeping units) and produces its line overseas. These manufacturers determine production quantities by relying on past seasons' selling results, current market conditions, line projections by door (number of stores sold) and feedback from preliminary presentations to buying offices and key accounts. Smaller companies can show the line, then go into production because of the more manageable size of their sales volume.

Many companies own their own facilities, but sometimes work is contracted out to a plant that may do work for several different companies. These plants may be located in the United States or overseas, depending on the production requirements. The production manager is responsible for overseeing the production of the product in the most efficient way possible. He or she will work in the plant, and there is often a production assistant in the main office (where the design staff and showroom are located) to act as a liaison between this office and the factories or mills. For off-shore production, fax machines facilitate communication between the place of production and the home office. Although the production process is overseen by the production manager, it is additionally guided by the merchandiser, designer, spec-tech or agent through on-site visits.

SALES

Samples of the line are the sales force's primary selling tools. The sales staff is responsible for promoting the line to the buyers. Textile companies sell to manufacturers, and manufacturers sell to retail buyers, store owners and market representatives from buying offices.

There are three types of fashion-industry salespeople: showroom salespeople, independent representatives and traveling, or road, salespeople. Showroom sales concentrates on selling a line for one manufacturer or textile company from a permanent showroom facility. Samples of finished garments or textiles are displayed in a showroom, often in a large building where many other companies making a similar product are located. In primary garment centers such as New York City or Los Angeles, certain buildings are designated "designer" buildings. Other buildings are mostly occupied by specialized areas of design, such as bridal or fur.

Independent representatives sell non-competing lines from several manufacturers that cater to the same customer base. For example, an independent-representative organization could specialize in the junior customer and sell junior dresses, junior coats, junior swimwear and junior intimate apparel from four different junior manufacturing companies. Independent representatives receive a percentage from each manufacturer for each order they sell to retailers. The majority of independent-representative companies are located in regional marts across the country—Dallas, Chicago, Florida and San Francisco, for example. This arrangement is beneficial to companies based in New York or Los Angeles who want exposure to buyers who cannot or will not travel.

Traveling, or road, salespeople take the merchandise to small retailers who do not shop the major markets (New York or Los Angeles) or regional marts. They either sell the line of only one manufacturer or of several non-competing manufacturers (a traveling independent representative).

All three types of sales staff provide valuable feedback to the design and merchandising staff regarding the response and desires of the buyers. In the increasingly large private-label sector, the design product is sold to buyers at adoption meetings, initially through board presentations and then via samples meetings.

JOB DESCRIPTIONS IN THE FASHION DESIGN INDUSTRY

Designing is a position of responsibility and vision. It encompasses creativity, technical knowledge, acute business instinct and diplomacy. However, the road to fame and runway shows is a long one, dotted with successful seasons as well as less successful ones. Most people start at the entry level, usually as assistant designers, and work their way up the ladder of experience. Failures teach more than successes. The experienced designer learns to turn mistakes into creative solutions and opportunities. Eventually all designers discover for themselves where they shine and what they like best. Taking inventory along the way helps identify your niche. Those who like supervising others gravitate toward managerial positions. Individuals who prefer "hands-on" tasks seek technical areas. Often the multi-skilled designer incorporates aspects of both, balancing all that is required.

Design positions are categorized below, starting with those requiring the most training and experience and working down toward entry level. Within some companies, design and merchandising hierarchies are firmly separated. The vice president of merchandising/design would be a former merchandiser, the director of design would be a former designer. In most companies, the two areas overlap, so advancement does not follow a strict departmental progression. Salary ranges are indicated. However, this can vary from company to company and according to the skills and abilities of the individual.

VICE PRESIDENT OF MERCHANDISING/DESIGN

Works with sales, design director, designers, production, advertising and public relations. Must have technical knowledge and expertise in design, merchandising, product development, sales and production. Must be able to understand and identify new and upcoming trends and be knowledgeable of fabric sourcing, importing and costing. Must be well organized and able to lead the design team. Works directly with the stores or with design staff to conceptualize an item or line. Conducts buy meetings, manages sample approval process, store communication and order follow-up. Overseas experience required. There are two types of merchandisers: creative and/or sales oriented. Salary range: $75,000–$150,000+.

ASSOCIATE MERCHANDISER

Figure 13.1
An aspiring designer at work in the design room of Christian Roth.

Assists the merchandiser. Must have strong organizational, verbal and communication skills, as well as good color sense, analytical skills, knowledge of garment construction, costing and fabric sourcing. Computer proficiency mandatory. Salary range: $40,000–$75,000.

ASSISTANT MERCHANDISER

Entry-level position assisting the merchandiser. Must have good organizational, verbal and communication skills, as well as good color sense. Follows up communications, faxes, etc. Computer knowledge mandatory. Salary range: $20,000–$30,000.

DESIGN DIRECTOR/HEAD DESIGNER

Highly creative designer who heads the design team. Possesses merchandising background, technical skills, fabric sourcing knowledge and is able to communicate with sales. Salary range: $70,000–$125,000+.

DESIGNER

Responsible for concepts, sketches, fabric and trends. Oversees all aspects of a design room, including design assistants, patternmakers, sample hands and artists. Possesses good illustration, flat and detailed sketch ability. Must have strong technical knowledge and be able to do preliminary fittings. Must be able to communicate ideas to his or her staff. Must know the current market and the competition. Possesses some computer skills. Salary range: $50,000–$75,000.

Figure 13.2

The walls of Donna Karan's design room are covered with sketches of concepts for upcoming lines.

ASSOCIATE DESIGNER

Formerly an assistant designer, but not yet ready to be a designer. Works together with the designer on all aspects of design. Must have technical knowledge, fabric/trim sourcing skills, good aesthetic and sketching ability for presentation boards. Must have good verbal/communication, organizational and computer skills. Must be able to flat sketch and spec. Salary range: $30,000–$50,000.

ASSISTANT DESIGNER

An entry-level position. Most graduates or novices start off at this level. Works together with the associate designer or with the designer. Shops trim market, makes appointments and sometimes accompanies the associate designer/designer on fabric appointments. Does follow-up work for the designer on samples, trims, fabric cuts, etc. Has a technical background and good sketching ability. Assists in creating presentation boards and has computer skills. Salary range: $20,000–$25,000.

TECHNICAL DESIGNER/SPEC-TECH

Must have strong patternmaking, fit and grading experience. Able to fit on a live model or mannequin. Must be able to do detailed flat drawings and write garment specifications. Communicates pattern corrections with domestic and overseas vendors. Has knowledge and ability to develop and review fabric and construction standards. Knows garment construction in order to inspect production. Product development background and ability to work with key accounts essential. Reports to the designer and production manager. Salary range: $28,000–$55,000.

CAD OPERATOR/DESIGNER

Must have flat sketching ability, good color sense and verbal communication skills. Knowledge of various computer-aided design (CAD) systems mandatory. Salary range: $35,000–$50,000; managers: $50,000–$70,000.

THE MARKDOWN ASSIGNMENT

This assignment promotes fashion awareness and brings the student into contact with essential merchandising and retail aspects of the fashion business.

After researching garments in a better department or specialty store, select one garment from three different categories and predict what you think will not sell or be marked down. The three distinct categories assist you in identifying these diverse design areas and customers. If higher priced garments are unavailable in certain stores, substitute different price points, such as moderate, better or bridge.

The three categories are:

1. Established Designer; i.e., Bill Blass, Oscar de la Renta, Geoffrey Beene

2. Sportswear Designer; i.e., Giorgio Armani, Donna Karan, Calvin Klein

3. Avant-Garde Designer; i.e., Commes des Garçon, Vivienne Westwood, John Galliano

On the form provided at the end of this chapter, include the following information: name of designer, sketch of garment, description/fabric/color, price, how many and reason why you think it will not sell.

The form contains space to track a single garment for a five-week period. Use three different forms, one for each category. Allow two to three weeks between store visits; use the same store for the assignment. After each visit indicate how many garments are left and their price. (If the garment has been marked down, the price will be lower. This may affect customer incentive to buy.)

Because garments are often shifted on the selling floor, talk to salespeople and/or buyers for additional feedback on how their garments are faring. Merchandisers are usually extremely supportive. In the past, students have reported that the buyer has taken them on a tour of the floor. This is an opportunity to learn additional information about the designers, store, etc. Several students met well-known designers in person while they were doing their trunk shows at the store.

When in the store, always ask permission before sketching garments or taking notes. Usually students get a positive response if they make it known that this is for a class assignment. A negative reaction is rare, but could happen. In this case, students should be polite and rely on memory for sketching and note-taking. You can always run to the restroom or leave the store to make a quick sketch. Relying on memory is excellent practice in itself. After several store visits, you will have all the information you need and may find a more sympathetic floor person. Dress appropriately when visiting the store (no jeans or sweats).

Visit a better department for this assignment, preferably a specialty store such as Bergdorf Goodman or Barney's where there is more control of merchandise inventory. Some students are initially intimidated by this caliber of store and express trepidation. However, this assignment helps to dissolve this barrier. Even the most reticent student can get past this and discover the importance of this resource.

Exercise (*continued*)

This assignment teaches the following:

- Awareness of fashion classifications and markets
- Pricing of garments within specific markets
- Inventory and size ratio
- Style identification i.e., the "look" associated with a designer
- Raised awareness and taste level through exposure to quality garments
- Customer wants/factors that effect purchasing power

Markdown Log Sheet

Designer Name: *DKNY (Donna Karan)*

Design Category: *Bridge Sportswear, Customer who*

wants to look trendy but not on the edge

Description/Fabric/Color: *Dupioni Silk, Mandarin Orange*

Price: *$385.00*

Why Garment Will Not Sell:

color was too bright

price was too high for casual clothing

fabric not practical for casual wear

silhouette unflattering

Sketch of Garment

	Week/Date	How Many?	Price
Week 1	*June 9*	*4*	*$385.00*
Week 2	*June 16*	*4*	*$385.00*
Week 3	*June 23*	*3*	*$385.00*
Week 4	*June 30*	*0 (removed)*	
Week 5			

Figure 13.3

A completed Markdown Assignment Log Sheet. Five weeks of "visiting" your chosen garments increases fashion awareness on many levels.

Illustration by Elliot Jusino-Serrano.

Markdown Log Sheet

Designer Name: _____

Design Category: _____

_____

Description/Fabric/Color: _____

_____

Price: _____

Why Garment Will Not Sell: _____

_____

_____

_____

_____

_____

Sketch of Garment

Week/Date	How Many?	Price
Week 1		
Week 2		
Week 3		
Week 4		
Week 5		

CHAPTER 14

A resumé is a marketing tool—a brief summary of your qualifications to sell yourself to prospective employers. It should attract attention and spark interest, impress an employer, and ultimately create an invitation for a personal interview.

A resumé is a marketing tool; a brief summary of your qualifications to sell yourself to prospective employers. Your resumé should reflect you—your experiences, interests, accomplishments, skills and education. It should attract attention and spark interest, impress an employer and ultimately create an invitation for a personal interview.

RESUMÉ PREPARATION

1. Spend ample time reviewing your background and past experiences so you know what skills, abilities and qualifications you have to offer an employer. Use the Career Preparation Worksheet to assist you. Include volunteer work, which is an important indicator of your skills and effectiveness. This can be especially valuable for those re-entering the work force.

   You will need to ask yourself several questions before beginning to write your resumé. Make an honest assessment of your likes and dislikes to write the best possible resumé for you. It is only human to gravitate toward the things we like and do best. Answering the following questions will help you clarify some of the important points:

   - Which skills or achievements give me the greatest satisfaction?
   - Which of my past jobs (including volunteer work) did I like best?
   - What are my main attributes?
   - What are my main liabilities?
   - Do I prefer a large or small company?
   - Do I prefer to work alone or am I a team player?
   - Am I most comfortable following direction or do I prefer supervising and motivating others?
   - Do I enjoy working with people or equipment?
   - Do I need the security of a regular salary or do I prefer the incentive of commission/bonus work?
   - Do I prefer a full-time job or freelance work?
   - Would I prefer a job that includes travel?

2. Select the appropriate resumé format—chronological or functional—to market you and your experience most effectively. If you start in one format, continue with that style throughout the entire resumé. A new resumé may not be necessary for every job you apply for. However, you may need to revise your resumé for a special interview, so keep several versions on hand. A computer is great for making revisions. You can keep several resumés on file and update and revise whenever necessary.

3. Typeset your resumé or produce it on a computer. Because they are in a creative profession, designers have more latitude in their choice of typefaces, or fonts, but be sure not to use anything smaller than 10-point. The serif types are considered to be more traditional, the sans serif types more contemporary. The typeface you choose should be both aesthetic and readable.

4. Have your resumé reviewed by an instructor, placement counselor or industry professional before distributing it. Many colleges offer workshops in resumé preparation if you are currently enrolled in a program or have recently graduated.

Professional advice can save you time, worry and, ultimately, disappointment.

5. Invest as much time as necessary to revise your draft. Proofread your resumé carefully before having it duplicated. Remember, the resumé is an extension of you. It promotes your image.

Paper

Choose an 8½″ × 11″ acid-free, 100-percent cotton or high-quality recycled paper in a color light enough for easy reading and a weight heavy enough for photocopying or faxing. Usually 24 lb. is best, though resumé cover stock is fine. Match stationery for cover letter, resumé, #10 envelopes and follow-up letters.

Fonts and Layout

Select a clear, readable font, avoiding those that are overly decorative. Use only one font for the resumé. View your name and important words in various fonts to see which you prefer. Generally, you'll want to keep the size either 10- or 12-point, with a larger size acceptable for your name.

Use various font styles (bold, underline, etc.) and punctuation sparingly; let the resumé speak for itself. Use black ink and a laser printer or high-resolution ink jet printer. Never use a dot matrix printer. Always have black-and-white copies available for photocopying and to respond to ads.

Select your resumé format (chronological or functional) and edit the information to one page only.

CHRONOLOGICAL RESUMÉS

RESUMÉ STYLES

Chronological resumés outline your background in a sequential time frame, with the most recent events listed first. This format is commonly used by recent college graduates with limited work experience.

Rules for the Chronological Resumé

1. Start with your present or most recent position and work backward, with most space devoted to recent employment.
2. Detail only the last four or five positions of employment covering the last 10 or so years.
3. Use year designations, not month and day. Give greater detail at the interview or on the application.
4. Don't show every major position change with a given employer. List two or three at most, including the most recent.
5. Do not repeat details/duties common to several positions.
6. Within each position listed, stress the major accomplishments and responsibilities that demonstrate your competency. Once the most significant aspects of your work are clear, it is generally not necessary to include lesser achievements.
7. Keep your next job target in mind, and as you describe prior positions and accomplishments, emphasize those that relate most to your next move up.
8. Do not include education in chronological order. If it is within the past five years, list it at the top of the resumé. If earlier than that, at the bottom. (This is not a hard and fast rule, however. Follow your own instincts whether to emphasize work or education.)
9. Keep the resumé to one page.

CHRONOLOGICAL RESUMÉ

Chloe DesJardins
47 Satin St.
Portland, Oregon 97531
206-555-5555

OCCUPATIONAL GOAL   *Assistant Designer*

EDUCATION   **Fashion Institute of Technology, State University of New York**
Associate in Applied Science degree, June 1996
Fashion Design major—Specialization: Sportswear

HONORS & AWARDS   Fashion Institute of Technology, Dean's List
Sportswear design selected for college fashion show
Recipient of the Helen Saunders Academic Scholarship

INTERNSHIP   **Harve Benard (bridge sportswear),** NYC
Fall 1996   *Design intern*
• Researched fabric and trims
• Organized and maintained fabric swatches
• Sketched and speced flats
• Provided design input on line development

WORK EXPERIENCE
December 1996 - May 1997   **Andy Johns,** NYC
Assistant Designer, moderate outerwear
• Prepared and cut first patterns
• Checked and corrected samples
• Maintained swatch book
• Assisted with selection of fabric trims

May 1995 - August 1997   **Designer (self employed),** Spring Valley, NY
• Established wedding/special occasion dress business
• Designed and constructed gowns
• Sourced fabric and trims
• Maintained all bookkeeping records

November 1995 - June 1996   **Macy's,** Wayne, NJ
Sales Associate, sleepwear
• Assisted customers with merchandise selection
• Arranged in-store display
• Operated point of sales register

October 1994 - February 1996   **McDonald's,** Spring Valley, NY
Assistant Evening Manager
• Supervised eight employees
• Assigned schedules and work loads
• Responded to customer complaints

SKILLS   Embroidery and beading layouts, handknitting and crocheting,
understanding of Spanish and German

FUNCTIONAL RESUMÉS

Functional resumés focus on your most important skill areas and summarize your work history by listing employers and dates of employment in a chronological fashion. This format is effective for those who have held a position with varied responsibilities for a number of years, for those with time gaps or for those re-entering the job market after a prolonged absence.

Rules for the Functional Resumé

1. Use four or five separate paragraphs or sections, each one highlighting a particular area of expertise.

2. List these paragraphs in order of importance, with the area most related to your present job target at the top and containing slightly more information.

3. Within each functional area, stress your strongest abilities and the accomplishments most directly related to the job you are now seeking.

4. You can include any relevant accomplishment without necessarily identifying which employment or avocational situation with which it was connected.

5. Include education toward the bottom, unless it was within the past three to five years. If it was in an unrelated field, include it at the end regardless of how recent.

6. List a brief synopsis of your actual work experience at the bottom, giving dates, employers and titles. If you have had no work experience or a very spotty record, leave out the employment synopsis entirely (but be prepared to talk about the subject at the interview).

7. Keep the length to one page.

GENERAL INFORMATION TO INCLUDE IN YOUR RESUMÉ

Name and Contact Information: Current address, zip code and phone/fax number (center at the top of page).

Professional Objective (optional): An objective is a concise statement indicating what career path or position you are seeking. It should indicate a sense of purpose and direction. However, there is great debate as to whether or not to include an objective. An objective is only effective if you are applying for a specific position in the industry. Stating a specific objective can limit your job possibilities and require several versions of your resumé. A resumé without a stated objective creates the opportunity for an employer to consider you for a broader range of job possibilities, sometimes even a higher position than you applied for.

Education/Training: Name of school, degree, major. For recent graduates with minimal industry experience, this section should precede "Work History." If you have two degrees, list the higher degree first, i.e., "Bachelor of Science, June 1993; Associate in Applied Science, June 1991." Include honors and a grade point average of 3.0 or higher, as these will enhance your image; list additional educational training and study abroad. It is not always necessary to list all the schools you have attended. An abundance of degrees, even from prestigious institutions, can be intimidating. You can always reveal your additional degree accomplishments if your interviewer is impressed by educational awards. Do not list high school education.

FUNCTIONAL RESUMÉ

FABIO FERNADEZ
22 Fashion Ave.
Superior, WI 00000
612-555-5555

OBJECTIVE	To obtain Summer 1998 internship
EDUCATION	The Shannon Rodgers and Jerry Silverman School of Fashion Design and Merchandising • Kent State University • Kent, Ohio Bachelor of Arts • December 1998 • Major: Fashion Design

SUMMARY OF SKILLS

Design
- Develop concepts, color stories, and silhouette
- Analyze market trends for research and presentation
- Source fabrics for appropriate applications
- Create original gouache applied designs
- Create graphs of knitwear

Technology
- Develop, manipulate, and construct patterns for illustrations and specification sheets
- Develop design and pattern through draping techniques
- Create production patterns with pattern charts and cost sheets
- Construct and fit garment
- Hand knit on single-bed machine

Visual Communications
- Develop design illustrations from concept sketches to final presentations
- Render in mediums of marker, colored pencil, gouache, and watercolor
- Create concept boards for design presentations
- Apply computer aided design to apparel industry (Microdynamics ADS)

HONORS

Shannon Rodgers Endowed Scholarship
Helen Joseph Armstrong Excellent Workmanship Award
Maintained Dean's List status
First Place Haute Goodwill Design Competition

PAST EMPLOYMENT

Fashion Bug • Superior, Wisconsin
Summer 1997; Sales Associate

Domino's Pizza • Superior, Wisconsin
1992-94, 1997; Assistant Manager

Kent State University • Kent, Ohio
Spring 1997; Secretary/Receptionist
Fall 1996; Food Service

Work History: If you are currently working or have recently been employed in the industry, "Work Experience" should precede "Education." Describe work experience in reverse order, with the most recent first. You may want to make a list of your work experience—full-time, part-time, summer jobs and paid and unpaid internships—before deciding which ones to include. Because you only have one page to tell your story, you want to be selective. Evaluate each job individually. Be prepared to alter this information if necessary to suit each interview. Volunteer work, activities or independent projects that relate to the types of positions you are seeking may also be included when applicable.

For all resumé formats, the basics to include are: job title, name of employing organization and dates of employment. When listing positions of short-term employment, group them rather than list each one separately.

Use phrases, not sentences, as this will save space and make the information easier to "pick out." You need not list every duty. Select your most important responsibilities and stress your specific accomplishments, rather than "describing" your job. Be factual and honest in your descriptions. Don't fabricate or embroider facts you can't substantiate.

Optional Information:

Honors, Awards, Exhibitions: These headings usually follow "Education" and should be included if they enhance your credentials.

Course Highlights: This section should be used only if you do not have enough relevant work experience. You can use this opportunity to emphasize specific courses that would enhance your job performance, such as CAD, marketing or production courses.

Extracurricular Activities: List school clubs. Be sure to indicate leadership positions held.

Interests/Hobbies: This section allows you to present yourself as an interesting, well-rounded individual. Make sure interests and hobbies relate to your career objective.

Skills: This section usually follows "Work Experience." Not to be used as subjective statements about yourself, the skills you include are rather measurable strengths, abilities and talents (proficiency in a foreign language, computer training, typing/word processing, etc.). These skills should go beyond those required for the applied position.

References: It is not necessary to list specific names and telephone numbers of references on a resumé, as this takes up valuable room. If you feel your references will be an important asset, write "References available upon request" at the bottom of the page. (Be sure your references are informed and available.)

The following are some job skills, power words and phrases that are key to a resumé. See Table 14.1 for a list of action verbs to further enhance your resumé.

FINESSING YOUR RESUMÉ

- Your ability to move swiftly and capably from task to task, one work environment to another, even across national boundaries.
- Your ability to master new concepts, ideas and practices.
- Versatility, flexibility, mobility.
- High learning curve, adaptive to change, innovative approach to problem-solving.

- Organizing and reorganizing new data, work systems and corporate processes; ability to integrate concepts.
- Entrepreneurial and risk-smart.
- Customer focused.
- Cross-cultural, diverse, second or third language fluency.
- Computer literate.
- Worked on special task forces, project teams.
- Think globally, act locally.
- Quality orientation.

Employers want to hire people who can:

- Work on a team.
- Energize and motivate others.
- Learn and use new things.
- Demonstrate versatility.
- Challenge old ways of thinking.
- Understand how to create profits.
- Display business savvy.
- Communicate directly and clearly, both written and verbally.
- Take calculated risks.
- Admit mistakes.
- Exhibit high personal standards.

We've looked at some important elements to include in a resumé; now here are a few "do's and don'ts":

RESUMÉ DO'S & DON'TS

Do use a simple, legible font, keeping capital letters and/or bold or italic type to a minimum.

Do use plain, clear English, avoiding hip language or "buzz" words. Reviewers tend to disregard that which is unfamiliar.

Do update your resumé and print a clean copy as often as necessary instead of just handwriting revisions.

Don't write "Resumé" at the top of the page.

Don't use personal pronouns (I, me, etc.) since it is understood the resumé is written in the first person.

Don't include self-serving evaluations.

Don't include photos or personal data such as age, height, weight, marital status, religion, ethnicity, etc. Potential employers may not obtain this information under Federal regulations.

Don't include names and phone numbers of references.

Don't state salary requirements or how much you earned on previous jobs.

Don't include addresses of firms, names of supervisors and reasons for leaving a position.

Don't apologize for deficiencies in qualifications or presentation of your resumé.

Don't use a resumé service to prepare your resumé. Their product can be too generic. Creating your own will help you "package" yourself.

TABLE 14.1 *ACTION VERBS*

Use effective phrases rather than full sentences to strengthen your accomplishments. Begin phrases with an action verb such as those listed below. Verbs communicate your abilities. Emphasizing action and accomplishments is more important than stressing job responsibilities. Your interviewer wants to hear what you have done, not a job description.

accomplished	discovered	maintained	reviewed
achieved	dispensed	managed	revised
adapted	distributed	marketed	revitalized
administered	diverted	maximized	rewrote
advised	doubled	measured	routed
analyzed	drafted	mediated	selected
applied	edited	modernized	served
appraised	eliminated	monitored	set up
approved	equipped	motivated	simplified
arranged	established	negotiated	sold
attained	evaluated	obtained	solved
averted	exceeded	operated	specified
budgeted	executed	ordered	streamlined
built	exhibited	organized	strengthened
calculated	expanded	oversaw	studied
certified	expedited	participated	succeeded
chaired	facilitated	performed	summarized
charted	forecasted	pioneered	supervised
checked	formulated	planned	supported
collected	founded	prepared	surveyed
communicated	gathered	presented	synthesized
compiled	generated	processed	systematized
completed	guided	produced	taught
composed	handled	programmed	tested
computed	headed	promoted	trained
conceived	identified	provided	translated
conducted	implemented	publicized	traveled
constructed	improved	published	trimmed
consulted	increased	purchased	tripled
contracted	influenced	raised	undertook
controlled	initiated	recommended	unified
converted	innovated	recruited	united
convinced	installed	reduced	unraveled
coordinated	instituted	referred	updated
counseled	instructed	regulated	upgraded
created	interpreted	renegotiated	used
delegated	interviewed	reorganized	utilized
delivered	introduced	repaired	verified
demonstrated	invented	reported	widened
designed	investigated	represented	won
detected	judged	researched	worked
determined	justified	resolved	wrote
developed	launched	responded	
devised	led	restored	
directed	located	revamped	

RESUMÉ STRATEGIES

Your resumé should arrive on a Tuesday, Wednesday or Thursday so it does not have to compete with the Friday backlog. If mailing locally, drop it in the mail Monday morning. From a greater distance, mail on Friday.

There is no need to use overnight delivery services if you are simply responding to an ad and haven't spoken directly to someone in charge of hiring. However, if you have spoken to them directly, your resumé, sent with a strong cover letter via FedEx or Express Mail, is sure to make a positive impression. Those cardboard envelopes get attention and are delivered and opened immediately. Be sure to pay for the service yourself; don't use your current employer's account.

Keep a list of the resumés you send, dates you sent them and contacts. Call your contacts within one week of the date your resumé should have arrived to be sure they received it. You may want to explain that you have received an offer of employment from another company and, before committing, would like to interview with their company. Ask to speak with the individual who is hiring. This gives you the opportunity to find out the name of the person reviewing resumés for the position you are applying for, since the person you initially speak with may be from Human Resources and screening resumés.

One of two things might happen. If all goes well, you may be given the name of the person interviewing and their extension. Or you may be met with a version of "don't call us, we'll call you." Be polite and thank the person in any case. No need to push too hard. Remember, they are in the driver's seat.

THE COVER LETTER

When mailing a resumé, send a cover letter to clarify and support it. A strong cover letter can single you out and personalize your message for an employer who must go through perhaps hundreds of resumés. Send the cover letter directly to an individual, and include his or her job title. Mailing simply to the company reveals a lack of investigative ability. The cover letter is your way of personally introducing yourself. Its "voice" should echo you. Think of it as a brief telephone conversation describing your attributes. It should communicate your potential value to the company, stimulate the employer's interest and create a sense of curiosity and desire to know more about you.

Write a new cover letter each time you send your resumé. Perfect spelling and grammar are essential. Poor language skills are not an excuse for errors here. Get help from counselors or instructors if your communication skills are lacking. Both written and verbal skills have a definite bearing on job hiring. You don't want to discourage them before you can show what you can do.

Personalize each letter. Avoid formula letters where you simply change the date and address each time. The lack of effort is evident in these generic letters and potential employers can easily spot them. The cover letter, like the resumé, should not be photocopied. Only originals are acceptable for this purpose.

The cover letter and resumé should be produced on complementary papers. If you prefer a tinted stock, investigate which ones can be fed through a laser printer. Either choose a uniform color for both or one that coordinates with the envelope. Designers tend to be less traditional about their choice of color, though white or eggshell are easiest to match and are always appropriate.

The format should be block style, as in a business letter. Have someone proofread your letter for typos and spelling errors. Pay special attention to the correct spelling of the interviewer's name and title. Sign your name in a color other than black, as black ink often looks like a copy rather than an original signature. Dark blue ink is said to produce greater attention in reader response.

A cover letter should never be lengthy. It should consist of a single page and include three to four concise, well-written paragraphs. Indicate you are enclosing the resumé for reference. Some designers also like to include an illustrated flyer or business card to pique further interest in their abilities.

SAMPLE COVER LETTER

Date

Sydney Superstar
Design Director (or contact name)
The Fabulous Fashion Company
777 Fashion Avenue
Fashion City, NY 00007

Dear Mr. Superstar:

It was an unexpected pleasure to meet you at the CFDA Awards in New York in February and a great thrill to be present when you accepted the lifetime achievement award for design. I have admired your clothes since the first time I picked up a fashion magazine. Attending the award ceremony afforded me my first opportunity to experience New York. The excitement and pulse of this great city is everywhere. After exploring Seventh Avenue, Fifth Avenue, Madison Avenue and Soho and attending the shows at Seventh On Sixth, I am determined to begin my design career in New York.

In our conversation you suggested I send you a resumé upon graduation. While at Kent State I studied under Professor Draper, who worked with you as critic and encouraged me to contact your firm. The fashion design program features strong emphasis on construction techniques, creative design interpretation and computer technology. Two internships with New York City-based Superior Sportswear and Knatty Knit Co. during the summer and winter break, respectively, helped me hone my computer skills and acquire further knowledge of these areas.

The sophisticated look of The Fabulous Fashion Company is well known through its distinctive advertisements in *W, Vogue, Bazaar, Elle*, and others. A retrospective of your designs last October helped me understand the long history and design point of view of the company leading into the future. My professional goal has long been to design for a quality designer company like the Fabulous Fashion Company.

As first prize winner of The Absolutely Fabulous Fashion Competition, I will be in New York during the second week in March to attend the Fashion Group International Paris/Milan presentation. I will telephone early Tuesday, March 3rd, to schedule an interview for the following week.

I look forward to meeting with you and thank you in advance for your consideration.

Sincerely,

Harriet Hopeful

The opening paragraph is critical since it must to get attention immediately. Mention an interesting point about the firm or, better yet, the reader. Being current counts, and the tone of the letter should indicate you are informed about the company. Briefly discuss a recent event or design innovation connected with the firm. If you have a mutual reference or connection, mention the name to create an association. If the person you are writing to has appeared in a recent article or won a professional award like the CFDA, show your awareness by acknowledging such. Of course, mention the purpose of your letter. Indicate whether you are responding to an advertisement for job placement or seeking an exploratory meeting for informational purposes.

Paragraph two might contain an interesting fact included in the resumé, tempting the reader to find out more. List your college, degree, year and area of focus. Internships and related part-time jobs are significant, especially for recent graduates. Keep it brief. This paragraph should convey the information in three to four sentences.

Paragraph three should say something special about you, while connecting your skills to the employer. This "hook" must entice the employer to want to meet you even if there is no position available. This is easier said than done. Research can be the key to creating a knowledgeable impression. Confidence, informed and valuable are qualities you want to project to potential employers.

The last paragraph should suggest an interview and/or a review of your portfolio. Mention you will be calling for a meeting. If you are planning to be in town a limited time only, specify dates and a contact number. Your telephone promise helps "break the ice" for further contact. Follow up on all your professional correspondence. (Use the Job Search Work Log in Chapter 15.) Each contact and experience adds up to slow and steady success in the job search process.

Taking a creative, clever approach might be just the right way to draw attention to your resumé and cover letter, especially if you have not had success with conventional means. For example, I know of a case where an applicant sent a resume and cover letter in a glass bottle. The cover letter was written like an S.O.S., emphatically stating how much the person wanted to be interviewed but hadn't been able to get to first base. Impressed by this unique approach, the employer immediately arranged a date for an interview.

Another eager candidate sent a broom, with a resumé attached. The note read something to the effect that, "I do floors as well as great design, please hire me." This unconventional approach demonstrates the lengths one might go to in order to get hired at their "dream" company. Perhaps these examples are extreme, but they do paint a stark picture about the job-search process. With the number of candidates competing for the same job, those who standout and can communicate their talents have a definite edge over other applicants. The interview process is tedious for the interviewer as well as the applicant. The interviewer must read through many resumés and cover letters where a sameness prevails. If an applicant strikes a humorous chord in the process, it will certainly get noticed.

CHAPTER 15

Interviewing can be a nerve-wracking
experience or an extremely positive one.
Good preparation can lessen the anxiety
and put you in control, ultimately shortening
your job search.

Organizing Your Job Hunt, Mastering the Interview

The more you know about yourself, the better your chance at identifying a job that will bring you ultimate success and satisfaction. Interviewing can be a nerve-wracking experience or an extremely positive one. Some say job hunting is one of the most traumatic events in our lives. Good preparation, however, can lessen the anxiety and put you in control. Leaving less to chance will increase your job possibilities and strengthen your confidence. Ultimately, good preparation will shorten your job search.

Generally, companies are looking for creative individuals with good organizational, time-management and communication skills. Most creative people think their creativity is enough to get them a job. This may be true—in rare cases. More often, however, when hiring assistants, designers look for creative people who will help them organize themselves better, who are neat and efficient, in short, composed people who can handle themselves under pressure and know how to manage their time while working under deadlines. Good communication skills are a must, as well as an energetic attitude.

Wanting a job is a start, but it's not enough. You must be willing to take a good look at yourself and approach the career game with a plan—the same way you would if you were given any project or assignment. Organizing your job search can be a valuable learning experience. This time, the subject is you.

GETTING STARTED

GET ORGANIZED

- Target companies in order of preference.
- Know what positions for which you're qualified.
- Prepare several resumés.
- Make your job search a real campaign; work at it daily.
- Use a work log (Fig. 15.1) to keep track of each interview.
- Keep copious notes.

INFORMATIONAL INTERVIEWING

This type of interview is an excellent way to make contacts and learn about the fashion industry. Before you begin, make sure you have several versions of your resumé, tailored for each recipient (see Chapter 14), as well as letters requesting exploratory meetings (Fig. 15.2). It's important to remember this type of interview is *only* a networking tool for developing a list of contacts—not a job request! To inquire about employment during an informational interview is a serious breach of protocol. These meetings are simply for gathering information about the industry, a company or a position. You can also seek advice, direction and learn about educational requirements and industry expectations.

Sample questions to ask during an informational interview:

- What are the major responsibilities of your job?
- What is the career path for someone in your position?
- What preparation, education and experience would prepare me for a job such as yours?
- How did you get started in the fashion field?
- What is an average day like?
- What is the potential for growth and advancement in your job?

Job Search Work Log

Contact; date called: _____

Left message: _____

Call back: _____

Name/Title: _____

Interview date/time: _____

Phone: _____

Send resumé: _____

Company Name: _____

Send cover letter: _____

Address: _____

_____

Second interview date/time: _____

Job Title/Description: _____

_____

Call back on: _____

Salary/Range: _____

Send thank-you note: _____

- What are the future trends in the fashion industry? Problems? Concerns?
- What skills should I be developing now?
- Does your position require any travel, overtime or opportunity for relocation?
- What do you like/dislike about your work?
- How is your company structured? To whom do you report? Do you have supervisory responsibilities?
- Could you suggest someone else I could speak with regarding the fashion industry?

Figure   15.1
Work Log.

Keep in mind that industry professionals have full schedules. Be sensitive to time and don't wear out your welcome by lingering or asking too many questions. You will have other opportunities to gather additional information at your next interview. Because they are busy people, they may want to schedule an interview at a breakfast meeting, after the work day, or even by phone. Be flexible. You may have to adjust your calendar to the convenience of your contact and the time allotted may be brief.

As you interview you will gain valuable information about careers within the fashion industry. Look for opportunities to take advantage of those who are genuinely interested in sharing their work-related experiences with you. These giving individuals remember when! Stay in touch with them.

Sample Exploratory Meeting Letter

Date

Ms. Freda Fashion
Design Director
The Fabulous Fashion Company
777 Fashion Avenue
Fashion City, NY 00007

Dear Ms Fashion,

I am writing at the suggestion of our mutual (associate, acquaintance, contact, etc.) Mr. Martin Manufacturer, who has known me for a number of years (has been acquainted with my family or has hired me for the past several summers or any information that will establish the connection). He recommended you as a source of information relative to my career goals.

I would welcome the opportunity to meet with you to explore the current marketplace and hear your suggestions and advice regarding how I might best use my skills and abilities to find an entry-level design position in the fashion industry.

I would appreciate any time you may have available in your busy schedule to speak with me. I will be calling your office in the next few days to set up an appointment for a brief exploratory meeting at your convenience.
I look forward to meeting you. Thank you for your time and consideration.*

Sincerely,

Janet Jobseeker

Contact Information:
Name
Address
City, State, zip code
Phone Number

Figure   15.2
Letter requesting an exploratory meeting.

**If you enclose your resumé (optional) add this sentence to your letter: "I am
enclosing my resumé for your reference."*

First, identify your skills, values, interests, personal and professional strengths and weaknesses. Formulate your short- and long-term goals and be ready to discuss this important information with your interviewer. Then familiarize yourself with companies that make the kind of clothes you want to design. This will help you present yourself as more knowledgeable at an interview. Libraries, stores, industry professionals, teachers and friends in the industry are excellent resources.

This sample (Fig. 15.3) is the type of letter you would send to initiate an appointment in response to an advertised job. And even if the interview doesn't net you the job, there are potential benefits, nonetheless. One is networking. Networking is the strategy of making contacts with people who can give you helpful suggestions or advice, identify potential positions, and be a support system for you. It is an important part of the job search process. Talk to as many people as you can who might potentially hire you or refer you to others who can.

Many positions are filled through personal referrals. As you network you will begin to develop your own list of people, professional groups and alumni. Don't forget friends, relatives, faculty members and counselors who may be able to give you job referrals.

PREPARING FOR A JOB INTERVIEW

ARRANGING INTERVIEWS

Be prepared by knowing exactly what you want to say and ask. Have your date book handy for interview scheduling. Industry professionals are busy people and may not be in when you call or return your call promptly. Don't allow your impatience or annoyance to come across if this is the case. Be courteous and understanding.

Aim for at least five calls a day or more if you have leads. If you get a negative response when you ask about a job opening, ask for other referrals to departments or divisions within the company. You might also ask for referrals to other people your contact might be willing to share. Keep notes about the people you have spoken with, their companies and their suggestions or contacts.

PRELIMINARY RESEARCH

Obtaining background information about the company you will be interviewing with is essential. It demonstrates your investigative skills and interest in working there. College and business libraries will have major references for this purpose, such as *Moody's, Standard* and *Poor's, Dun & Bradstreet, Davison's Textile Bluebook, Standard Dictionary of Advertising Agencies, Madison Avenue Handbook, Sheldon's Guide to Retail Stores* and *Resident Buying Offices, The Encyclopedia of Associations* and a variety of directories for many areas of the fashion industry.

Knowing the product or range of products a company makes is important for intelligent discussion at the interview. Familiarize yourself with their specific market/price point, the target customer, stores where their merchandise is carried, floors or location of merchandise, seasonal fabrics and color stories, silhouettes and distinctive details.

Possible questions you may be asked:

- What are your short-term goals?
- What are your long-term goals?
- What are your hobbies or interests other than fashion?

Sample Advertised Job Response Letter

Date

Name
Director of Personnel (or contact name)
The Fabulous Fashion Company
777 Fashion Avenue
Fashion City, NY 00007

Dear Mr. or Ms. (insert name),

I am responding to your recent advertisement in the January 1st issue of *Women's Wear Daily*. I believe I am an ideal candidate for the advertised position given my experience, credentials and background.

As a recent graduate of (school name), I have gained knowledge in (explain how your acquired knowledge relates to the job advertised.) During my years at (school name), I worked as an intern for the Super Sportswear Corporation, where I functioned as (explain what you did) and learned a great deal about the industry. (If you did several internships, include them here as well and briefly discuss your job functions.)

My training and internship experiences have been invaluable assets to my career development. I would very much like the opportunity to discuss them further with you. I am enclosing my resumé for your reference, and I am available for an interview (if you are planning to travel in for the interview, specify dates and a contact number where you can be reached in town). My references can be furnished upon request.

Thank you in advance for your consideration. I look forward to hearing from you soon.

Sincerely,

Janet Jobseeker

Encl.: Resumé

Figure   15.3
Letter sent in response to an advertised job.

- What magazines do you like and why?
- What do you see currently in stores that you think is absolutely great?
- What do you love to do best?
- What do you do to relieve stress and how do you handle pressure?
- Why did you choose this company?
- Who are our competitors?
- Give at least four things you can offer the company or why you'd be an asset. (Sell yourself!)
- How long would it take for you to know whether this job is for you?
- What is your opinion about our product?

Sample questions to ask:

- What kind of assistant are you looking for? Design, technical, etc.
- What is the job description and what are the tasks required?
- Where is your production done and if there is travel involved, how much?
- What are the growth opportunities within the company?
- Are there salary reviews and how often, cost of living increases, bonuses?

Evaluate your portfolio contents for relevancy to the company you are going to see. Generally, companies prefer to look at designs in the category and price point they manufacture. Many firms, such as those that have licensees, manufacture a wide range of products and may have divisions in several price points. Find this out in your preliminary research.

Determine the rhythm or "flow" of your portfolio. Sketches should be large and detailed to amply show garments. Small sketches are fine for the croquis book, but not for finished presentations. Include a theme or storyline, as opposed to assorted sketches.

Include actual fabric swatches to help demonstrate your knowledge of quality and price. Demonstrate your ability to coordinate fabrics and select colors for a specific season.

Make sure your portfolio is well organized, with a beginning, middle and end. Be neat and don't show anything you need to apologize for.

If necessary, create one or two specific projects geared toward the company you are going to see. Taking this initiative is a strong indicator of your interest in working for that company.

THE INTERVIEW

Prepare everything the night before: portfolios, croquis book, presentation boards, resumé and leave-behind piece, the works! Get a good night's sleep. Know what you are going to wear from head to toe.

WHAT TO WEAR

First impressions count for a lot. Dress like a professional and you will make an excellent first impression. This may be your first and only shot, so go for it! Personal grooming and neatness are a must. If you want to

✔✗

GROOMING DO'S & DON'TS

Do make sure nails are clean, length not too exaggerated.	Don't overdo it.
	Don't wear low necklines.
Do make sure garments are pressed and clean.	Don't wear very short skirts.
Do keep it simple if you have budget constraints.	Don't wear too high a heel.
Do accessorize tastefully, i.e., minimal jewelry, etc.	Don't wear too much makeup or perfume.
	Don't dress too sexy. You don't want to get the job for the wrong reasons.
Do choose a bag or purse with ample room, not one that's over-stuffed.	
Do check shoes for heels in need of repair. Invest in a great pair of shoes, if you can afford it.	

✔✗

Exercise

DRESS FOR SUCCESS

As you are about to begin your job hunt, questions will arise concerning how to dress for each interview. Confusion often reigns. Should I wear clothes made by the design firm I am interviewing with? Should I dress in the "look" of that company? What can they tell about me from the way I dress for an interview? And how important is dressing anyway in the job search process?

Everyone has asked themselves these questions at one time or another. Logic, thorough thinking, information gathering and planning can help where interview dressing is concerned. In the fashion business, your style of dress and putting yourself together communicates your fashion awareness and ingenuity. The right clothes can help you feel more secure and confident, which will help you present yourself more positively at an interview.

This exercise creates awareness of appropriate interview dressing for the entry-level beginner by analyzing grooming, hair, makeup, accessories and clothing for each interview.

You have $50 to spend for each of the following interviews. You may also borrow an item from a friend to supplement your wardrobe. The companies selected for this assignment have three distinct images that might prompt different clothing decisions. The three companies you will be interviewing with are:

- Calvin Klein
- Anna Sui
- Chanel

Write a paragraph for each company interview, describing the image of each company, and how you would dress for that interview. Include descriptions for hairstyle, makeup, accessories and clothing. You may also want to include what you think would not be appropriate dress and why. Use visual descriptions such as sketches and photos to bring clarity and humor to the report (Fig. 15.4). Be especially aware of your rationale for your clothing choices. This is an informal report so you can intermingle the visuals with the written report.

If this exercise is done on an individual basis, as a non-classroom exercise, you may want to pass it by a placement counselor, instructor or industry professional for feedback.

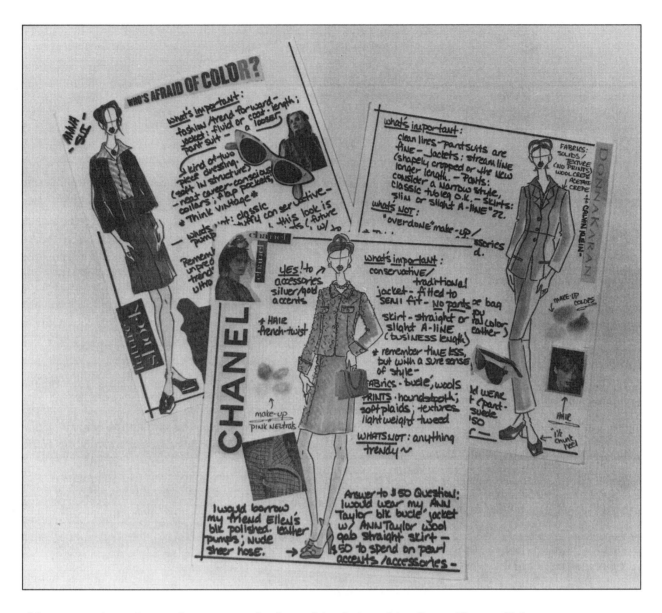

Figure   15.4
Dress For Success Exercise.

This example shows one student's rationale for interview dressing. Note that the companies selected for this assignment have three distinct images that might prompt different clothing decisions. The informality of this report allows for intermingling visuals with written comments that help you to think out and organize your own professional image.

Sketches by Dionne Muncy.

shine at your interview, make sure you also have shiny hair, a shiny face and shiny shoes.

Dress according to the company or designer with whom you are interviewing. For example, at Calvin Klein, minimal styles in neutrals are best. For Anna Sui, a slightly more individualistic approach may be appropriate, but don't go overboard.

Designers tend to dress casually on the job. Often your interviewer may be casually dressed, but remember he or she already has the job.

TIME MANAGEMENT

- Don't plan too many interviews on the same day. Schedule interviews far enough apart to allow time for travel, etc.
- Know exactly where you are going, from cross street to floor number. Rehearse the route you will take to get there: train and bus schedules, number of blocks, garages in vicinity, etc.
- Take along company addresses and phone numbers.
- Know who you will be interviewing with and his or her position.

- Be on time! Punctuality is required, not optional. (It's always better to be early. Have juice or coffee in a coffee shop nearby.)
- If you are delayed (only a natural disaster is excusable), call and reschedule. Don't simply fail to show up. Use common courtesy.
- Go alone. If you must go with a friend, have them wait for you away from the offices.

PRESENTING YOURSELF

Present yourself in a relaxed and confident manner. This facilitates the flow of the conversation. Relax by exercising moderately the night before or earlier that day. Exercising just before the interview can ruin a well-groomed appearance. Or try deep breathing, allowing physical tension to go. Meditation is also excellent for relieving stress. Visit the restroom before the interview to freshen up.

Once you're sitting in the office, facing your interviewer:

- Introduce yourself.
- Greet your interviewer with a firm, dry handshake.
- Be confident, not cocky.
- Leave any "attitude" outside the door.
- Sit up straight in the chair, be alert and show them what you've got! How you present yourself physically and verbally says a lot about who you are.
- Be sensitive to what the interviewer wants. Let him take the lead. Sometimes interviewers like to talk briefly before reviewing your portfolio.
- You're on! Talk about yourself enthusiastically. A time lapse often indicates it is your turn to continue.
- Ask questions if you are unclear what is expected.

PRESENTING YOUR PORTFOLIO

When the interviewer is ready to see your portfolio, place it where they indicate. If the format or orientation requires a set-up, offer to assist in getting it ready for viewing. Talk the portfolio through. Explain your point of view, inspiration, influences, design ideas, etc.

Rehearse your presentation several times, so your communication is fluid. Use correct fashion terminology to reinforce your knowledge.

If feedback is given, be appreciative of their comments even if you don't agree. Write down important suggestions for future reference.

GENERAL TIPS

Every interview results in valuable information that can help in the job search process. Bring a pad and pencil to jot down information. Don't rely on your memory.

If you've initiated the interview, be clear what you hope to get out of it, i.e., help and suggestions, advice, direction, prospective job leads or contacts.

Conversely, if you are responding to an ad, allow them to take the lead. If the company or exact job description was not mentioned in the ad, find out about the company and what the job entails. These facts will help you respond and know whether the job is for you.

Don't be over-eager. Remember, you are interviewing them as well. Look for follow-up clues. For instance, if they ask whether you would be interested in meeting the design director, or doing a special project for them. Listen for when they will be making a final decision. Ask if you can call them, knowing how busy they are.

Don't fake an answer. If you don't know something, say so and offer to get the information requested. You can follow up with either a phone call or include it in your thank-you note.

Don't smoke, even if the interviewer does. Don't slouch. Good posture reflects confidence and physical energy.

Avoid bad grammar and lazy pronunciation, such as "ain't," "cool," "didja" for "did you," as well as double negatives and curse words.

Should you be asked to interview over a meal, brush up on your table manners and etiquette. Avoid difficult to eat foods (e.g., spare ribs, spaghetti) that can mar your neat appearance and make conversation difficult. Order a soda or juice, no liquor. You need to be alert and fresh. Remember, you are not out with friends. Avoid being overly familiar.

Again, no smoking, even if they do. If a menu in foreign language is a problem, ask the waiter for a recommendation or take you host's lead and order similarly. Show manners with the restaurant personnel.

If you were invited, you are the guest, so they will pay for the meal. Thank them for their hospitality at the end of the meal, as well as in a follow-up note. Even an informal sandwich in the office says something about your style; remember you're still "on."

AFTER THE INTERVIEW

- Send a thank you note, preferably handwritten, after an interview or referral (Fig. 15.5).
- Supply references if requested.
- Keep an updated list of contacts.
- Follow-up good contacts by staying in touch with them even after you get a job. You might want to invite certain contacts to events or projects you will be involved with later on.
- Stay in touch by sending Christmas cards or congratulations on achievements. Newspapers, magazines, trade papers and alumni newsletters are good sources.

SALARY NEGOTIATION

Your ability to negotiate your salary depends upon your qualifications for the position, plus the salary information you have about the company or the industry. You should enter an interview with an idea of what the appropriate wages are for the job you are considering. Knowing a specific figure or salary range for candidates at your level of experience will allow you to intelligently discuss the salary issue. Advertised positions will usually indicate a weekly or annual salary range. Classified ads, trade papers and industry publications can help you become familiar with salaries in your chosen profession and level. Those employed in the fashion field, as well as placement counselors, can also give you appropriate guidelines. Remember, too, that the benefits of any job are not just monetary. Growth, career opportunities, benefits/bonuses and the professional environment can make up for a low starting wage.

The ability to negotiate your salary is a challenge faced by many entry-level professionals. Factors involved in the process include the industry you intend to enter and the specific position within that indus-

Figure 15.5

Thank-you note sent after an interview or referral. (No copy is sent to the contact, but you might phone your contact to mention the meeting and that you sent a thank-you.) A handwritten note has a personal touch. Since you have already met the person, you no longer have to maintain pre-meeting formalities. Keep the note concise and gracious. You want to show your appreciation without taking up too much of their valuable time. Aesthetics are important. Choose an attractive card or stationery. Let it be a positive reminder of you!

Sample Thank-You Note

Date

Dear Mr. or Ms:

I would like to take this opportunity to thank you for the valuable information and advice you offered during our recent meeting. It was very generous of you to take time from your hectic schedule to share your insights and to provide me with additional contacts in the industry.

I will be following-up on the leads you suggested and I will gladly keep you informed of my progress. (Send copies of all correspondence. To personalize the letter, make a specific reference to something that he or she said or observed or recommended that will serve as a reminder of your meeting.)

Again, many thanks for your encouragement. (You may want to mention your contact referral by saying you appreciate his/her suggestion of meeting you.) Our meeting was most worthwhile and I appreciate your support.

Best Regards,

Janet Jobseeker

---

try, current supply and demand, the general economic climate, size of the company, how you compare with other candidates, whether you have received other offers and the position of the person making the offer to you.

If your skills are in short supply, you have a definite edge in the negotiations. Conversely, if there are many qualified candidates interviewing for one position, companies are not likely to bargain easily. Can you determine if you are their prize candidate or just a good choice? Is your degree from a respected school in your field? Do you have an impressive grade point average? Academic qualifications are usually not the primary consideration in the fashion industry. Work experience, skills and abilities count for a lot and can be your trump card in negotiations. If your prospective employer indicates you are superior, your bargaining position is strengthened. Be alert for clues.

In negotiating salary and benefits, emphasize mutual benefits. In other words, compromise. In the bargaining process, everyone wins with compromise. You gain financial reward and self-esteem and your employer gains a committed and loyal staff member.

THE THREE PHASES OF NEGOTIATION

Analysis

Examine why you want to negotiate the offer. "My friends always nego-tiate" or "I really should not accept the first offer," are not sufficient reasons. Do your homework and you'll know if the offer is fair or not. Employers respond to what the market indicates someone with your qualifications is worth, not on the basis of your needs or wants. Know the going rate for the position in your geographic area, as well as the history and structure of the organization in which you are interested.

Although salary is usually the primary target, benefits are part of remuneration. The company's package may include health and life insurance, vacations, tuition reimbursement and relocation expenses. Other negotiables include your starting date, amount of out-of-town travel and expenses.

Planning

Play devil's advocate. Try to imagine the interviewer's assumptions and instincts about your motives. And conversely, your assumptions about his or hers. Decide what will satisfy you. Prioritize your options. You won't get everything you ask for, but know what is most important to you.

Be sure you understand the offer, including benefits. Ask questions to further clarify any points you may not understand. Demonstrate a willingness to come to terms. Avoid a "my way or you lose" position. Negotiation is a cooperative, rather than a competitive process.

Discussion

Negotiate in person whenever possible. Avoid telephone negotiations, as you're under pressure to make a quick decision over the phone. If you receive an offer by telephone, request a face-to face interview or arrange a later appointment by phone so you have time to plan a strategy.

Be prepared for some give-and-take in order to achieve a solution that is mutually acceptable.

NEGOTIATING DO'S AND DON'TS

Do listen carefully; be alert. Comprehend what is being said.

Do emphasize points of agreement.

Do come to the table with trust and a willingness to compromise.

Do be open to exchanging a salary increase for another kind of benefit.

Do be confident. Know what you want.

Do know when to stop.

Don't be antagonistic or argumentative.

Don't interrogate the interviewer.

Don't interrupt. Listen intently.

Don't negotiate based on your problems or needs. Emphasize your strengths and skills.

Don't bargain with a chip on your shoulder.

Don't underestimate yourself. Higher expectations reap higher rewards.

FREELANCE WORK

As a beginner, you may have the opportunity to work as a freelancer before committing to a full-time job. Seasoned designers often choose to freelance because they prefer the freedom and flexibility. Freelancing involves a different mind set. Generally, there are no benefits and you are paid by the job. Some freelance designers sell their sketches door-to-door, while others work at a company, designing or doing portions of a total job. This latter can range from designing a graphic to creating an entire collection.

If you choose the freelance route, be clear as to what the company expects of you. Here are some general things to consider:

- Will you be designing a whole collection or a portion?
- When must the work be completed? Is the time frame reasonable, or do they think you are a miracle worker?
- Ask to see their current line before you start. What sold well and what did not?
- Find out who will be draping, patternmaking and sewing the samples.

Negotiate payment based on your job responsibilities. Most likely, you would not get into detailed negotiations until your second interview. However, it's a good idea to have a ballpark figure of what the job pays, so less time is wasted all around. Put figures in writing in a contract form (this is usually done when the responsibilities include designing a collection and supervising the sample making, production, follow-up work, etc.) The contract should be itemized and specify payment for each task or designing phase, including the time allotted. This might include: fabric/trim sourcing, color story, flat sketches with or without specs, presentation boards and follow-up work such as supervising the sample making, production, consultation, etc. The above should be retained on an hourly consultation basis. Bill weekly. Smaller bills pass through more quickly than larger ones and are "easier to swallow."

For longer projects, ask that payments be made in installments. This demonstrates good faith and enables the freelancer to purchase any necessary supplies. A popular payment schedule is one-third when the contract is signed, one-third upon delivery of sketches and one-third when samples are checked. Or, when there is less involved, one-half when the contract is signed; one-half upon delivery of sketches. Always establish the amount and time of payment for freelance work beforehand, so there are no misunderstandings.

FREELANCE DO'S & DON'TS

Do be punctual for the interview.

Do talk your portfolio presentation through, demonstrating good communication skills and fashion vocabulary.

Do get their input on what you prepared for them. This is valuable for your next interview.

Do offer to supply references. It makes you more credible.

Don't leave sketches or allow your portfolio to be reviewed without you being present.

Don't discuss other freelance accounts. Maintain confidentiality.

Don't be overly aggressive.

Don't be over-anxious for the job.

Francois Freelancer
77 Avenue de la Mode
Paris, TX 75460

214-555-5555

S.S. #999-99-9999

INVOICE

Invoice # _____

Date: _____

Billed to: _____

_____

_____

_____

Delivery method: _____

Job description: _____

_____

_____

_____

Total due:

Thank you.

Figure   15.6

A freelancer might use an invoice similar to this one when billing clients. It is often best to bill regularly, rather than letting the amount owed accumulate, and include an invoice number to refer to when following up.

CHAPTER 16

Now you are ready to start your career. All your hard work and long hours spent preparing your portfolio and resumé have finally paid off. You've landed your first job!

The First Job: Building Your Career

Illustration by Steven Stipelman.

Now you are ready to start your career. Your training and education are about to be put to the real test. All your hard work and long hours spent preparing your portfolio and resumé have finally paid off. You've landed your first job! Yet with it comes many questions and fears about what to expect—and what will be expected of you.

Remembering why you were hired will bring a lot into focus. Your talent and enthusiasm for fashion were undoubtedly major factors in the company's decision to hire you over another candidate. Now that you have the job, don't allow these qualities to wane. Every day you will need to reinforce your employer's confidence in you. Be committed and caring about what you do and the rest will take care of itself. Make your goals about creating a standard, rather than meeting one.

At your final interview, you probably discussed the duties and responsibilities that go with your job. Review them to be clear as to what is expected of you. Every job incorporates "hidden" tasks you may not be aware of until they arise. Going-with-the-flow indicates flexibility and initiative to an employer. However, let your instincts be your guide. Be sure you are comfortable with what is asked of you, within reason.

Know the commitments that your employer has made to you. Every job is a two-way street involving commitment from both employer and employee. Be honest and forthright in voicing your expectations of your mutual agreement.

ON-THE-JOB SURVIVAL

It is natural to be nervous when starting a new job. Try to relax and do your best. A proven way to get rid of the jitters is to concentrate on the task at hand instead of looking at the job as a whole. You will gradually ease into your new work setting. It will probably take less time than you think to make the adjustment. Feeling comfortable with your new co-workers, and they with you, may take time, but don't let that bother you. Honesty and sensitivity go a long way. If you are having serious problems adjusting to the new situation or an individual, talk to your supervisor.

A sense of humor and enthusiasm are considered assets by most employers. Quarreling, hostility and anger have no more place in the workplace than laziness, dishonesty, tardiness or sloppy work. Each person contributes to the success of a company and should be treated with politeness and respect. "Excuse me" and "thank you" are common courtesies. Show others you respect them and you will be treated in kind.

Keeping some basics in mind can help get you off to the right start:

- Get to work on time and put in a full day. Industry professionals close to showing their collection often work extended hours, even weekends. Jobs have regulated hours, careers do not.
- Avoid being absent or late. Irregular attendance patterns are frowned upon in the business world.
- If you are unable to go to work or will be late, call your supervisor as soon as possible and explain why. Demonstrate responsibility and that you take your job seriously.
- If you need to take time off, make arrangements in advance with your supervisor.
- Minimize personal phone calls during work hours.
- Organize your personal life so that it does not interfere with work.

Deadlines are a constant in the design business. Everyone is always juggling one or more deadlines. Because time is at a premium, listen carefully and be alert. Have an awareness of the immediate needs and goals of your division, and how it serves the company as a whole.

Because everything is due "yesterday," pay close attention when given instructions regarding jobs and assignments. Sometimes, out of nervousness, people find it difficult to focus. You may catch only part of the instructions. This is very common, especially among those starting a new job. Simply ask your supervisor questions you feel are necessary to do the assignments properly. If you miss part of the instructions, don't ask a co-worker because you're too embarrassed to ask the supervisor to repeat the information. Remember, he or she gave you the assignment and wants the work done in a specific way. Someone else will just be guessing or giving you their interpretation. Keeping a work journal or notebook can help you remember assignment instructions and track details. No one has total recall. Get in the habit of taking notes and keeping lists. It will save you time and insecurity about remembering job-related tasks.

At the beginning, it is common to make mistakes. Mistakes are made by everyone, professionals as well as beginners. Mistakes are an important part of the learning process. In a way, your first job is like a paid apprenticeship. And although you may not be making a lot of money, you will be gaining a great deal of knowledge, often through your first mistakes. Here, you have the opportunity to make them on the company's time and expense, which is part and parcel of training a beginner. Never try to hide or ignore a mistake or let sloppy work pass. Do not argue about fault or blame, but rather try to define what the problem is, what caused it, and what can be done to correct or resolve it. An understanding of the problem can prevent it from happening again. If you make a mistake, let your supervisor know so that it can be corrected in time. If you find you can't complete an assignment in the time allowed, tell your supervisor as soon as you realize it. Don't wait until the last minute. Take responsibility. Demonstrate that you are concerned, take pride in your work, and recognize the importance of deadlines. Meeting them will yield a great sense of satisfaction and accomplishment.

When you start a new job, you may not get to do the specific work you were hired for immediately. Show your new employer how good a worker you are by doing a good job with the tasks you are assigned to do. Approach your assignments with energy and enthusiasm. And be alert as to what others are working on at the same time. Be willing to take on extra assignments if necessary, as long as you think you can handle them. Be ready to help with jobs you don't normally do or those with which you are unfamiliar. This may require working overtime and could be an excellent learning opportunity. Everything you learn makes you more valuable and, eventually, more marketable as a designer. Employers genuinely appreciate employees who demonstrate good work ethics.

EMPLOYER/EMPLOYEE RELATIONSHIPS

It is not easy for anyone to admit they have made a mistake. No one likes to be wrong, especially among their peers. This is also true of supervisors. If you think your supervisor has made a mistake, talk it over privately, in a calm manner. Try to understand their point of view. Accusations only prompt defensive reactions. Often broaching the subject of an error in the form of a question makes it seem more reasonable and rational. Sometimes, by talking to others who work with your supervisor, you can get insight on how to get along with him or her. If you are having ongoing difficulties, talk over the problem with your supervisor directly and suggest solutions or ask for advice. If all this fails, try talking to someone in the personnel department.

Take an analytical and fair approach. Difficulties usually arise when there is a breakdown in communication between two people. Know what your responsibilities are and whether you are meeting them. Don't get angry with your supervisor for telling you to follow company rules. This is part of his or her job. Your initial approach and tone of voice is very important. Remember, many issues can be settled positively through tact, diplomacy and cooperation.

When doing assignments, try not to waste time or materials unnecessarily. Employers appreciate those who do a job well and cost-effectively. Work at a good pace. Those who work too quickly tend to make more mistakes than they normally might. Through practice you will increase speed and maintain accuracy. This is one of the bonuses of on-the-job learning. If you are given more than one assignment at a time, check with your supervisor about which one should be tackled first. Prioritizing work is the core of efficient time management.

Avoid socializing with your co-workers during working hours. From the employer's point of view, they are paying you for working, not socializing. This includes personal phone calls, as well. The workplace requires a professional business persona. Your time away from the office and at home is your own. Organize your personal life so that it does not interfere with your work. Show your employers you know the difference.

Once you become acclimated to your job and surroundings, you may see something that needs to be done that you can handle. Check with your supervisor first before assuming the task. In most cases, taking this initiative will be recognized and appreciated. Sometimes, though, work is delegated to others for purposes of efficiency or deferred because further information is still needed. Since you may not be privy to any of this, make inquiries before attempting to take on assignments.

Keeping an orderly work station contributes to on-the-job efficiency and productivity. Before leaving for the day, clean and organize your desk top so you are ready for the next day. Clean up after each stage that requires different tools and materials, and put them away in their proper places. Keep the contents of drawers and supply closets orderly and sorted, especially if shared by others. Creating organized discipline instead of organized chaos makes your work environment more pleasant while you are there.

In addition, each company may have a standard for environmental decoration in the workplace. You may be permitted to display personal objects, photos or artwork on your desk. However, some companies have restrictions about these things, as well as color preferences for paper clips or even cut flowers and plants. Ask your supervisor about your company's environmental preferences or restrictions.

MAKING IT WORK

Although every job is important, it is important to keep it in perspective. Other areas such as family, friends, school, hobbies and travel will all help balance what goes on in the design room and workplace. You will make mistakes on your first and even on your next job. Learn from them and own up to them. You will be respected for taking responsibility for your errors and being adult about acknowledging them. Observe those with experience and skills that you respect. Notice how they work and handle job situations. These individuals are excellent role models. Their leadership qualities are distinctive and set them apart. They can help you shape your career.

A key ingredient in building a career is setting high standards. Take pride and respect your own work. Strive for the highest level of quality. Don't leave it to someone else to set the standard for you. Successful design professionals consistently have high expectations for themselves. This does not mean they succeed each and every time they set out to accomplish a goal. The late president of F.I.T., Marvin Feldman, once said, "If you achieve everything you set out to accomplish, you probably are not aiming high enough." In addition, make sure your expectations are accompanied by a determined discipline to undertake the work necessary to create a high level of accomplishment.

Only you can define the expectations and achievements of your career. Others can offer information, give advice, even offer you jobs, but it will be up to you to design and develop your own career. Your career will be the total sum of your efforts. What goals do you envision for yourself? What do you consider to be a successful career for you? Designing those goals and that vision is the most important design you will create . . . for your future.

Glossary of Frequently Used Apparel Manufacturing Terms

Each industry has a special "language" all its own. The fashion industry is no exception. Knowing the vocabulary is extremely helpful in the job search, as it communicates awareness of the various areas that contribute to the manufacturing of apparel. The terminology included here is divided into three categories: apparel, manufacturing and textile. Although they are divided here for easy reference, frequently you will find there is a cross-over between categories. On-the-job experience will increase your familiarity with these terms and expand your vocabulary to include new ones.

APPAREL TERMS

Applique: Emblems, cut fabric shapes, figures or motifs that are superimposed and sewn or fused to garment components.

Body: Perfected pattern for a style that has been fitted and graded.

Bundle: A stack of cut garment sections, folded and/or tied, sorted and grouped according to pattern size.

Classic: A fashion style that has been accepted; a staple or basic.

Croquis: A small sketch of a design from which a garment is developed.

Coordinates: Jackets, blouses, pants and skirts designed to be produced, sold and worn together as a group.

Double ticket: Apparel that is manufactured to be sold to both junior and missy sizes, i.e. 5/6, 7/8, 9/10, 11/12.

Edging: Trim used to accentuate style lines, outline shapes or compartmentalize blocks of color; piping, lace, ribbon, fringe, tape, picot trim, etc.

Emblem: Cut-out, embroidered design with finished edges; patch, insignia or badge.

Embroidery: An art form that uses close or overlapping stitches to form intricate, three-dimensional surface designs to embellish piece goods, trims or garments.

Findings: Materials used in garments other than piece goods; trims, threads, closures, labels, etc.

Finishing: Process required to give a garment its final appearance; thread trimming, wet processing, garment dyeing and final pressing.

First pattern: Original paper pattern created from the designer's sketch, draft or drape and specifications.

Fit model: Person of sample size used to test garment fit and comfort.

Fit sample: First-garment prototype.

Fluff: A garment considered to be a "fashion" item rather than a key item basic. Its novel style draws interest and excitement to the line.

Fusing: The process of bonding fabric layers with an adhesive by the application of heat and pressure.

Gauge: Distance between needles; related to number of wales per inch on knitted fabric; distance between stitching lines made by multi-needle sewing machines.

Graded pattern: Individual patterns of a garment proportioned to a set of standardized body measurements for each size.

Hard body: Tailored item of clothing. Fabric used is usually woven, the design might have shoulder pads and /or a lining.

Interlining: Materials that are fused or sewn to specific areas inside garments or garment components; provides shape, support, stabilization, reinforcement, hand and improved performance

Key item: A basic article of clothing that may be manufactured inexpensively for different seasons and will generate a lot of sales, season after season.

Knockoff: Close reproduction of the design of an existing textile or apparel item.

Ligne: Unit of measure for buttons.

Line: Manufacturer's or designer's collection of styles in a given season.

Lining: Materials that increase aesthetics and performance by supporting and/or enclosing the interiors of garments or garment components.

Marker: A cutting guide made up of the outline of all production pattern pieces for a particular style in one or more sizes. Pattern pieces are always arranged for fabric economy.

Ornamental stitching (OS): Stitching on a single ply for decorative purposes.

Overedge stitch: Thread encompassing the cut edge of the fabric piece; machine trims fabric as overedge stitches are formed.

Pattern grading: The process of increasing or decreasing the dimensions of a pattern at specific points according to certain grade rules of proportional change.

Production pattern: Perfect, final patterns that meet all quality and production requirements, including seam allowances and markings.

Preproduction sample: A garment sample submitted to buyers for approval before production begins.

Production sample: First-run garment produced for inspection of garment quality.

Rub-off/rubbing: A line-for-line copy of a style made from an original sample, rather than a pattern.

Sample garment: The first or trial garment made from the muslin pattern or paper pattern.

Soft body: Clothing made out of soft fabric such as silk, nylon, soft knits, etc.

Sloper: A basic pattern, either whole or in part, from which other designs are created.

Underpressing: Pressing during garment assembly; facilitates production and increases quality level.

MANUFACTURING TERMS

Assortment: Range of choices offered at a particular time; usually determined by style, size, and color.

Branded line: A firm that manufactures and sells under its own label i.e., Liz Claiborne, Chaus, etc. (need more examples).

Branded name: A word, term or logo used for identification.

Chapter 9802 (Item 807): Provision in the Harmonized System of Tariffs that allows products to be partially made in the United States, exported for further manufacturing processes, and imported with tariff assessment based on value added.

Manufacturers receive tax benefits for manufacturing goods that have been cut in the U.S. and sent overseas for production. "807" is used to identify overseas countries, as that is the number on the application form used when items are returned to this country.

Contractor: Firm that provides sewing, cutting, finishing or other specialty services.

Costing: Process of determining the costs of producing each style in a product line.

FOB (Freight on Board): Final cost of a garment before leaving its country of origin; includes cost of fabric and trim, cutting, assembling, finishing and production.

LDP (Landed Duty Paid): Final cost of bringing a garment into the country, including FOB, duty, freight, commissions, insurance etc.

Lead time: The amount of production time required after all order details have been confirmed.

Licensee: A company that has purchased the permission to manufacture merchandise and sell it under the label of a well-known designer. This applies to apparel, accessories, cosmetics, domestics and home furnishings, i.e., Christian Dior, Anne Klein, Ralph Lauren, etc.

Line development: The process of determining the styles, fabrications, colors and sizes to be offered for sale. Based on sales history, goals and forecasts; framework for line development as well as the budget allocated for a particular season.

Mass market: Usually includes the middle-income class and part of the lower- and upper-income classes.

Moderate price: Goods sold at average prices for a product category.

Off-price: Practice of selling goods at less than regular retail price.

Off-shore production: Manufacture of products outside the continental United States.

Private label: A brand owned by a retailer or manufacturer, which is sold to a buyer (a retail chain or catalog), who then markets the merchandise under its own label.

Quota: Regulates quantities of goods that can be traded internationally.

Supplier: Source, resource or vendor.

Target customer/market: A customer or group of customers identified through a process of market segmentation that have similar wants and needs for certain products or services.

Unit production system (UPS): An overhead transporter system that moves individual units from work station to work station for assembly; a type of line layout that provides centralized production control.

Vendor: Supplier of goods to be used or sold; also called source or resource.

Vertical operation: A company that manufacturers fabric and then uses fabric to manufacture their own apparel.

Wholesale price: List price less trade discounts.

TEXTILE TERMS

Automatic stripes: A repeated stripe more than 1-1/2" wide.

Color cards: Reference material supplied seasonally by textile manufacturers/forecasting firms to assist with color selection.

Colorways: Choosing a range of colors for apparel designs that contrast and complement each other. Colorways are done for solids, prints, stripes and yarns.

Confined line: Fabric that is designed and manufactured and sold to one company. The purchaser will be the only apparel manufacturer using it.

Converter: Buys greige goods from mills, contracts the dyeing, printing, and/or finishing, and sells finished goods.

Count: Numerical designation of yarn size (cotton count); the number of warp and filling yarns in a square inch of woven fabric.

Directive dye: A less expensive dying process in which greige goods are prepared and then dyed. Color is less intense than reactive dye.

Engineered print: Planned print layout that corresponds to where print falls on garment.

Engineered stripe: Strategic placement of stripes for where designer wants it to fall on garment.

Fabric jobber: Buys fabric in comparatively small quantities from mills, converters and apparel manufacturers for resale.

Fabrication: The method used to produce the material; woven, knitted, molded, cast, etc.

Fancies: Special or fashion fabrics; structural design fabrics such as brocade, pique, etc.

Feeder stripe: A repeated stripe less than 1-1/4" wide.

Heat-transfer print: Image is transferred from pre-printed paper to a fabric by application of heat and pressure.

Lab-dips: A sample of dye mixtures that are created to approximate the actual color standard required. The firm purchasing the fabric usually approves a lab dip prior to the manufacture of goods.

Lab test: Fabric testing for endurance, color and specifications.

Ounce: Unit of weight for measuring denim and knits.

Piece goods: Bulk fabrics.

Ply: Single strand of yarn; single layer of fabric.

Pounds: Unit of weight measure for yarn.

Punch: Used as a verb, punch refers to a circular section taken from a knitwear garment for accurate measure of weight.

Reactive dye: A more expensive process in which greige goods are prepared and then dyed. Result is a more intense color that will not bleed.

Re-color prints or stripes (re-pitching): Selecting different or more current colors for an existing printed or striped fabric.

Screen printing: Process of applying a dye or pigment paste through a mesh stencil to produce a surface design.

Screen prints, embroideries, appliques: Various methods of embellishments for apparel designs.

Variegated stripe: A graduating stripe from narrow to wide in repeat.

Weigh-in: Term used to describe color balance in either garment colorways or textile patterns.

Yarn-dye: Most often used to describe stripe and jacquard fabrics. Yarns are dyed before knitting or weaving of fabric.

Appendix A

FASHION INFORMATION RESOURCES

FASHION FORECAST SERVICES

*Doneger Design Direction
463 Seventh Avenue
New York, NY 10018

*Here & There
1412 Broadway
New York, NY 10018

K Kids and Company
102 Barry Scott Drive
Fairfield, CT 06430

*Nigel French
270 Madison Avenue
New York, NY 10016

*Norma Morris Design Products
110 West 40th Street, Suite #306
New York, NY 10018

*Pat Tunsky, Inc.
1040 Avenue of the Americas, 23rd Floor
New York, NY 10018

*Promostyl USA
80 West 40th Street
New York, NY 10018

*Stylists Information Service (SIS)
575 Main Street
Roosevelt Island, NY 10044

*The Fashion Service (TFS)
1412 Broadway, Suite #1410
New York, NY 10018

*Denotes company provides color services, as well.

*Trend Union
90 Riverside Drive, Suite #9D
New York, NY 10024

COLOR SERVICES

Color Association of the U.S. (CAUS)
409 West 44th Street
New York, NY 10036

Cotton Inc.
1370 Avenue of the Americas, 34th Floor
New York, NY 10019

Color Portfolio
201 East 17th Street
New York, NY 10003

E. I. Dupont de Nemours
1251 Avenue of the Americas
New York, NY 10020

Huepoint
39 West 37th Street
New York, NY 10018

Pantone Color Institute
590 Commerce Avenue
Carlstadt, NJ 07072

Scotdic
488 Seventh Avenue, Suite #8A
New York, NY 10018

The Wool Bureau
330 Madison Avenue
New York, NY 10017

AMERICAN FIBER COUNCILS AND LIBRARIES

American Wool Council
50 Rockefeller Plaza
New York, NY 10020

Hoechst Celanese Corp.
3 Park Avenue
New York, NY 10016

Cotton Inc.
1370 Avenue of the Americas, 34th Floor
New York, NY 10019

E. I. Dupont De Nemours
1251 Avenue of the Americas
New York, NY 10020

International Linen Promotion Commission
200 Lexington Avenue, Suite 225
New York, NY 10016

Mademoiselle (fabric library)
350 Madison Avenue
New York, NY 10017

Mohair Council of America
499 Seventh Avenue, 1200 N. Tower
New York, NY 10018

Spectrum Dyed Yarns, Inc.
1450 Broadway
New York, 10018

Vogue (fabric library)
350 Madison Avenue
New York, NY 10017

The Wool Bureau
330 Madison Avenue
New York, NY 10017

FABRIC/COLOR SHOWS

Ideacomo, Italy
Interstoff, Germany
International Fabric Expo, New York
Le Semaine du Cuir, Paris
Moda-In, Italy
Pan-Am, Miami
Premier Vision, Paris
Texitalia, New York
The Yarn Fair, New York

COSTUME COLLECTIONS

U.S.
Metropolitan Museum of Art, New York
Brooklyn Museum, New York
Museum at FIT, New York
Boston Museum of Art, Massachusetts
Philadelphia Museum of Art, Pennsylvania
Los Angeles County Museum of Art, California
Chicago Historical Society, Illinois
Kent State University, Ohio
Ohio State Universtiy, Ohio

Overseas
Kyoto Costume Institute, Japan
Musée de la Mode et du Costume, Paris
Musée des Arts de la Mode, Paris
Victoria and Albert Museum, London

RESOURCE DIRECTORIES

Designers use two major directories to locate resources such as fabric, yarn and trim suppliers, print studios and swatch libraries. These guides are valuable tools for the designer:

The TIP Resource Guide
Fashiondex

TRADE PUBLICATIONS

California Apparel News
Women's Wear Daily (WWD)
Daily News Record (DNR) (Men's Fashions)
Fashion Reporter
Tobe Report
W

FASHION MAGAZINES

American
Elle
Glamour
Harper's Bazaar
In Style
Mademoiselle
Marie Claire
Mirabella
New Woman
NY Women
Paper
Self
Teen
Vogue
European
Collezoni Donna (Italian)
Depeche Mode (French)
Donna (Italian)
Elle (British, French, German, Italian, Spanish)
Fashion Collections GAP
Glamour (Italian)
Harper's & Queen (British)
Harper's Bazaar (Italian)
Harper's Bazaar Alta Moda (Italian)
Joyce (French)
L'Officiel de la Couture (French)
Marie Claire (French, Italian)
Moda (Italian)
Tattler (British)
Vogue (Australian, British, French, German, Italian, Spanish)

Appendix B

ART SUPPLIES FOR FASHION DESIGNERS

Pencils

Used for a variety of sketching purposes, for both preliminary and finishing techniques, pencils are available in a variety of leads. The degree of hardness in drawing pencils is indicated by a standard code stamped on every pencil. Degrees range from 6B (very soft) and "blackest," through 9H (extremely hard) and "lightest." B leads allow for the most variation in line pressure. H leads have less of a tendency to smudge and are used when a lighter touch is needed. Ultimately, your choice of pencils should be based on the type of result desired as well as your own natural pressure or "hand."

Faber Castell Ebony Drawing Pencil: Round, soft and jet black intensity.

Mongol Writing Pencils: No. 2 HB standard pencil with eraser; allows for medium pressure.

Venus Drawing Pencils: Available in a versatile degree range B, HB and H.

Koh-I-Noor Rapidomatic Drawing Pencil #5635/0.5mm Leads HB or 2B: Automatic or retractable holders are available in a variety of lead types and thicknesses. Give controlled, clean, precise results and are preferred by many designers.

General Charcoal Pencil: Pure charcoal encased in pencil form. Infrequently used for portfolio purposes, as charcoal has a tendency to smudge.

Colored Pencils: Versatile in that they can be used alone or in combination with other media.

Berol Prismacolor Colored Pencils: A thick lead pencil with excellent intensity, both waterproof and light-resistant.

Berol Eagle Verithin Colored Pencils: Verithin hard pencils have less intensity and won't run under moisture.

Mongol Colored Pencils: "Paint with pencils" by going over colors with a moist brush. This watercolor type pencil can be used wet or dry.

Erasers

Faber Castell Pink Pearl Eraser: For erasing smudges and shading pencil drawings.

Koh-I-Noor Soft Vinyl Eraser: Soft, non-abrasive composition for removing graphite from tracing paper.

Berol Eraser Pencil: Self-sharpening, paper-wrapped eraser in a pencil shape. Available in New Way (for pencil) or Klenzo (for ink).

Faber Castell Kneaded Eraser: For general page clean-up and shading pencil drawings. Can be cleaned by manipulating it with your hands.

Sharpeners

Panasonic KP-33—The Point-O-Matic: Sturdy, long lasting and excellent for maintaining graphite and colored pencil points. First choice in design studios.

Panasonic KP-2A Portable Battery-Operated Pencil Sharpener: The battery-operated sharpener is a good substitute when portability is important. Freelance designers find the smaller size and weight practical when carrying supplies.

Baumgarten's Pencil Sharpeners: Hand-held sharpeners made from metal or plastic.

Sandpaper Pads: Provides a hard and sturdy surface for sharpening a variety of pencils. More popularly used for sharpening charcoal or crayon.

Magic Markers

Most frequently used in industry due to their quick application and almost instant drying ability. Markers come in a variety of nib sizes, making them suitable for different purposes. For general coverage over a large area, use flat or rounded, broad-tip markers. For smaller areas and fine detail work, fine-tip markers are preferable. There are several brands of multi-nibbed markers, which ensure a perfect color match since the nibs use the same color cartridge. These markers come in a wide spectrum of colors, as well as a range of both warm and cool grey tones.

Chartpak AD Marker: A single-nib marker capable of three distinct line weights with a shift of the wrist. Available in 130 permanent colors.

Design Art Markers and Design Art Markers 2: The former is available in three single-nib styles including broad, pointed and ultra-fine. Design Art Markers 2 are double-ended markers featuring a flat, broad tip on one end and a pointed tip on the other.

Prismacolor Double-Ended Art Markers: Contains both a broad and fine line nib, yet can produce four line widths. Available in 144 non-toxic colors.

The Tria System: Pantone by Letraset Color Markers and Inks; a three-nibbed marker featuring broad, fine line and ultra-fine points. Available in 293 Pantone colors with refillable ink cartridges. Utilizes a universal color system that matches papers and fabrics.

Outline Markers

Can be used to outline and define garments in a variety of techniques. These markers come in a broad range of nib and tip widths, varying from bold to extra fine. Many designers prefer a bold outline to emphasize the silhouette of a garment, and a fine line for rendering seams and garment details. These markers are available in black and in limited colors.

Pro-Art Elegant Writer Calligraphy Fine Line Markers: These pens are fairly easy to handle and are excellent for achieving a varied line by rotating the pen while drawing. Capable of both a bold and fine line in one flat nib.

Berol Boldliner #F30: An excellent outline marker for strong definition and silhouette emphasis. The flexible point allows for line variation as well.

Sharpie Fine-Point Marker #3000: Has a thick, rounded tip, preferred as an outline pen for figures and flats. Quick drying, water resistant and non-toxic.

Pilot Precise and Pilot Razor Point Markers: Fine line markers that can be used for both outlining and inside garment detailing (stitching, pockets, buttons). Available with felt tip or roller-ball nibs.

Sakura Pigma Pens: Available in a wide range of precision nibs. The extra-fine tips (.005mm and .08mm) are excellent for rendering garment details. Contains waterproof pigment ink.

Marvy Le Pen 0.3mm: Micro-fine tip excellent for fine detail work. These pens replaced the Rapidograph for achieving fine detail results without clogging or mess.

Paint Sets

Used less frequently in the industry, painting techniques tend to be time-consuming compared with the immediacy of markers and pencils. Most companies prefer their designers to use media that will get quick results while adapting to the fast pace of the industry.

However, both watercolor and gouache are still preferred by some designers and educators, because of their great teaching value. The painting process literally teaches how colors affect one another when mixed together, and it is capable of creating many variations in transparency which cannot quite be duplicated by other media.

Painting sets are available in discs, tubes or bottles, ranging from 6 to 60 colors per set. Colors can be purchased individually as well.

Sakura Special Watercolors: Smooth, rich colors in tubes, they carry the non-toxic seal.

Grumbacher Deluxe Opaque Watercolor Set: 24 Quality opaque pan watercolors with brush. Non-toxic.

Luma Brilliant Concentrated Lightfast Watercolors: Available in ink bottle form, these highly concentrated, lightfast watercolors will not fade and are popular with textile designers.

Pro Art Liquid Tempera Paint: Opaque, non-toxic, water-soluble poster paint. Fast drying to a matte finish.

Winsor & Newton's Designers' Gouache: Available in sets of 12 to 60 colors and individual tubes, this opaque, water soluble medium is excellent for a variety of fabric rendering needs. It can be thinned to a transparent wash or used full-strength to create opacity. Because it does not separate, colors can be mixed and stored in containers for future use. Excellent when maintaining color-match consistency is essential.

Steig "Pro" White: Opaque, for use on all surfaces, paper, photo or acetate. Excellent for making corrections on finished art work.

Brushes

Used in conjunction with watercolor, tempera or gouache, brushes range from the smallest size (000) to the largest (14). Each brush has a series number, categorizing its use for oil, acrylic or watercolor. The most expensive are made of finest sable, the middle price-range features a combination of sable and synthetic, and the least expensive are made of acrylic bristle or camel hair. Each price range offers points that are flat, round or bright (a combination of both).

The true test of any brush is the water test. Saturate the brush in water, remove it and flick it to test the point's resiliency. If it bounces back up, pointing straight in the air, without the hairs separating, the brush is worth its weight.

Grumbacher Pure Red Sable Series 197: Most expensive, made of pure red sable.

Winsor & Newton Sceptre Watercolor Brushes: Medium priced, made of a combination of sable and synthetic. Multi-purpose.

Loew Cornell Brushes Series 795: Least expensive, made of synthetic nylon.

Bamboo Brushes: Some designers prefer brushes in bamboo handles. Considered "all purpose," they have a sharp tip, resiliency, and are extremely flexible, adapting to a variety of media.

Papers

A variety of papers are available for different uses in the portfolio, for both preparatory and finished work, and may be purchased in pad form or individual sheets. Several factors can determine the papers you select: a favorite technique, desired special effect, personal media preference, demonstration of a special skill, etc. The most popular sizes for fashion portfolios are 11 x 14 and 14 x 17 as they are practical for job hunting and can be placed on most desks for easy viewing.

Decorative Papers: These papers come in a wide range of colors and textures and can be used to create a variety of effects, both for direct drawing purposes or as an attractive background to enhance a presentation. These papers are distinguished by their novelty surfaces: coated/shiny, metallic foil, floral, marbleized, mirrored, Taieri imbedded fiber and corrugated.

Bristol Board: Available in two types of finishes— vellum-kid, which has a slight tooth and more grip; or plate, when a smooth surface is preferred. This sturdy, opaque paper is versatile and can be used for drawing and mounting with a variety of media.

Tracing Paper: Essential in portfolio preparation. Most often used in combination with pencil or outline pens. Extremely pliable, never used for finished presentations.

Vellum: A translucent paper with more body than tracing paper. Excellent for two-sided rendering i.e., with colored pencils on the top side and marker on the reverse. May require backing of solid white or colored papers to eliminate haziness.

Bienfang Marker Paper Graphics 360 and Extra Bright 340: Available in two finishes—one with a slight tooth, the other smooth. Created for mainly marker techniques, but may also be used in combination with other media, i.e. pencils. Not appropriate for watercolor or other wet media due to its thin weight and lack of absorbency.

Watercolor Paper: Varies in weight (light 90#, medium 140#, heavy 300#) and is available in three surface textures: cold press with a slight tooth, hot press with a smooth surface and rough. Media other than watercolor can be used on watercolor paper for less conventional techniques.

Canson Watercolor Paper #1059: A basic watercolor paper with a slight tooth. Encased in a spiral pad.

Precision Drawing Tools

For accuracy and a crisp, sure, line quality, many designers prefer the results they get using rulers, curves and templates. These tools take the guess work out of drawing garments and details. Especially good for flat sketching.

Plastic Ruler with Graph Grid: Excellent for measuring and lining-up work.

Plastic French Curves: Excellent for creating precision in drawing curved shapes in garments or textiles. Available in a variety of sizes.

Plastic Template Stencil: Available with circles or a combination of circles and geometric shapes and details. Excellent for precision drawing of garment details.

ART SUPPLIES FOR PRESENTATION BOARDS

Foam-Core Board: This lightweight board comes in 1/8", 3/16"(called 1/4") and 1/2" thicknesses and is available in sizes ranging from 20 x 30, 32 x 40, 40 x 60, 48 x 48 and 48 x 96. Because of its light weight and ability to resist warping it is ideal for cut-outs and mounting. Foam-Core comes in a variety of colors and metallics as well as all-white, all-black and black/white. Custom colors can be specially ordered with minimum quantities.

Bainbridge Board: Used for smaller presentations, this board is more weighty than Foam-Core. Available in sizes 15 x 20, 20 x 30, 22 x 30, 30 x 40. It comes in both smooth and medium surfaces and is ideal for all types of illustration media and adhesives.

Decorative Papers: Novelty papers are perfect for creating an attractive background to enhance a presentation board. Available in a wide range of colors and textures, they can produce a dramatic and eye-catching effect.

Adhesives

Best-Test Rubber Cement: An excellent adhesive for all paper pasting purposes. Cleans up easily.

Pro-Art Rubber Cement Pick-Up: A crepe-latex square that lifts up and removes dried rubber cement.

Bestine Rubber Cement Thinner: For thinning and reducing rubber cement and frisket work.

Post-it Removable Adhesive Glue Stick: A non-messy product perfect for gluing small-sized papers or fabric, especially those that are transparent and porous. Non-toxic

3M Remount Repositionable Adhesive: Holds firmly, yet lets you remove or reposition your artwork as many times as you want. Non-staining, non-yellowing, will not soak through and bonds quickly to a variety of surfaces.

Scotch Brand Adhesive Transfer Tape: An instant-bonding, permanent rubber cement adhesive on a protective liner. Excellent for transferring adhesive to fragile surfaces such as tissue or fabric. Will not soak through.

Studiotac By Letraset: A pad of special sheets coated with a powerful adhesive. Art work is pressed down onto the adhesive sheet. It can be repositioned again and again.

Cello-Tak Double Sided Mounting Adhesive Film: Used for dry mounting, adhesive is sandwiched between two protective release sheets. The longer the film remains in contact, the more permanent the bond. Leaves no adhesive residue. Non-toxic.

Pro Art Drafting Tape: Holds drawings in place on any surface. Useful for temporary jobs where tape must be removed without lifting the surface to which it was applied. Good in preparatory stages.

Velcro Tape: These tapes have a pressure-sensitive adhesive backing for instant mounting and removal. Hook-and-Pile tapes are sold separately by the yard or in 25-yard rolls. Excellent for adding or removing sketches or swatches from a presentation.

Wax Coater: Applies an even, heated-wax coating to the back of artwork surfaces, allowing artwork to adhere smoothly to a surface. Can be repositioned if necessary.

Cutting Tools

Utility Mat Knife: Heavy duty cutting knife for thick surfaces such as board or Foam-Core.

Fiskar Lightweight Scissors: Used in free-form cutting of lightweight materials.

Pinking Shears: Used for creating a pinked edge for either fabric or paper swatches. Prevents fraying.

X-Acto Knives: Available in grades for light, medium, and heavy work. These tools feature different handle grips and come complete with blade. Best for precision cutting of light-weight materials.

Razor Blades: Single-edge blades can be used for a variety of general paper cutting purposes.

Lettering and Borders

Letraset Instant Lettering: Available in hundreds of typefaces and point sizes. Excellent for titling or labeling presentation boards. Because of its tendency to peel, it is advisable to photo-copy before mounting.

Brother P-Touch: Generates lettering onto a transparent sheet with a peel-off adhesive backing for fast and easy application.

Computer Generated Lettering: Appropriate for presentation board titles and labels. Can be used directly from printer to board. Will not peel off.

Letraline Tapes: Available in over 1,000 different sharp-edged corners, borders, and transparent, opaque and patterned tapes. Gives a polished, professional result.

ART SUPPLY SOURCES

Art Materials
2728 Lyndale Ave. S.
Minneapolis, MN 55408
catalog orders: 612-872-8088

Art Station Ltd.
144 West 27th Street
New York, NY 10001
catalog orders: 212-807-8000

Artists Connection
catalog orders only: 800-851-9333

Brewer-Cantelmo
(custom portfolios)
350 Seventh Ave.
New York, NY 10001
212-244-4600
http//www.brewer-cantelmo.com

Daniel Smith Fine Art Materials
4150 1st Ave. S.
Seattle, WA
catalog orders: 800-426-6740
dsartmtrl@aol.com

Dick Blick Art Materials
34 store locations across the Midwest
catalog orders: 800-447-8192
info@dickblick.com
http//www.dickblick.com

Flax Art and Design
1699 Market Street
San Francisco, CA
catalog orders: 800-547-7778

Pearl Paint
308 Canal Street
New York, NY 10013
catalog orders: 800-221-6845
(catalog costs $1.50)

Sam Flax
425 Park Ave.
New York, NY 10021
catalog orders: 800-628-9512